From Resource Rich to Resource Smart

From Resource Rich to Resource Smart

Opportunities for Latin America and the Caribbean in the Energy Transition

Guillermo Beylis and Nancy Lozano Gracia, Editors

WORLD BANK GROUP

Contents

Boxes

Figures

Map

Tables

Foreword

In an era marked by profound global shifts, the transition to a lower carbon economy offers the Latin America and the Caribbean (LAC) region new opportunities for growth and more and better jobs. The region boasts a higher contribution of renewables (hydro, solar, and wind) in its electricity grid than any other; it is well endowed with critical minerals essential to new technologies; and it is rich in biodiversity and fertile lands. However, history suggests that leveraging these advantages for broad based and sustainable growth is neither automatic nor a foregone conclusion. It will require far-reaching reforms and strategic interventions, what some have called "green industrial policies."

From Resource Rich to Resource Smart: Opportunities for Latin America and the Caribbean in the Energy Transition offers a comprehensive exploration of the elements of such policies needed to transition the region from its legacy resource-driven model to one characterized by resource and environmental efficiency, and innovation.

The report begins by emphasizing the importance of measuring efficiency in both economic and environmental dimensions and introduces the concept of the *economic-environmental production possibilities frontier*. It then outlines actions to maximize both values across three stages: catching up with the frontier, shifting the frontier outward, and creating new frontiers. To this end, it examines three promising "representative" sectors (land and forests, mining, and green hydrogen) to illustrate the vast opportunities available, but also the policy interventions and innovative capabilities necessary to realize this potential. It identifies key market failures, among them asymmetric information, coordination failures, and externalities, and then proposes three areas of policy intervention—the three I's (institutions, investment, and innovation)—where advances are needed if LAC is going to translate its resource riches into smart development.

Great uncertainty surrounds the energy transition and even the fundamentals of the international trade order. However, we believe LAC is living a moment of great opportunity when it could not only thrive, but also lead. We hope that the insights and robust framework offered by this report will serve as a valuable resource for policymakers, industry leaders, and stakeholders committed to advancing the region's economic development in harmony with environmental stewardship.

Benoit Bosquet
Regional Practice Director
Sustainable Development,
Latin America and the
Caribbean Region,
World Bank

William F. Maloney
Chief Economist
Latin America and the
Caribbean Region,
World Bank

Maria Marcela Silva
Regional Practice Director
Infrastructure,
Latin America and the
Caribbean Region,
World Bank

Acknowledgments

This report was prepared by the Office of the Chief Economist for Latin America and the Caribbean at the World Bank. It was led by William F. Maloney (Chief Economist), Guillermo Beylis (Senior Economist), and Nancy Lozano Gracia (Program Manager). The core team included Javier Aguilar (Senior Mining Specialist), Pierre Audinet (Lead Energy Specialist), Mariana Conte Grand (Senior Economist), Sara Diane Turner (Economist), and Joeri Frederick de Wit (Senior Economist).

Important contributions were provided by Sofia de Abreau Ferreira (Lead Social Development Specialist), Andrea Georgina Frassetto (Social Specialist), María Celeste Piñera (Social Specialist), Olle Östensson (Mining Specialist), Paulo De Sa (Mining Specialist), Edward William Bresnyan (Lead Agriculture Economist), Paula Restrepo Cadavid (Lead Economist), Vladimir Tafur Hernandez (Land Specialist, Consultant), Ivone Astrid Moreno Horta (Senior Land Administration Specialist), Samuel Kaspar Rosenow (Economist), Aicha Lompo (Consultant), and Jacob Wessel (Consultant).

David Hynes, Stephanie La Hoz Theuer, Santiago Ramírez Niembro, and Maia Hall from Adelphi contributed to the background paper, "Opportunities for Carbon Credits Markets in Land Use and Forests in Latin America and the Caribbean." Peter Hawthorne from Hawthorne Spatial, LLC, contributed to the background paper, "Improving Land Use for a Prosperous, Low-Carbon Latin America," extending modeling developed by the Natural Capital Project team, led by Stephen Polasky (University of Minnesota) and Mary Ruckelshaus (Stanford University) for the "Nature's Frontiers" report. Data on global and regional Integrated Assessment Modeling scenarios for decarbonization were provided by Luiz Bernardo C. S. Baptista and Rebecca Draeger de Oliveira. Olle Östensson contributed to the background paper, "Energy Transition Minerals in Latin America and the Caribbean." Luis Miguel Diazgranados, Nathalia Gama, Felipe Bonilla, and Justine Zitouni from Hinicio worked on the green hydrogen scorecard and country deep dives. Michael Mortiz, Ann-Kathrin Klaas, David Wohleben, and Nada Fadl from Energiewirtschaftliches Institut an der Universität zu Köln carried out work on green hydrogen cost analysis. Both analysis were used in the background paper, "Green Hydrogen in Latin America and the Caribbean".

The report greatly benefited from comments provided by Genevieve Connors (Practice Manager, Environment), Diego Arias (Practice Manager, Agriculture), Richard Damania (Chief Economist, Planet), Ana Paula Cusolito (Senior Economist), James Cust (Senior Economist), Franz Drees-Gross (Regional Practice Director), and Surbhi Goyal (Senior Energy Specialist).

Excellent administrative assistance was provided by Jacqueline Larrabure (Senior Program Assistant), Maria Caridad Gutierrez Cordoba (Senior Program Assistant), and Samia Benbouzid (Senior Program Assistant).

The team benefited from the guidance of Benoit Bosquet (Latin America and the Caribbean Regional Practice Director, Planet) and Maria Marcela Silva (Latin America and the Caribbean Regional Practice Director, Infrastructure). The report was edited by Erin Rupprecht Aylor and Benedict Mander.

About the Editors and Contributors

Editors

Guillermo Beylis is a Senior Economist in the Office of the Chief Economist, Latin America and the Caribbean, at the World Bank. He specializes in labor markets, with a focus on skills, gender, and inequality. He has published on many topics, including energy economics, digital transformation, informality, inequality, and labor market skills. He holds an MA and a PhD in economics from the University of California, Los Angeles, and a BA and an MA from the Universidad Torcuato di Tella, Buenos Aires, Argentina.

Nancy Lozano Gracia is a Program Manager at the World Bank's Institute for Economic Development. She has over 20 years of experience in economic policy and research, working across sectors with a focus on sustainable development and devising innovative tools and data to improve the understanding of sustainable development challenges and help identify priorities for action. She is also the Colead of the Global Solutions Group on Spatial Economics and Analytics of the Urban, Resilience, and Land Global Practice. She holds a PhD in applied economics from the University of Illinois and master's degrees in environmental and agricultural and resource economics from the University of Maryland and the Universidad de los Andes, Colombia.

Contributors

Javier Aguilar is a Senior Mining Specialist at the World Bank, where he leads mining policy reform engagements in Latin America and contributes to global initiatives on sustainable extractives and local economic development. With two decades of combined experience at the International Finance Corporation and the World Bank, he has provided strategic and operational leadership on mining governance, institutional reform, and community investment, with a focus on critical minerals and sustainable development. His work spans Eastern Africa,

South and Central America, and Central Asia. Prior to joining the World Bank, he worked in private consultancy at KPMG and as a founding partner of SAXgr, and he served in the Bolivian government as Undersecretary for Social Investments. He is an economist and holds a master's degree in local and regional development from the International Institute of Social Studies of Erasmus University, Rotterdam.

Mariana Conte Grand works as a Senior Economist for Environment, Latin America and the Caribbean Region, at the World Bank, and she is also a Professor at the University of CEMA in Buenos Aires. At the World Bank, she worked on the Argentina and Paraguay Country Climate and Development Reports and other analytic pieces on fire damages valuation, the impact of heat on health, sentiments and productivity, the quantification of exposure, and the vulnerability of trade-climate regulations for the region. She has published in books and academic journals, including *Ecological Economics*, *Ecological Indicators*, *Environment and Development Economics*, *Environmental Economics and Policy Studies*, and the *Journal of Benefit-Cost Analysis*. She was also a lead author of the *Fifth Assessment Report of the Intergovernmental Panel on Climate Change* and contributed to the Harvard Project on Climate Change. She holds a PhD in economics from the University of California, Los Angeles.

Sara Turner is an Economist for Environment, Latin America and the Caribbean Region, at the World Bank. Her work focuses on analyzing the economic impacts of climate change on the region and evaluating policy options to reduce these impacts. In her current role, she has led analytic work on costing infrastructure resilience to hurricanes, floods, and landslides in the Eastern Caribbean; has assessed the impacts of flooding on well-being in Argentina; and has contributed to the World Bank's Country Climate and Development Reports in Argentina, the Dominican Republic, Peru, and the Eastern Caribbean states of Dominica, Grenada, St. Lucia, and St. Vincent and the Grenadines. Before joining the World Bank, she completed her PhD at the Pardee RAND Graduate School in Los Angeles, California.

Joeri de Wit is a Senior Energy Economist in the Latin America and Caribbean Region for the World Bank. Since joining the World Bank in 2013, he has focused on developing knowledge on the topics of renewable energy, energy efficiency, power sector reform, energy subsidy reform, and industrial decarbonization. He holds a PhD in resource economics from the University of California, Davis, and master's degrees in economics from Erasmus University, Rotterdam, and the University of Chicago.

Executive Summary

Opportunities in the Energy Transition

The transition to a lower carbon global economy opens a window of opportunity for dynamic growth and job creation in Latin America and the Caribbean. Moving toward a net zero economy requires new products, energy sources, markets, and production processes. Crucially, the region is well positioned to take advantage of changing consumer demands and advancing technology. Global efforts to ensure that prices reflect carbon emissions favor a region with abundant renewable resources and green power grids because these assets boost the potential for greenshoring by attracting energy-intensive industries. The Latin America and the Caribbean region boasts not only almost a quarter of the world's standing forest but also ample renewable freshwater resources and fertile land, which are critical for both global decarbonization goals and regional economic growth. Furthermore, the energy transition depends heavily on mineral resources, such as lithium and copper, which the region has in abundance.

But such bountiful natural wealth is no silver bullet for development. To capitalize on the region's competitive advantages, its governments must develop a comprehensive set of policies that transform the region's legacy resource-driven model into one driven by resource and environmental efficiency and greater productive and innovation capabilities. This report examines three sectors that, while not comprehensive, nonetheless span a broad range of the opportunities presented to the region: land and forests that are both rich in biodiversity and represent an engine for growth; mining as both a legacy sector and one that is potentially entering a new phase; and green hydrogen (GH_2) as representative of a new industry. By studying these sectors closely, the report identifies several market failures—information asymmetry, lack of coordination, externalities, misaligned incentives, and more—that are relevant to all emerging sectors in the green transition. This exercise, in turn, gives rise to a tripartite policy framework to structure what might loosely be called a "green industrial policy" that focuses on necessary advances in the "three I's": institutions, investment, and innovation. Stronger institutions are needed to develop a new set of rules and regulations as well as a system of compatible incentives;

All dollars are US dollars unless otherwise indicated.

investment is required in infrastructure and key public goods to strengthen competitiveness and coordination; and innovation, through effective national innovation systems (NISs), is essential to engage the region in adopting, disseminating, and developing technologies.

Environmental and Economic Efficiency

Success in the new economy will require accounting for the environmental value or cost embedded in production processes. Therefore, this report uses a conceptual framework in which efficiency is measured in two dimensions: both the economic value and the environmental value generated by the use of resources. This idea is encapsulated in what the report describes as the economic-environmental production possibilities frontier (EE-PPF), which represents the outcomes that maximize both economic and environmental values.

The report proposes actions along the EE-PPF in three increasingly complex stages: catching up, shifting outward, and creating new frontiers. Examination of the three sectors chosen—land and forests, mining, and GH_2—illustrates the specific challenges associated with each stage.

First, Latin America and the Caribbean must catch up with the existing EE-PPF by increasing efficiency in allocating resources and long-term planning to manage natural capital more sustainably. For far too long, the region has grown by depleting its natural capital rather than by investing in the technology and productive practices that would improve overall efficiency and protect its riches. Analysis in this report indicates that Latin America and the Caribbean is the world's lowest-ranking region in terms of economic efficiency in land use, suggesting there are significant environmental and economic gains available for the region by catching up to the EE-PPF.

Second, Latin America and the Caribbean must shift the EE-PPF outward, particularly in sectors expected to grow during the transition, by upgrading existing production processes with more sustainable technologies. Often, despite high environmental efficiency, products still impose significant environmental costs, so producers will need to upgrade processes to remain competitive. The mining sector serves as a great example for the region. Despite the sector's importance in several countries, opportunities for technological upgrades and innovation have been squandered in the past, leaving Latin America and the Caribbean with weak innovation systems and exports dominated by primary unprocessed goods.

Third, Latin America and the Caribbean needs to cultivate new sources of (green) economic dynamism through innovation in products and technologies, thereby creating new markets. With the right enabling environment and strong capabilities, lagging countries will be able to leapfrog ahead of developed countries by quickly adopting, diffusing, and improving on emerging technologies. Currently, Latin America and the Caribbean underperforms in innovation because countries focus more on trade protectionism and subsidies than on competition. As an example, the region has an opportunity to leverage its huge potential in renewable energy sources (RES) into new products such as GH_2 and its derivatives.

Seizing the Window of Opportunity: Three Illustrative Examples

Land and forests: Leveraging natural capital for greener markets

The initial example aims to cast light on the challenges associated with catching up with the existing EE-PPF by increasing efficiency in allocating resources and long-term planning. Latin America and the Caribbean's land and forests are critical both for global decarbonization goals and for regional economic growth and poverty reduction, while they also provide important ecosystem services. Yet Latin America and the Caribbean is the world's lowest-ranking region in terms of economic efficiency in land use. High rates of deforestation, coupled with pressures from agriculture on land and forest resources, are jeopardizing environmental assets. Nevertheless, the Latin America and the Caribbean region has great potential to improve land-based economic outcomes without harming environmental objectives: Better land allocation and management could increase annual income from agriculture, grazing, and forestry by approximately $94 billion. Alternatively, the region could sequester 25 billion additional tons of carbon dioxide equivalent per year (worth around $1 trillion) without harming economic production. More sustainable and efficient land use will require a combination of strategies, given diverse and sometimes conflicting pressures, while managing risks and trade-offs will need creative and collaborative responses from all concerned.

- **Institutions** must be strong to protect natural capital and its benefits. Weak land rights, including carbon rights, pose a major barrier, leading to weaker enforcement of regulations, reduced credit, and lower investment, while also driving poverty and food insecurity. Land speculation, cattle pasture expansion, forest conversion for subsistence and commercial crops, and clearing for mining are driving high rates of deforestation. Further, deforestation is exacerbated by weak enforcement of environmental laws and regulations.

- **Investments** and supportive public policies are important. Despite the obvious long-term benefits, transitioning between different uses of land to make it more efficient has high costs, especially in Latin America and the Caribbean, where costs fall disproportionately on the poor. Investments will be needed in information systems, agricultural technologies, and monitoring and enforcement.

- **Innovation** is also key, with research and development (R&D) investments and new technologies supporting the transition to more efficient land allocation. The direction of agricultural innovation and the strength of governance can lead to contrasting effects on deforestation. Innovation in tracking and tracing products, combined with improved monitoring of deforestation, can ensure continued access to existing markets while opening doors to new markets.

Minerals to support the energy transition: Upgrading existing production processes

This second example is intended to show what Latin America and the Caribbean can do to tackle the next stage of development by shifting the EE-PPF outward, which requires upgrading existing production processes with more sustainable technologies. Growing global demand for the region's abundant energy transition minerals will create opportunities for adding more value to serve both regional and global markets, and to develop downstream products like batteries. Latin America and the Caribbean must upgrade current production systems to expand the EE-PPF, improve efficiency and competitiveness, and ensure continued access to international markets. Emissions from mining remain high, environmental footprints are large, and social risks run deep. As for all industrial processes in the region, innovation is required to make mining more environmentally and socially sustainable, and Latin America and the Caribbean must broaden its participation in global value chains to leverage its natural resources.

- **Institutions** must be strong to avoid the large environmental and social (E&S) costs of increased production. A lack of strong regulatory frameworks and strong enforcement mechanisms could aggravate negative externalities affecting land, flora and fauna, water management, and local communities. High levels of socio-environmental conflicts in mining cause production delays. But sustainable mining offers an opportunity to generate revenues that enable greater investment in infrastructure and community benefits. Institutions are also needed to ensure macroeconomic stability, mitigate volatile commodity revenues, and avoid procyclical spending, as well as to prevent coordination failures and promote value chain development, both upstream and downstream.

- **Investments** in information and complementary public goods and services are needed to incentivize exploration, enabling future production to expand. A good geological knowledge base is key, while transparent and efficient legal regimes, including fast authorization procedures, are essential for new exploration investment. Complementary infrastructure investment is also needed to support greater and more sustainable production, such as by connecting mines to RES and digital services.

- **Innovation** can help increase the use of clean energy, which remains low owing to concerns about energy intermittency, high switching costs, and regulatory limitations. More innovation to limit water use and assure its quality is also needed. The radical innovations needed to boost productivity, profitability, and environmental performance will require highly connected innovation ecosystems.

Leveraging green energy to support new markets: Green hydrogen

The last example used in this report provides insights into how Latin America and the Caribbean can confront the third stage of leveraging new economic opportunities: innovation and the creation of new markets. This stage involves creating a new EE-PPF that didn't exist before—in this case, GH_2. The potential for the region to become a green energy powerhouse is huge given its abundant supply of renewable energy. Latin America and the Caribbean can leverage this advantage by focusing innovation on new electricity-intensive uses, such as producing GH_2. The experience of GH_2 illustrates the challenges of developing new markets with a nascent technology: Despite its great potential for accelerating the green transition, the extent of its growth remains unclear. But there is great optimism for the potential of GH_2 in Latin America and the Caribbean, both as a means to decarbonize domestic economies and as a source of export revenue. Three factors will determine the region's comparative advantage. First, the abundance of RES can enable lower costs and strengthen international competitiveness; second, geography can influence trade patterns by affecting transportation modes and costs; and third, the weighted average cost of capital is another key component of the cost of producing GH_2.

This report developed a scorecard for Latin America and the Caribbean's GH_2–enabling environment to assess the level of market potential, bottlenecks, and policy action areas: Chile has the most supportive ecosystem of all, followed by Colombia, Uruguay, and Brazil. Governments must play an important role in removing barriers to the development of GH_2, including high production costs, to align enabling environments with ambitions and to remove uncertainty.

- **Institutions** are required to reduce market risk and stimulate private sector investment. That means establishing regulatory and policy frameworks to address problems like information asymmetry. Internationally compatible standards and certification are also lacking. Regional coordination on regulatory frameworks to facilitate cross-border trade could help markets achieve scale. Long-term policies to lower the costs of capital could also have an important effect on the viability of GH_2 projects.

- **Investments** could strengthen Latin America and the Caribbean's comparative advantage. To avoid compromising the decarbonization of the grid, a massive and rapid scale-up of renewable power will be needed. Large upfront investments in infrastructure for transport, storage, and conversion of GH_2 to connect market actors could resolve coordination failures and create positive externalities associated with network economies.

- **Innovation** requires government support customized to national strengths and needs. Improving GH_2 technology is complex, requiring sophisticated capabilities from firms and well-designed policies to support R&D. While regional GH_2 innovation is lagging, emerging leaders such as Brazil, Chile, and Colombia are investing in R&D with a focus on the energy transition.

The Way Forward: Institutions, Investment, and Innovation

To lay the foundations for sustainable and inclusive growth, the Latin America and the Caribbean region must focus on ongoing, fast-paced changes in prices, regulations, preferences, and technology. If the region is to advance successfully through the three stages surrounding the EE-PPF, it must decarbonize production, export sustainable goods, and invest in green NISs. Although each sector faces specific obstacles, there are clearly common challenges that jeopardize all sectors. Market failures that must be addressed across the board include asymmetric information, coordination challenges, and the management of externalities and lack of public goods. These failures often lead to underinvestment, preventing markets from reaching scale to compete with traditionally produced goods. Therefore, regardless of the sector in question, the transition to a new economic development model almost inevitably means addressing the three I's (institutions, investment, and innovation).

Institutions

In the new economy, solid institutions are crucial for addressing market failures and the inefficient allocation of resources. The right policy and regulatory frameworks must be built to guide and incentivize actions while protecting people and the environment. Externalities must be addressed through the establishment of clear property rights and strong regulatory frameworks. This effort will enable private sector participation and attract international investment, especially with supportive public policy—like taxes and subsidies—and effective enforcement of rules and regulations. Institutions can also resolve failures of coordination and asymmetric information by providing needed transparency, reliable information systems, and better communication between public and private actors. Better access to information will lead to better policy decisions and more effective implementation.

Establish new rules for a new economy

Given the negative externalities of certain economic activities, a new set of "rules of the game," effective enforcement, and public policies that shape the right incentives are needed to protect the value of natural capital. Clear property rights are a prerequisite for addressing externalities and efficiently allocating resources—particularly in land and carbon credit markets. Land titling helps enforcement, credit, and investment in productive activity, while undesignated land is especially vulnerable to deforestation. To improve land rights, cadastral databases need to be updated and more land titles granted to local communities. Strong environmental frameworks are needed to protect standing forests and support regeneration of degraded lands. Legal frameworks could incorporate ecosystem services as part of the standards for regulating E&S evaluation of projects.

New rules can make existing production processes more efficient and sustainable, especially in the mining sector, given the increasing demand for energy transition minerals and the environmental impact of their production. Latin America and the Caribbean has made good progress on including E&S impact assessments of mining projects in legal frameworks. Policy can also support the decarbonization of production by promoting renewable energy. The development of new markets and technologies also requires regulatory frameworks to define how they will function. Here, there is great social value in policy experimentation and regulatory learning. The emerging carbon credit markets are a good example of a new market with diverse regulatory approaches globally, with as-yet unclear outcomes. Policy makers must balance the value of learning about policy effectiveness with the need to provide stability and clarity to market actors in order to stimulate investment.

Coordinate to accelerate the transformation

Coordination between diverse stakeholders is imperative. Policy makers can play a key role by establishing institutions that foster communication, align incentives, and induce coordination. Enhancing coordination within the public sector—both horizontally and vertically—can align incentives and reduce the unintended consequences of policies, addressing market inefficiencies. A regional approach could help develop capabilities faster and more efficiently, enabling sectors to achieve scale and savings on learning and enforcement costs, while making monitoring and verification more efficient.

Coordination between governments and firms is also key. But developing new technologies requires an effective NIS, in which companies, universities, and research centers interact. In mining, coordination between public and private actors (and local communities) has led to improved governance and sustainable development strategies. When new technologies emerge, coordination can prevent markets from failing. Demand and supply must be fostered simultaneously; again, the right regulatory frameworks and an effective NIS are important. The GH_2 market shows how national and regional coordination can help develop a new technology.

Increase sustainability through incentives, from enforcement to subsidies

Protecting property rights and E&S regulations is only part of the equation. Governments should invest in monitoring and enforcement technologies and services, while legal frameworks should establish economic penalties that reflect the value of natural capital and ecosystem services. A high probability of getting caught will limit negative externalities and the misallocation of resources; deforestation can decline rapidly if monitoring and enforcement are strong. Governments can also shape incentives by designing subsidies and taxes that align private and social values.

Land use and forest markets are riddled with externalities, causing serious inefficiencies. But some countries in Latin America and the Caribbean, like Costa Rica, have addressed deforestation challenges by establishing a consistent set of incentives. Adjustments to the valuation of land can rectify discrepancies between private and public valuations rebalancing incentives in favor of conservation. In addition, making agricultural cash transfers conditional on sustainable techniques and integrating forest technical assistance into agricultural extension programs could help increase the use of sustainable forest management principles. Furthermore, new digital monitoring, reporting, and verification (MRV) technologies could unlock new opportunities for carbon credit markets. Efforts to adjust incentive systems will need to be sensitive to the ways in which they operate in different contexts. Policies designed to reduce incentives for relying on extensive, deforestation-linked agricultural systems will differ from those designed to increase incentives to adopt more productive, capital-intensive agricultural systems. At the same time, policy makers will need to be mindful of the effect of productivity gains in agriculture on incentives to deforest—agricultural productivity gains in some regions of the Amazon may increase incentives to deforest in that area, even if overall deforestation declines nationally (Hanusch 2023).

Focus on inclusion to ensure that no one is left behind

The resource-driven development model of Latin America and the Caribbean has often compromised Indigenous communities and vulnerable populations. Not only could these communities be better protected, but inclusion may even be economically desirable for the region. Increased land use efficiency requires complementary actions to avoid having the costs of maximizing carbon storage fall disproportionately on the poor. The management of forests by Indigenous peoples, within a stronger general framework for land rights, can help reduce deforestation and support inclusion. Similarly, strong community involvement with both the public and private sectors in mining could be replicated elsewhere, as could policies to address gender disparity in employment. But efforts at the regulatory and project level must be aligned with existing agreements.

Investment

Governments must make complementary investments in infrastructure and other productive public goods. Markets are still incomplete and imperfect, and the social benefits of developing them will not be incorporated into private decisions. Such investments can help lock in private investment and lower technological and political risks, while creating more productive and competitive markets. Complementary public goods could also reduce informational asymmetries and coordination failures by strengthening linkages between actors in a particular sector. Latin America and the Caribbean's infrastructure is deficient, even without considering the energy transition: The region needs to invest about 3 percent of gross domestic product in water and sanitation, energy, transport, and telecommunications infrastructure every year through 2030.

Harness the power of information to enable green markets

Poor information is an important obstacle for the green economy. Public access to information could help the region design better policies, protect vulnerable populations, foster more research and innovation, and empower the private sector to make better investments. Consumers may prefer to pay for "green" products yet lack information; producers could respond by using input suppliers that can meet new standards. By imposing new information requirements in international trade, credible certification mechanisms allow producers to capture "green premiums," input suppliers to gain market share, and producers to develop new technologies and products.

In the new economy, the sustainability of goods and services is another dimension of quality. Standards can minimize uncertainties over quality; adhering to them and obtaining certification by internationally accredited bodies will be crucial. Better information also supports innovation and stimulates productivity, sustainability, and more efficient use of resources. Establishing a baseline for resource use and for the environmental impact of production can improve sustainability policies. Meanwhile, governments could develop better regulations to internalize externalities and could become more effective at monitoring and enforcement.

Build a "green" national quality infrastructure to support greener, internationally recognized local markets

Governments must invest in a "green" national quality infrastructure (NQI), a key public good for reducing informational asymmetries. First, that means acquiring the necessary capabilities, such as creating quality certification processes. Then, governments should establish standards and perform conformity assessments. Reliable public information systems and effective MRV can support enforcement efforts and incentivize the efficient use of natural resources. Given increased demand for sustainable products in international markets, this quality assurance can help ensure continued access. Advanced information and MRV systems are also key to unlocking new markets: Uncertainty over new technologies can hamper long-term offtake agreements. An effective green NQI is also a prerequisite for technological innovation and for upgrading production processes.

Use investments to complement and coordinate policies

To prevent undeveloped markets due to a failure to coordinate investments, governments can create institutions or provide enabling infrastructure or public goods that raise the productivity of private investments. Complementary investments in public infrastructure—including basic transport, logistics, or digital infrastructure—can make exports more competitive and maintain production value chains with a low carbon footprint. Quality infrastructure paired with abundant, reliable, and affordable renewable energy can be a magnet for new investments, leveraging recent trends in greenshoring. In the mining sector, the proximity of many mines to solar energy sources may require government investments in transmission lines or energy storage solutions; investments in roads and logistics can also leverage potential. Alternative transportation—such as rail networks for mines or river transportation in the Amazon— also should be considered.

Coordinating investments could lower deployment costs for infrastructure. Network industries can contribute by making their own infrastructure available to telecom operators to install parallel digital networks. This action could also improve the effectiveness of enforcement agencies; for example, digital MRV tools could help prevent illegal deforestation. Reliable, affordable, and high-quality connectivity requires that governments facilitate not only the "hard" infrastructure (like internet cables or data centers), but also the complementary "soft" infrastructure, such as a labor force skilled in digital capabilities or technology centers and business associations.

Innovation

Currently, Latin America and the Caribbean underperforms in both innovation efforts and outcomes, even considering the region's income level. But with the right enabling environment and a capacity to quickly adopt, adapt, invent, and diffuse emerging technologies, Latin America and the Caribbean will get the chance to leapfrog ahead of developed countries. That result requires building a green NIS that promotes interaction among all those involved in the development, distribution, and application of new technologies, including governments, the private sector, public research institutes, and universities. An effective NIS can help firms improve the allocation of resources by developing new production processes and technologies that can expand production while also reducing the environmental impact. Crucially, a strong NIS is essential to opening new markets. Investing in sharpening the capabilities of both governments and firms is key. Policies supporting innovation need to be matched with the capabilities of firms so that they can climb the "capabilities escalator," on which firms advance from basic production capabilities to the ability to adopt and adapt technologies, and finally to invent.

Strengthening government capabilities

The type, responsibilities, and coordination of the agencies and organizations that design and implement innovation policy are crucial, but Latin America and the Caribbean cannot just copy from advanced countries. The same applies to the policies themselves, which also require clear rationales, goals, and objectives, taking into account government implementation capacity. But some important principles can be adapted to the local context: Boards of directors should represent diverse interests; staff must have the right skills; incentive structures must prioritize quality and output goals; long-term funding and commitment from governments are key; and policy design must be consistent over time. A dynamic feedback loop framework—from design to implementation, to evaluation and back to design—is recommended.

Strengthening private capabilities

There are striking contrasts between and within the region's countries when it comes to NIS maturity and innovation capabilities. Most firms in Latin America and the Caribbean are generally at the lower end of the capabilities spectrum, with just a few—especially in the agriculture technology sector—reaching the highest levels. Policies targeting firms should match existing skills, and mechanisms are needed to gradually strengthen capabilities, especially for laggards.

Catching up to the frontier: Moving from basic production to adoption of new technologies

For firms at the bottom of the capabilities escalator, innovation policy should focus on basic managerial and organizational practices, process improvements, and machinery upgrades, with little investment in R&D. It is important to promote the diffusion of best practices and the adoption of technology. Governments can help not only by providing digital infrastructure, but also by developing apps and services that improve productivity and sustainability. Further, government can help workers develop digital skills to use new technology and can provide incubators and accelerators for entrepreneurs. Pricing and compensation mechanisms that include the right incentives are another area where governments can guide the private sector. Crucially, investments in science, technology, engineering, and mathematics skills; green NQIs; and business environment reforms should be made in parallel.

Pushing the frontier: Moving from adoption to invention

More advanced firms should have well-established technology centers to keep up with the latest developments. An effective NIS should help firms not only to adopt global innovations, but also to develop home-grown innovations that confront local challenges. A cooperative approach is needed with a highly connected innovation ecosystem that includes firms, suppliers, government, industry associations, academia, and incubators. Technology extension centers and business associations are more effective when they are the result of public-private partnerships, and successful institutions tend to be subnational and close to specific sector clusters. Governments can also provide services that help local firms connect internationally, such as export promotion agencies.

Arriving at the new frontiers: Leading in invention and new technology

At the technological frontier, innovation policy should focus on enabling advanced development capabilities and invention. Three types of instruments can promote R&D. First is tax incentives, yet they primarily benefit larger firms and promote limited NIS interaction. While easy to implement, authorities must be aware and carefully monitor such incentives. Grants, the second instrument, are preferable to tax incentives, especially when paired with mentoring or technical assistance. Their effectiveness varies, however, but they have shown to have input and behavioral additionality in several cases. Third, public research institutes support both applied and basic R&D, but they require significant technological capabilities and are most effective when they have clear goals.

The GH_2 sector illustrates the complexity of challenges at the R&D stage well—it is costly and has uncertain outcomes, although costs will likely fall through economies of scale, innovation, and learning. Carbon credit markets are another good example, in which a government learning framework using a regulatory sandbox could help inform policy makers about their effectiveness and possible adjustments. The most potent investment is an NIS capable of bringing new technologies to the world.

An Attainable Goal

Latin America and the Caribbean has long been a region of great promise, yet lasting prosperity has remained elusive. As a new window of opportunity for the region to advance presents itself in the form of the energy transition—perhaps the region's best chance yet given its unparalleled natural resources—this report aims to make a contribution to smoothing the path toward inclusive economic growth. The insights provided here are intended to help the region progress toward what the report calls the EE-PPF, and to push that boundary outward even further. Although the three sectors of land and forests, mining, and GH_2 are intended merely as examples, they nevertheless yield valuable lessons for the wider economy, framed here around the three I's of institutions, investment, and innovation. If applied comprehensively, it is expected the region's goal of enduring prosperity will become an attainable one.

Reference

Hanusch, M., ed. 2023. *A Balancing Act for Brazil's Amazonian States: An Economic Memorandum*. Washington, DC: World Bank. https://doi.org/10.1596/978-1 -4648-1909-4.

Abbreviations

AFOLU	agriculture, forest, and other land use
AI	artificial intelligence
APS	announced pledges scenario
CBAM	Carbon Border Adjustment Mechanism
CCS	carbon capture and storage
CIESIN	Center for International Earth Science Information Network
CCS	carbon capture and storage
CO_2e	carbon dioxide equivalent
CORFO	Production Development Corporation (Chile)
COVID-19	coronavirus
CWON	Changing Wealth of Nations
DFPs	deforestation-free products
DLE	direct lithium extraction
E&S	environmental and social
EE-PPF	economic-environmental production possibilities frontier
EITI	Extractive Industries Transparency Initiative
EMBRAPA	Brazilian Agricultural Research Corporation
ESG	environmental, social, and governance
ESMAP	Energy Sector Management Assistance Program
ETMs	energy transition minerals
ETS	emissions trading system
EU	European Union
EU-28	European Union before the United Kingdom departed
EU CBAM	European Union Carbon Border Adjustment Mechanism
EVs	electric vehicles
FAO	Food and Agriculture Organization (United Nations)
FCEV	fuel cell electric vehicles
FILAC	Fund for the Development of Indigenous Peoples of Latin America and the Caribbean

FPIC	free and prior informed consent
GDP	gross domestic product
GH_2	green hydrogen
GHG	greenhouse gas
$GtCO_2e$	gigatons of carbon dioxide equivalent
GW	gigawatt(s)
H_2	hydrogen
ha	hectare
HLI	Hydrogen Lighthouse Initiative
IBAMA	Institute of Environment and Renewable Natural Resources (Brazil)
ILO	International Labour Organization
INCRA	National Institute of Colonization and Agrarian Reform
IRA	Inflation Reduction Act
ISO	International Organization for Standardization
IUCN	International Union for Conservation of Nature
k^2	square kilometers
kg	kilogram(s)
$kg/CO_2\ eq/kg\ H_2$	kilograms of carbon dioxide per kilogram of hydrogen
$kg\ H_2$	kilograms hydrogen
kWh	kilowatt-hour
LAC	Latin America and the Caribbean
LCOH	levelized cost of hydrogen production
MGAP	Ministry of Livestock, Agriculture and Fishing (Uruguay)
MMT	million metric tons
MNC	multinational corporation
MRV	monitoring, reporting, and verification
Mt	metric tons
$MtCO_2e$	metric tons of carbon dioxide equivalent
MtCu	metric tons of copper ore
NDC	Nationally Determined Contributions
NIS	national innovation system
NQI	national quality infrastructure
NZE	net zero emissions
O&G	oil and gas
OECD	Organisation for Economic Co-operation and Development
PES	payments for ecosystem services
PNH_2	National Program of Hydrogen (Brazil)

PPA	private purchase agreement
PPF	production possibilities frontier
PPP	purchasing power parity
PRI	public research institute
PRODAF	Program for Rural Development and Family Agriculture (Argentina)
PV	photovoltaic
R&D	research and development
RCA	revealed comparative advantage
RE	renewable energy
REE	rare earth elements
RES	renewable energy sources
RMI	Responsible Minerals Initiative
SEA	Environmental Assessment Service (Chile)
STEM	science, technology, engineering, and mathematics
tCO_2e	tons of carbon dioxide equivalent
TFP	total factor productivity
TWh	terawatt-hours
UK	United Kingdom
UNEP	United Nations Environment Programme
UN-REDD	United Nations Collaborative Program to Reduce Emissions from Deforestation and Forest Degradation in Developing Countries
US	United States
USGS	United States Geological Survey
WACC	weighted average cost of capital
YLB	Yacimientos del Litio Bolivianos

All dollar amounts are in US dollars unless otherwise indicated.

Introduction

Window of Opportunity

Building a net zero economy is a daunting task that requires a major technological and institutional shift. A decarbonized world needs new products, technologies, energy sources, processes for making existing goods, and markets. Essentially, goods and services that were not previously within the scope of the market economy are now being valued and priced.

For policy makers in Latin America and the Caribbean, this shift is a historic opportunity for economic and technological catch-up. In Schumpeterian economics literature, this is known as a window of opportunity (Perez and Soete 1988). In effect, exogenous changes in conditions enable firms to catch up with industry leaders and, once they have developed the right capabilities, even "leapfrog" them. Although there are several types of windows of opportunity, the transition toward net zero is characterized by a technological shift and changes in demand that level the playing field for all countries (Lee 2019).

Success in the new economy, then, requires that the environmental value or cost that is embedded in goods and production processes be explicitly accounted for. Sustainability or carbon footprints can be interpreted as an extra dimension of the quality of a product for which consumers are now willing to pay. Therefore, this report uses a conceptual framework with two dimensions (Damania et al. 2023): both the economic *and* the environmental value generated by the use of resources. The economic-environmental production possibilities frontier (EE-PPF) can then be defined as all the production outcomes that jointly maximize the economic and environmental values in any given economy. One axis represents the traditional notion of productivity or economic efficiency; the other represents environmental efficiency.

This report maps this framework onto three specific sectors—land use and forests; mining; and green hydrogen (GH_2)—which serve simply as examples to illustrate and assess the challenges and opportunities that the broader economy faces as the world embarks on the green transition. An exhaustive survey of the impact of the transition on all sectors is unnecessary for the purposes of this report; lessons from the experience of these three sectors can be drawn, modified as appropriate, and applied elsewhere.

Needless to say, it will be challenging for Latin America and the Caribbean to take advantage of these opportunities and to leverage them to foster sustainable and inclusive growth. Far-reaching global changes are occurring as the Latin America and the Caribbean region continues to struggle with low growth rates that are insufficient to tackle poverty and inequality.[1] The issue goes beyond factor accumulation (capital and labor), which has actually contributed to reducing the income gap with the United States. The problem, instead, is driven by sluggish growth in total factor productivity, which measures the efficiency of the factors of production (Fernández-Arias 2014). So not only does the Latin America and the Caribbean region still need to become more economically efficient; on top of that, it must now also solve new sustainability challenges.

The good news for the region is that its rich natural capital provides a competitive advantage in this new economy. Latin America and the Caribbean boasts more than 23 percent of the world's standing forests,[2] large reserves of lithium and copper (USGS 2023), and enormous potential in additional renewable energy (RE) generation on top of an electricity matrix that is already considerably cleaner than those in other regions. The region is clearly well positioned to leverage the green transition.

A quick review of the region's development history makes it clear that, by itself, the region's natural wealth is not enough to generate inclusive and sustained growth. The new possibilities emerging are no different: they will require the design of appropriate incentives, policies, and investments, as well as the development of productive and innovation capabilities. Success in this new economy requires a deep transformation of the Latin America and the Caribbean region's legacy resource-driven model, with actions along three steps: first, catching up to the EE-PPF; second, shifting the frontier outward, particularly in sectors that are expected to grow significantly during the transition; and third, cultivating new sources of (green) economic dynamism through innovation in products and technologies, as well as creating markets for newly valued environmental services (figure I.1).

The first step requires a determined focus on improving economic and environmental efficiency, allocating resources more effectively, and crafting long-term plans to manage natural capital more sustainably. For far too long, the region has grown by depleting its natural capital rather than by investing in the technology and productive practices that would improve overall efficiency and protect its riches. Unmanaged expansion of the agricultural frontier, for example, results in deforestation, while the overuse of fertilizers causes water pollution and overtaxing of freshwater resources. Both problems significantly reduce the productivity of surrounding areas while harming soil quality and hydrological cycles.

Figure I.1   Opportunities for a Deep Transformation: Three Possibilities

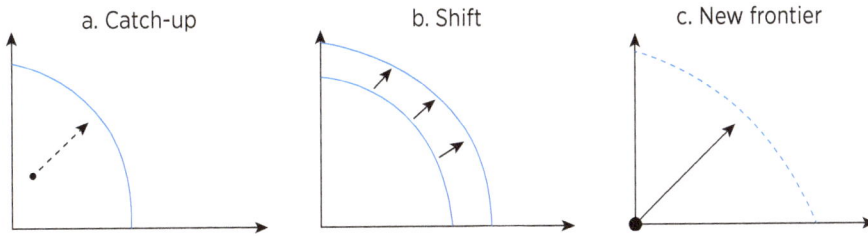

Source: Original figure for this publication.

The second step is to upgrade existing production processes through technologies that lower carbon content and make products more sustainable. Often, despite high environmental efficiency, products still impose significant environmental costs. These costs are particularly concerning for products for which demand is likely to grow during the transition. As this report shows, changes in consumer preferences and production technologies will channel global demand toward greener inputs and intermediate goods (McMillan, Rodrik, and Verduzco-Gallo 2014). Producers will need to upgrade processes to remain competitive, but opportunities like these have been squandered in the past. The commodity supercycle of the 2000s generated extraordinary rents that were rapidly distributed to consumption instead of investment and technological upgrades. As a result, the region remains a technological laggard with weak innovation systems, a lack of connection to global value chains, and export baskets heavily dependent on primary nonmanufactured commodities.

The third and final step is to recognize—and act on—the fact that the ground is now fertile for new markets to emerge. The green transition will be a period of intense innovation, during which new technologies can quickly displace old ones. The underlying opportunity, then, is for countries with the right enabling environment and strong capabilities to leapfrog ahead of developed countries by quickly adopting, diffusing, and improving on emerging technologies. Currently, Latin America and the Caribbean underperforms in innovation, even considering its income level (Cirera and Maloney 2017). Average expenditures on research and development (R&D) in the region are 0.6 percent of gross domestic product (GDP) annually. Even for the regional leader, Brazil (which spends about 1.6 percent of GDP on R&D), the outcomes are underwhelming. The current development model has limited innovation by focusing more on unconditional trade protections and subsidies than on competition.

The challenges associated with these three steps are illustrated through a discussion of the three selected sectors. This report uses the land use and forests sector to analyze the first step in more detail, mining for the second step, and GH_2 for the third. In this way, the report seeks to throw light on some of the opportunities that are emerging during the green transition, and it points at what it will take for the region to capitalize on its natural capital and competitive advantages. Clearly, there are many more latent opportunities for the region that are not covered in this report. The examples highlighted, however, showcase several development challenges the region will face, and they provide lessons and insights applicable to the development of the broader net zero economy.

In the case of the initial example used to elucidate the first step, new analysis finds that Latin America and the Caribbean is the world's lowest-ranking region in terms of land use efficiency for agriculture, livestock, and forestry. Moreover, while most countries in the region are performing relatively well on environmental efficiency, high rates of deforestation, coupled with pressures from agriculture on land and forest resources, are putting pressure on environmental assets. Latin America and the Caribbean's comparative advantage in this sector lies in its rich natural capital: almost half of its surface is covered by forests (FAO 2020), and it accounts for 23 percent of all forests worldwide (ECLAC 2021). The importance of the agriculture, forest, and other land use (AFOLU) sector also lies in the vital ecosystem services it provides and its ability to reduce vulnerability to physical climate risks at the local level;[3] it is therefore critical to the livelihoods of local communities and for climate adaptation strategies (IPCC 2022). The region has the largest reserves of arable land in the world, including some undeveloped areas that could be sustainably used for agriculture (Morris, Sebastian, and Perego 2020). A decline in productivity growth over the past decade and stagnating shares of global agricultural trade undermine the region's position as a major agricultural producer and have resulted in increasing reliance on input intensification and, to a lesser extent, land expansion for agriculture.

As for the second step, the mining sector, particularly for lithium and copper, provides an excellent illustration of the challenges. The green transition will increase demand for minerals that are abundant in the region (such as copper and lithium), creating opportunities for further value addition to serve both regional and global demand. Yet even the most technologically advanced mines still impose significant environmental burdens. To manage increased production in a way that is both environmentally and socially sustainable, extractive activities will have to be rethought, and innovation will be needed to push the EE-PPF outward.

At the same time, for the mining sector to better leverage natural resources into productive value chains, it will be necessary to integrate sustainability and inclusion targets into production processes. Productive linkages can also help economies diversify and increase the sustainability and complexity of export baskets. Particularly for sectors that stand to benefit from the green transition, such as copper and lithium mining, there are opportunities to evolve along the supply chain, from exporting primary commodities to producing higher value-added inputs and goods needed for the energy transition (solar panels, wind turbines, batteries, electric vehicles, and so on). So far, Latin America and the Caribbean has forgone opportunities for diversification and growth that other countries, such as the United States and Japan, have seized very successfully (Maloney and Valencia Caicedo 2022; Maloney and Zambrano 2021; World Bank 2022).

For the last of the three steps, this report examines the large potential of the region in RE and the development of GH_2, since it provides a timely example of the challenges of developing a completely new market with nascent technology. The global move toward decarbonization has highlighted the need to prioritize an increased share of renewables in the energy mix of all countries, and GH_2 can help accelerate this transition. Currently, hydrogen (H_2) is primarily used in industrial processes to produce other goods, such as ammonia. While at present H_2's use as an energy carrier is marginal, its role in the global energy mix is likely to increase significantly—although it remains unclear by how much. This uncertainty stems from the technology's relatively nascent stage of development and the difficulty in predicting future demand, which will depend on global progress in decarbonization. These are common challenges facing the emergence of all new markets.

In identifying the actions needed to catch up to the EE-PPF, upgrade production processes to expand the EE-PPF, and lay the foundations for new markets to flourish, this report proposes a tripartite framework to evaluate challenges and opportunities for action: institutions, investment, and innovation.

Strong **institutions** will be necessary to develop the green economy. A new set of rules and regulations, as well as a compatible system of incentives, will be key to cementing an environmental dimension into the development model. Reliable monitoring, reporting, and verification systems and credible traceability and certification mechanisms are also essential inputs. Credible monitoring can (a) help ensure that resources are allocated efficiently and (b) support the growth of new markets and prove that processes have been upgraded to cleaner technologies. This monitoring will be necessary to reduce perceived risks and uncertainty and to enable the capture of green premiums, the avoidance of carbon-related import taxes, and compliance with deforestation-free regulations that could otherwise limit market access. Equally important is institutional design that can help address externalities and coordination failures as well as incentivize the upgrading of production processes and the emergence of new markets.[4]

Governments can also enable the new economy by **investing** in key infrastructure and other public goods. To gain competitiveness in sustainable products, the private sector will require good-quality public infrastructure. The construction and maintenance of roads and railways can increase efficiency in markets such as critical minerals. By sending the right signals and providing mechanisms for risk reduction, public investments through careful strategic planning can solve coordination failures that often plague new and emerging markets. The significant shift in demand for skills across sectors means that governments must help prepare the required labor force. From strengthening the region's scientific and engineering knowledge base to developing government capabilities to design and enforce regulations in new markets, to fostering the necessary managerial and entrepreneurial skills, governments have an important role to play.

To seize this window of opportunity, countries must be able to adapt to a moving EE-PPF by developing national **innovation** systems and productive capabilities for the new economy. At first, they can adopt and disseminate foreign technologies, but developing the capabilities that will then allow them to innovate and develop local technologies will be crucial to set the stage for future growth.

This report contains five chapters. The first chapter discusses the "greening winds" that are reshaping economies around the world, reviewing recent changes in regulation, preferences, and technology. The second chapter focuses on the challenges faced in the sectors of land use and forests, mining, and GH_2, which are intended as examples that yield lessons for all sectors. The final three chapters discuss the actions needed to address those challenges in three priority areas: institutions, investment, and innovation.

Notes

1. Over the past two decades, Latin America's resource-driven model of development has not delivered long-term, sustainable, and inclusive growth; only a short-lived growth acceleration was observed during the commodity supercycle of the 2000s. Over the past decade, the region has produced an average growth rate of 2.2 percent, inequality remains high (ranging from a Gini coefficient of 0.505 in Central America to 0.417 in the Southern Cone), and poverty has barely budged, hovering around 30 percent (poverty measured at the $6.85 poverty line, 2017 purchasing power parity; PPP)
2. World Bank calculations from the Changing Wealth of Nations (CWON) dataset, 2021.
3. Ecosystem services are defined as the direct and indirect goods or services provided to humans by a natural system. Examples include water purification; water cycle regulation; flood risk protection; pollination; food production; medicine; recreation; therapeutic, spiritual, or religious uses; soil formation; and habitat formation.
4. Throughout this report, *externalities*, unless otherwise noted, refers to both positive and negative externalities, both of which must be managed effectively.

References

Cirera, X., and W. F. Maloney. 2017. *The Innovation Paradox: Developing-Country Capabilities and the Unrealized Promise of Technological Catch-Up*. Washington, DC: World Bank.

Damania, R., S. Polasky, M. Ruckelshaus, et al. 2023. *Nature's Frontiers: Achieving Sustainability, Efficiency, and Prosperity with Natural Capital*. Environment and Sustainable Development Series. Washington, DC: World Bank. http://hdl.handle.net/10986/39453.

ECLAC (Economic Commission for Latin America and the Caribbean). 2021. *Forest Loss in Latin America and the Caribbean from 1990 to 2020: The Statistical Evidence*. ECLAC Statistical Briefings no. 2, July 2021.

FAO (Food and Agriculture Organization of the United Nations). 2020. *Global Forest Resources Assessment 2020: Main Report*. Rome: Food and Agriculture Organization of the United Nations.

Fernández-Arias, E. 2014. "Productivity and Factor Accumulation in Latin America and the Caribbean: A Database." Inter-American Development Bank, Washington, DC. https://publications.iadb.org/en/productivity-and-factor-accumulation-latin-america-and-caribbean-database.

IPCC (Intergovernmental Panel on Climate Change). 2022. *Climate Change 2022: Impacts, Adaptation and Vulnerability*, edited by H.-O. Pörtner, D. C. Roberts, M. Tignor et al. Cambridge: Cambridge University Press. https://doi.org/10.1017/9781009325844.

Lee, K. 2019. *The Art of Economic Catch-Up: Barriers, Detours, and Leapfrogging*. Cambridge: Cambridge University Press.

Maloney, W. F., and F. Valencia Caicedo. 2022. "Engineering Growth: Innovative Capacity and Development in the Americas." *Journal of the European Economic Association* 20 (4): 1554–94.

Maloney, W. F., and A. Zambrano. 2021. "Learning to Learn: Experimentation, Entrepreneurial Capital, and Development." Policy Research Working Paper 9890, World Bank, Washington, DC.

McMillan, M., D. Rodrik, and I. Verduzco-Gallo. 2014. "Globalization, Structural Change, and Productivity Growth, with an Update on Africa." *World Development* 63 (C): 11–32.

Morris, M., A. R. Sebastian, and V. M. E. Perego. 2020. *Future Foodscapes: Re-imagining Agriculture in Latin America and the Caribbean*. Washington, DC: World Bank.

Perez, C., and L. Soete. 1988. "Catching-Up in Technology: Entry Barriers and Windows of Opportunity." In *Technical Change and Economic Theory*, edited by G. Dosi, C. Freeman, R. Nelson et al., 458–79. London: Pinter Publishers.

USGS (US Geological Survey). 2023. *Mineral Commodity Summaries 2023*. United States Geological Survey. Reston, VA: US Geological Survey. https://pubs.usgs.gov/periodicals/mcs2023/mcs2023.pdf.

World Bank. 2022. "Consolidating the Recovery: Seizing Green Growth Opportunities." LAC Semiannual Report (April). World Bank, Washington, DC. http://hdl.handle.net/10986/37244.

PART I

The Window of Opportunity

The green transition is reshaping economies around the world. Both globally and locally, consumer preferences have moved towards products that utilize sustainable and low-carbon production methods. Companies are adapting by decarbonizing their supply chains, enhancing product traceability, and ensuring their suppliers do not contribute to deforestation. Some nations are implementing regulations to promote decarbonization and foster more sustainable, environmentally-friendly markets potentially affecting international trade dynamics. Chapter 1 of this report describes these 'greening winds' in more detail.

This exogenous change in conditions represents a historic window of opportunity for Latin America and the Caribbean. Countries that can meet the demand for lower-carbon-footprint products—both new ones and older ones— will gain market share and potentially capture green premiums. As countries and firms seek to achieve net zero commitments, new markets, products, and technologies may appear; the nations and companies that adopt new technologies and adapt to the new environment will gain a competitive advantage.

Chapter 2 reviews three sectors that cover a broad range of opportunities in the region: land and forests which are rich in biodiversity and have growth potential; mining which has historical significance and may be entering a new phase; and green hydrogen (GH_2) as representative of a new industry. By closely analyzing these sectors, the report identifies several market failures—information asymmetry, lack of coordination, externalities, misaligned incentives, and more— that are relevant to all emerging sectors in the green transition.

CHAPTER 1

Greening Winds Are Reshaping Economies

Guillermo Beylis, Nancy Lozano Gracia, and Sara Diane Turner

Changes in prices, regulations, and preferences around the world are reshaping economies and will determine Latin America and the Caribbean's opportunities under the green transition. For their future emissions, about 76 percent of countries have declared some form of net zero goals,[1] some of which include concrete plans while others are still at a declaration level. Notable announcements since 2021 include China's target of carbon neutrality by 2060, India's goal of net zero emissions by 2070, and Indonesia's net zero emissions target of 2060. In Latin America, a similar share of countries (73.5 percent) has pledged some kind of net zero target.[2] If all stated goals (National Determined Contributions, long-term strategies, and net zero targets) were met in full and on time, that would be enough to hold global temperature increases to about 1.7°C in 2100 with respect to preindustrial levels,[3] bringing the world closer to reaching the stricter 1.5°C goal of the Paris Agreement.[4] As the damaging impacts of climate change become more evident, countries around the world are increasingly acting to decarbonize their economies, and changes in prices, regulations, and preferences are shaping how world economies move toward a greener development path.

More policy makers are recognizing that reducing greenhouse gases (GHGs) will require that a price be put on carbon emissions; markets to enable carbon pricing are growing rapidly. The share of global emissions covered by carbon taxes and emissions trading systems (ETSs) has grown from 7 to 23 percent over the past 10 years; such initiatives can be seen in 39 countries and 33 subnational jurisdictions (World Bank 2023). Also, 37 carbon crediting initiatives have been implemented, 14 of which are at the national level.[5] Global revenue from carbon pricing instruments exceeded $100 billion in 2023, with more than 70 percent of that revenue coming from emissions trading schemes rather than carbon taxes (World Bank 2023). The market continues to expand and diversify, emerging markets are beginning to take a more active role in developing carbon pricing instruments, and the supply across markets is becoming more sophisticated.

In 2020, Mexico became the first country in Latin America and the Caribbean with an operational ETS, and New Zealand announced its intention to become the first country to put a price on agricultural emissions in 2025—a pilot that, if successful, will dramatically expand the proportion of emissions covered by pricing systems.

Some countries are using regulations to support decarbonization and more sustainable, greener markets. These regulations have the potential to reshape international trade. Two recent examples led by the European Union (EU) are the implementation of the first phase of the Carbon Border Adjustment Mechanism (CBAM) and the deforestation-free products (DFP) regulations.[6] (See box 1.1 for effects on Latin America and the Caribbean.) The CBAM was designed to ensure that the carbon price of imports is equivalent to the carbon price of domestic production. CBAM's transitional phase, which started on October 1, 2023, and will run through the end of 2025, includes only imports of cement, iron and steel, aluminum, fertilizers, electricity, and hydrogen. The transitional period's objective is to provide an opportunity for all stakeholders to learn how to measure and report on the embedded carbon in products and to understand their needs in terms of CBAM certificates. The permanent system will become effective on January 1, 2026, at which point importers will be required to report the quantity and embedded GHGs of goods imported into the EU the previous year and to submit the required CBAM certificates for those goods. The price of CBAM certificates will be calculated from the weekly average auction price of EU ETS allowances expressed in euros per ton of carbon dioxide (CO_2) emitted.

Box 1.1

CBAM and DFP Regulations: Impacts on Latin America and the Caribbean

Recent work using 2019 data from the World Bank's World Integrated Trade Solution data dissemination and analytical tool (Conte Grand, Schulz-Antipa, and Rozenberg 2023) finds that the European Union Carbon Border Adjustment Mechanism (EU CBAM) will have a minor impact on countries in the region, primarily because of Latin America and the Caribbean's limited industrial profile. Less than 0.5 percent of this region's exports are exposed under the EU CBAM. Within that area, Brazil, Chile, and Costa Rica have the highest exposures to the EU CBAM, with approximately 0.4, 0.3, and 0.1 percent, respectively, of total exports of CBAM goods to the EU. The main products affected are iron and steel for Brazil and Costa Rica and fertilizers for Chile.

box continued next page

Box 1.1

CBAM and DFP Regulations: Impacts on Latin America and the Caribbean *(continued)*

Argentina, Brazil, Honduras, Paraguay, and Uruguay are the most exposed to the EU deforestation-free products (DFPs) regulation. Estimates indicate that 17 percent of Honduras's exports of palm oil and cocoa go to European markets, while the EU is a large market for beef and soy exports from Southern Cone Common Market (Mercosur) countries. In countries such as Peru, although overall exposure is lower, the impact may be stronger because whereas only 1 percent of total exports are subject to the DFP regulation, 51 percent of coffee exports and nearly 43 percent of cacao exports go to EU markets, suggesting significant impacts for these specific sectors.

On September 26, 2023, nine countries in Latin America and the Caribbean submitted a letter to the World Trade Organization Committee on Agriculture expressing their concern about the regulation's potential impact. The countries noted that the assessment and benchmarking system is likely to generate trade distortions and diplomatic tension and to unfairly penalize producers in developing countries. They also criticized the short time frame and unilateral nature of the regulation's development and adoption, as well as its significant compliance costs.

Without adequate safeguards, these regulations may also have unintended effects on the poor and vulnerable in affected countries, through exclusion from global value chains and increased conflict and land expropriation among landholders with properties of different sizes.

The DFP regulation is designed to reduce the EU's contribution to global deforestation and forest degradation. The directive, which was enacted on June 29, 2023, gives importers 18 months to implement the new rules, with some extended adaptation periods given to small firms; thus, for most companies, the rules will apply on December 30, 2025. In essence, the new regulation requires companies doing business in the EU market to conduct due diligence to confirm that products have not been sourced from land that was deforested or degraded after December 31, 2020. The process involves three steps: gathering information on the geographic location from which products are sourced, assessing the risk of noncompliance, and taking mitigating actions to ensure that the risk is negligible. A lower risk assessment will be associated with a simpler due diligence process.[7] This mandate also requires companies to verify that their goods are compliant with any applicable legislation in the products' country of origin. Currently, the EU DFP regulation applies to wood, rubber, palm oil, soy, beef, coffee, and cacao.[8]

Preferences are changing around the world, with sustainable and low-carbon modes of production increasingly valued by a variety of market actors. Globally and locally, consumer preferences have shifted toward greener products. Market studies of global sustainability and surveys of consumer preferences find that interest in sustainable products and willingness to pay more for them are both increasing. In a 2020 McKinsey US consumer sentiment survey, more than 60 percent of respondents expressed willingness to pay more for a product with sustainable packaging (Singh 2025). A more recent assessment of the actual spending behavior of US consumers suggests that products making environmental, social, and governance (ESG)-related claims averaged 28 percent cumulative growth in sales between 2017 and 2022, compared to 20 percent growth for products with no such claims, providing evidence of a shift in household preferences (Frey et al. 2023). Within Latin America and the Caribbean, there is also a high level of awareness and concern about the impact of climate change and an uptick in individual efforts to promote more sustainable living. In the region, consumers' awareness of climate change and its impacts is higher than the global average (Gomes 2021). Consumers there are also the most likely to believe that everyday and individual actions can have a positive impact on the environment (Araya and Zuniga 2021). A 2020–21 public opinion survey found that deforestation was a key environmental issue of concern globally but Latin Americans and Europeans expressed the most concern about the issue. In Colombia, 84 percent of respondents stated that it was a very serious issue, compared with 73 percent in Brazil (GlobeScan 2021).

Because of evolving consumer preferences, a growing number of countries are introducing regulations that place a high value on strategies for sourcing energy transition minerals with strong environmental and social credentials. For example, a European battery regulation formally approved by the European Parliament and the Council of Europe in July 2023 sets tight due diligence rules for companies that trade or sell specific mineral products in the EU to ensure that they have a low carbon footprint and are compliant with robust environmental and social procedures.[9] EU manufacturers must verify the sources of chemical precursors used for batteries placed on the EU market and must require the suppliers to certify that their products have a low carbon footprint and are compliant with robust ESG practices.

Firms are responding to these changing preferences by decarbonizing their supply chains, improving traceability of their products, and ensuring that their suppliers are not contributing to deforestation. More than 2,000 global companies (34 percent of the global economy) have set a science-based target for emissions reduction (SBTi 2023). Of these firms, 70 percent are aligned with a 1.5°C commitment for scope 1 and 2 emissions.[10] The CDP–Accountability Framework Initiative report for 2022 found that 44 percent of 675 reporting companies had a policy of no deforestation/no forest conversion for some or all of their production and sourcing (CDP and Afi 2022). However, there is still a long road ahead to turn firms' commitments into an actual reduction in deforestation, and early reviews already point to challenges of implementation (Bager and Lambin 2022). Recent work suggests that the probability of companies' success in becoming more sustainable and avoiding greenwashing is linked to several factors, including the following: the recognition that costs in the short run might be necessary, even if returns can be expected later on; the presence of ethical leadership; the establishment of long-term, close relationships along the supply chain; the definition of specific policies and guidelines for sustainability; and the assessment and reporting of sustainable practices (Inês, Diniz, and Moreira 2023).

As part of their decarbonization strategies, firms—particularly in energy-intensive industries—may reconsider the optimal location of their manufacturing plants. *Greenshoring* is a concept related to environmental sustainability and corporate social responsibility. It is a play on the words *green* and *offshoring*. Offshoring typically refers to the practice of relocating certain business processes or operations to another country, often to reduce costs. Greenshoring, however, refers to the practice of relocating business processes or operations specifically to reduce environmental impact and promote sustainability. Currently, the energy produced through renewable sources is very costly to transport beyond the local electricity grid (C. Hausman 2024). This suggests that countries with clean, safe, affordable, and abundant energy may have a comparative advantage in hosting energy-intensive industries. Greenshoring is a growing trend among companies seeking to align their business operations with environmental and sustainability goals.

Nations that value their competitiveness in global markets are acting now to incentivize greener production practices all along the value chains of the goods and services that are most critical to their economies (box 1.2). Countries that can meet the demand for lower-carbon-footprint products—both new ones and older ones—will gain market share and potentially capture green premiums. In the transition toward net zero, nations that can innovate—broadly understood as being capable of adopting, adapting, imitating, and inventing—in the space of decarbonization and sustainability will be at an advantage. As countries and firms seek to achieve net zero commitments, new markets, products, and technologies may appear; the nations and companies that adopt new technologies and adapt to the new environment will gain a competitive advantage. The Latin America and the Caribbean region could guide its innovation efforts toward solutions based on renewable electricity, leveraging its clean energy matrix and huge potential to add further renewable capacity. Development of green hydrogen, for example, is an innovative method that produces hydrogen through green electricity, which may help power hard-to-abate industries (such as cement, steel, aviation, and shipping). Similarly, the region can invest in developing technologies that electrify production processes, further contributing to decarbonization of downstream industries. Gaining a foothold in these potential markets requires countries to develop national innovation systems focusing on decarbonization and sustainable production.

Box 1.2

Current Role of Green Value Chains in Latin American and the Caribbean's Manufacturing Chains

How can the strengths and opportunities of Latin America and the Caribbean in global green value chains be assessed? Revealed comparative advantage (RCA) is an economic metric used to determine and quantify the relative trade performance in a certain class of goods or services of a country. RCA compares the exports of a commodity from a country with the total exports of that country and with the corresponding exports of a set of countries. There is no universally accepted threshold for determining a strong RCA. The higher the RCA, the stronger the country's trade competitiveness for that product. Past research suggests that RCA has predictive power for understanding the evolution of export products and economic complexity in a country over time (Mealy and Teytelboym 2022). (Use of this metric in conjunction with others, such as the portions of exports and markets, can help identify strengths and opportunities for the Latin America and the Caribbean region to increase its role in manufacturing more lucrative components in value chains for decarbonization, including solar photovoltaic, wind, and batteries.) The economic complexity of a country can be assessed by analyzing the characteristics and mix of products a country makes. It is expressed as an index of the diversity and complexity of the total goods a country produces with a comparative advantage. Economic complexity is highly correlated with current levels of income and has been found to be predictive of future economic growth rates. The income of countries with higher economic complexity ratings than would be predicted by their gross domestic product tends to grow faster (R. Hausmann 2024).

box continued next page

Box 1.2

Current Role of Green Value Chains in Latin American and the Caribbean's Manufacturing Chains *(continued)*

At the product level, complexity comprises the number of countries that manufacture a particular commodity and the economic complexity of those countries (product complexity index). This measure is expressed relative to a particular basket of goods of interest (either total products or a subset, such as items associated with energy transition).

Countries in Latin America and the Caribbean rank relatively poorly overall in production of high-complexity manufactured goods, especially those in high demand for the energy transition (specifically in wind, solar photovoltaic, and battery technologies). This region exports primarily lower-value-added natural resources and imports higher-value green tech products from Asia, Europe, and the United States. The market shares in Latin America and the Caribbean for green technologies lag those of global leaders, and countries in the region make fewer green products that are currently competitive relative to regional and income group comparators (figure B1.2.1). Measures of economic complexity place countries in Latin America and the Caribbean in the middle of such rankings, with only a few countries significantly improving their positions by beginning to increase the share of complex products they make (R. Hausmann 2024). Only three countries in this region improved their rankings by more than 20 places in the past 20 years: Costa Rica, the Dominican Republic (which moved from the third quartile to the second), and Paraguay (which moved from the fourth to the third). Meanwhile, five countries declined in their overall economic complexity rankings by more than 20 places: Argentina, Bolivia, Brazil, Panama, and Peru.

A similar pattern of relative regional weakness can be observed when only green supply chains are considered. For the Latin America and the Caribbean region, in global rankings of green complexity, Mexico performs best, with just under 60 products showing RCAs of greater than one (indicating economic competitiveness), but that is still far less than those of global leaders such as China and Germany, which make more than 100 green products in which they have a comparative advantage. Similarly, market share of green products in countries in Latin America and the Caribbean lags that of global leaders, at less than 2 percent of the total market across products.

box continued next page

Box 1.2

Current Role of Green Value Chains in Latin American and the Caribbean's Manufacturing Chains *(continued)*

Figure B1.2.1   Income Group and Regional Comparison of Latin America and the Caribbean's Competitiveness in Green Value Chains

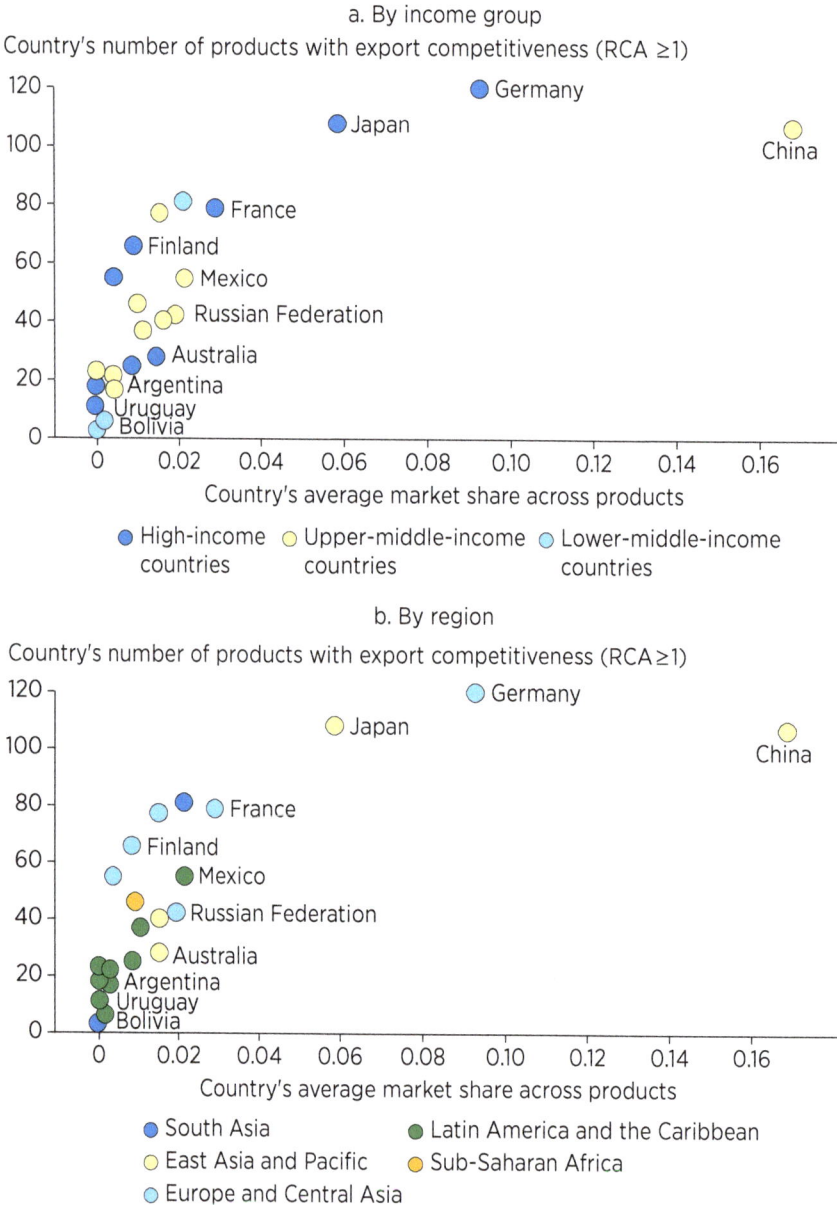

a. By income group

Country's number of products with export competitiveness (RCA ≥1)

Germany
Japan
China
France
Finland
Mexico
Russian Federation
Australia
Argentina
Uruguay
Bolivia

Country's average market share across products

● High-income countries   ○ Upper-middle-income countries   ○ Lower-middle-income countries

b. By region

Country's number of products with export competitiveness (RCA ≥1)

Germany
Japan
China
France
Finland
Mexico
Russian Federation
Australia
Argentina
Uruguay
Bolivia

Country's average market share across products

● South Asia   ● Latin America and the Caribbean
○ East Asia and Pacific   ● Sub-Saharan Africa
○ Europe and Central Asia

Source: World Bank calculations based on data from Andres and Mealy 2023.

Note: RCA = revealed comparative advantage.

Notes

1. As clearly explained elsewhere (Energy & Climate Intelligence Unit, https://eciu.net /analysis/infographics/our-climate-goals), there are various types of net zero goals. Some refer to carbon dioxide (CO_2) or greenhouse gas net zero (*net* refers to the difference between removals and emissions), while others refer to carbon neutrality (in such a case, emissions could be compensated with purchases of carbon offset credits in order to reach net zero).
2. For example, Argentina announced its goal to become carbon neutral by 2050, whereas Uruguay has a net zero target for CO_2 for the same year.
3. International Energy Agency, "Credible Pathways to 1.5°C," 2023, https://www.iea.org /reports/credible-pathways-to-150c.
4. A similar conclusion is reached by Climate Action Tracker ("The CAT Thermometer Explained," 2024, https://climateactiontracker.org/global/cat-thermometer/), which projects an "optimistic" increase of about 1.9°C by 2100, when in 2023, that increase is already 1.3°C.
5. An ETS is a system in which emitters can trade emission units to meet their emission targets. The two main types of ETSs are cap-and-trade and baseline-and-credit. In the former, there is an absolute limit on the emissions, and emission allowances are distributed for free or through auctions. In the latter, baseline emissions levels are defined, and credits are issued to entities that have reduced their emissions below this level. Those credits then can be sold to others exceeding their baseline emission levels. A crediting mechanism designates the GHG emission reductions from project- or program-based activities, according to an accounting protocol and their own registry, and can be sold either domestically or in other countries.
6. The DFP regulation was expected to come into force for traders and operators in December 2024; for small and medium enterprises, it was set to take effect on June 30, 2025.
7. That is, if the product is sourced from a country benchmarked as having low deforestation risk, the last step will not be necessary.
8. Regulation (EU) 2023/1115 on DFPs.
9. See Reuters, "EU Lawmakers Approve Legislation to Make Batteries Greener," June 14, 2023, https://www.reuters.com/sustainability/eu-lawmakers-approve -legislation-make-batteries-greener-2023-06-14/.
10. Industrial emissions are categorized into three groups depending on the origin. Two of these scopes are referenced in this section. Scope 1 emissions are direct emissions from sources controlled by the company (for example, transport emissions), while scope 2 emissions cover emissions that arise from the energy used to produce goods and services by the company.

References

Andres, P., and P. Mealy. 2023. Green Transition Navigator. https://www.green-transition -navigator.org.

Araya, J., and J. Zuniga. 2021. "Navigating Sustainability in Latin America." Euromonitor International, April 13, 2021. https://www.euromonitor.com/article/navigating -sustainability-in-latin-america.

Bager, S. L., and E. F. Lambin. 2022. "How Do Companies Implement Their Zero-Deforestation Commitments." *Journal of Cleaner Production* 375: 134056.

CDP (Carbon Disclosure Project) and AFi (Accountability Framework initiative). 2022. "From Commitments to Action at Scale: Critical Steps to Achieve Deforestation-Free Supply Chains." CDP, London, and AFi, New York. https://accountability-framework.org/fileadmin /uploads/afi/Documents/News/CDP_AFI_Forest_Report_2022_2022_05_23.pdf.

Conte Grand, M., P. Schulz-Antipa, and J. Rozenberg. 2023. "Potential Exposure and Vulnerability to Broader Climate-Related Trade Regulations: An Illustration for LAC Countries." *Environment, Development and Sustainability: A Multidisciplinary Approach to the Theory and Practice of Sustainable Development* 26 (3): 6195–220.

Frey, S., J. Bar Am, V. Doshi, A. Malik, and S. Noble. 2023. "Consumers Care about Sustainability—And Back It Up with Their Wallets." McKinsey's Consumer Packaged Goods Practice. McKinsey and NielsenIQ. https://www.mckinsey.com/industries /consumer-packaged-goods/our-insights/consumers-care-about-sustainability -and-back-it-up-with-their-wallets#/.

GlobeScan. 2021. "Study Finds That Deforestation of the Amazon Rainforest Is a Serious Concern Worldwide." GlobeScan, October 26, 2021. https://globescan.com/2021 /10/26/study-finds-that-deforestation-of-the-amazon-rainforest-is-a-serious -concern-worldwide/.

Gomes, K. 2021. "In Latin America, Going Green(er) Is Good for Business." Kantar, June 25, 2021. https://www.kantar.com/inspiration/sustainability/in-latin-america -going-greener-is-good-for-business.

Hausman, C. 2024. "Power Flows: Transmission Lines, Allocative Efficiency, and Corporate Profits." NBER Working Paper Series 32091, National Bureau of Economic Research, Cambridge, MA. https://www.nber.org/system/files/working_papers/w32091 /w32091.pdf.

Hausmann, R. 2024. "Export-Led Growth." Growth Lab Working Paper Series no. 231, Harvard University, Cambridge, MA.

Inês, A., A. Diniz, and A. C. Moreira. 2023. "A Review of Greenwashing and Supply Chain Management: Challenges Ahead." *Cleaner Environmental Systems* 11 (December): 100136.

Mealy, P., and A. Teytelboym. 2022. "Economic Complexity and the Green Economy." *Research Policy* 51 (8): 103948.

SBTi (Science Based Targets initiative). 2023. "SBTi Monitoring Report 2022: Looking Back at 2022 and Looking Forward at 2023 and Beyond." SBTi, London. https:// sciencebasedtargets.org/resources/files/SBTiMonitoringReport2022.pdf.

Singh, A.K. 2025. "Principles and Characterization of Sustainability Assessment." In *Quantitative Assessment of Sustainability and Sustainable Development*, 19–61. Berlin: Springer Nature. https://doi.org/10.1007/978-3-031-83852-1_2

World Bank. 2023. "State and Trends of Carbon Pricing 2023." World Bank, Washington, DC. https://openknowledge.worldbank.org/handle/10986/39796.

CHAPTER 2

Seizing the Window of Opportunity: Three Illustrative Examples

Javier Aguilar, Mariana Conte Grand, Sara Diane Turner, and Joeri Frederik de Wit

Introduction

Given its richness in both renewable and nonrenewable natural resources, Latin America and the Caribbean is uniquely placed to leverage the window of opportunity opened by the green transition. First, for example, one of the region's greatest advantages is its high levels of natural capital like forests, renewable freshwater resources, and fertile land. If properly managed, these resources can act as carbon sinks and a source of additional exports, based on an already dominant position in the trade of agricultural and food products. Almost half of the region's surface is covered by forests, representing 23 percent of worldwide forest cover.[1] It is also endowed with some of the highest levels of renewable freshwater resources in the world[2] and is an important region for global biodiversity—65 percent of countries in this region perform above the global average on environmental performance and protection of species and habitats.[3] Latin America and the Caribbean's landscapes also provide key sources of economic growth in the form of land for agricultural production. The region has 11 percent of the world's arable land, (FAO 2023), including some underdeveloped areas that could be used for sustainable agriculture. The region is also the world's largest net exporter of food and agricultural products, serving as the primary source of globally traded agricultural products such as avocados, sugarcane, and soy; for all of these, it represents over half of global production.[4]

Second, Latin America and the Caribbean is rich in mineral resources that are key inputs for some of the technologies that are driving the energy transition. The region holds over 47 percent of global reserves of lithium, a key component of battery-based energy storage, as most electric vehicles (EVs) use lithium-ion batteries. Additionally, the demand for copper, which is also abundant in the region (over 36 percent of global reserves), is also expected to increase significantly, at a rate of 1.6 percent annually to 2050 (IEA 2023a). Copper is used extensively in electricity networks and is essential in all electricity-related technologies. Some of the region's countries also have significant endowments of other energy transition minerals (ETM) such as cobalt, graphite, nickel, and rare earth elements (REE).

Third, Latin America and the Caribbean begins from a favorable starting point to manage the energy transition toward a low-carbon system. With an electricity generation matrix based mostly on large-scale hydropower and complemented with natural gas, the region already has one of the greenest electricity grids in the world. Further, the region has great potential for generating abundant and reliable green electricity. It is blessed with vast potential in nonconventional renewable energy (RE), including geothermal, wind, solar, tidal, wave, biomass, and small hydroelectric plants. Northwest Argentina, Chile, and Mexico contain deserts with some of the highest solar radiation in the world.[5] Northern Colombia and the Patagonia region have the potential to generate large amounts of wind energy.[6] Such significant potential in low-carbon energy production can be an important lever to attract energy-intensive industries from around the world.

Together, these factors suggest that Latin America and the Caribbean may have a comparative advantage in the green economy that would open the door for new growth and export opportunities. Fully embracing green policies could enable producers to capture green premiums on their products, expand to new markets, and avoid carbon-adjustment taxes as well as anti-deforestation import bans or restrictions. Additionally, building the capabilities and institutions that facilitate low-carbon technology adoption will enable the region to approach the technological frontier and, with the right policies and incentives, to become an innovator itself. In the following sections, this chapter provides an illustration of the proposed conceptual framework through a discussion of the opportunities and challenges in the three selected sectors—land and forests, mining, and green hydrogen (GH_2)—which are intended only as examples. The lessons learned from each example are potentially applicable to all sectors, depending on their specific stage of development and their relation to the economic-environmental production possibilities frontier (EE-PPF).

Land and Forests—Leveraging Natural Capital for Greener Markets

Box 2.1 presents an overview of the challenges to institutions, investments, and innovations regarding land, forests, and other natural resources in the region.

Box 2.1

Key Bottlenecks to Developing Greener Markets From Land and Forests

Moving closer to the economic-environmental production possibilities frontier can bring benefits in terms of increased production and sustainability. Better allocation and management of land, water, and other inputs could increase annual income from agriculture, grazing, and forestry by approximately $94 billion.

- *Institutions*: Incomplete land registries, unclear tenure, and partially implemented land regulations and environmental frameworks restrict the ability of governments to optimize land use patterns and perpetuate the exclusion of vulnerable populations. Misaligned incentives and weak enforcement of regulations further undermine sustainable land use in the region.

- *Investments*: Lagging investments in information systems for monitoring, reporting, and verification have limited effective monitoring of deforestation in many countries and contribute to misallocation of land.

- *Innovation*: Slow uptake of innovation technologies in the agricultural sector has limited productivity growth and challenges food security and market access.

Latin America and the Caribbean is Fertile Ground for Growth and Ecosystem Services

Although Latin America and the Caribbean is rich in a wide variety of natural capital, this section focuses on the opportunities for the region specific to land and forests, resources that are of critical importance to achieving global decarbonization goals. As has been noted, almost half of the region's surface is covered by forests (FAO 2020), accounting for 23 percent of all forests worldwide (ECLAC 2021). Latin America and the Caribbean also possesses some of the highest levels of renewable freshwater resources, and six of the region's countries are listed among the 17 most biodiverse countries in the world.[7] Total growing and biomass carbon stock in the region is estimated at 573.3 gigatons of carbon dioxide equivalent ($GtCO_2e$), the majority of which is stored in tropical forests and represents almost 24 percent of global carbon stock.[8] The importance of the agriculture, forest, and other land use (AFOLU) sector also lies in the vital ecosystem services[9] it provides, and its ability to reduce vulnerability to physical climate risks at the local level.[10] It is therefore critical to the livelihoods of local communities and an essential input to the region's climate adaptation and mitigation strategies (United Nations Framework Convention on Climate Change 2023).

Latin America and the Caribbean's landscapes are also key sources of economic growth, providing land for agricultural production for food and energy. The region has the largest reserves of arable land in the world, including some undeveloped areas that could be sustainably used for agriculture (Morris, Sebastian, and Perego 2020). Agriculture plays a fundamental role in the region's economies, accounting for more than 5 percent of gross domestic product (GDP) and over 10 percent of employment in more than 19 countries. Agroindustry makes an even more important contribution to output and employment in many countries in the region. Agroindustry accounts for over 9 percent of total gross output and is an effective driver of increased domestic output, providing a boost comparable to or greater than that provided by construction and tourism, across a sample of five Central American and Caribbean countries (López Marmolejo, Eggers Prieto, and Ruiz-Arranz 2023). Latin America and the Caribbean is also the largest net exporter of food and agricultural products in the world. The region is a primary source of globally traded agricultural products, producing over half of the global production of avocados, coffee, sugarcane, and soy (Morris, Sebastian, and Perego 2020). Some countries in the region are globally significant exporters of specific agricultural products. For others, agricultural exports contribute a significant percentage of total exports (approximately 75 percent in Uruguay, for example), even though the absolute value of such agricultural exports is relatively lower than in the agriculture export heavyweights (Morris, Sebastian, and Perego 2020).

Land use plays a critical role in Latin America and the Caribbean economies, both as a driver of economic development and as a poverty-reduction tool. Although, overall, the population in the region is highly urbanized, and poverty is increasingly urbanized post-pandemic, poverty rates in rural areas nonetheless remain higher than in urban areas, with 47 percent of the region's impoverished people still living in rural areas. Agriculture and land use is particularly important as a source of food and income for the rural poor: more than half of the region's agrifood production comes from its 17 million family farms. Land is often one of the few productive assets (along with household labor and assets from the surrounding environment) available to the rural poor (Barbier and Hochard 2018). Further, despite progress on poverty over the past several decades, food security remains an ongoing challenge.[11]

Existing forests and grasslands also play important roles in regulating temperature and rainfall and provide key ecosystem services on which agriculture depends. Intermingling agricultural and natural landscapes is common in Latin America and the Caribbean and can provide important benefits for productivity (Kremen 2015). Currently, the region is the world's largest provider of ecosystem services and has significant potential to serve as a key source of carbon sequestration to help mitigate the impact of climate change (Morris, Sebastian, and Perego 2020). Ecosystem services beyond carbon sequestration also provide significant benefits, contributing $1.2 trillion to regional wealth in 2018, equal to approximately $1,947 per capita.

The region's inefficient use of land is leaving economic and environmental benefits on the table

New analysis for this report finds that Latin America and the Caribbean is the world's lowest-ranking region in terms of economic efficiency in land use for agriculture, livestock, and forestry. The analysis first seeks to quantify the economic and environmental value of current land use inefficiencies at the country level; second, it identifies the necessary changes that would bring countries closer to the optimal allocation of land uses. In this report, land use efficiency refers to the degree to which a country is allocating its land use to maximize that land's potential. At a landscape or country scale, land use efficiency means that a country is allocating its land in a way that best achieves the goals of sustainability and economic benefit, given the country's endowment of land assets. In other words, in an efficient system, land that is most suited to carbon storage is used for that purpose, while land with higher potential for agricultural production is used for agriculture. The efficiency frontier, then, indicates the optimal land allocations that maximize economic output and environmental value. Values below the frontier would indicate the presence of unrealized productivity gains or unrealized environmental benefits that could be achieved either through reallocation of land or by increasing productivity on that land, for example, through improvements in agricultural practices and technologies. Box 2.2 provides additional details on this methodology.

Box 2.2

Introducing the Concept of Efficiency Frontiers

This report develops new analytics using the framework introduced in the global report "Nature's Frontiers" (Damania et al. 2023), which uses spatial-weighted optimization to identify a range of land allocations that maximize environmental and economic values, called an efficiency frontier (see the yellow line in figure B2.2.1). A novel feature of the analysis is that it is multidimensional, considering multiple management objectives. Environmental value

box continued next page

Box 2.2

Introducing the Concept of Efficiency Frontiers *(continued)*

includes carbon and biodiversity, while economic value includes agriculture, grazing, and forestry. The analysis also compares the current land use pattern (point Z) to the potential maxima to identify how closely country land use patterns match the modeled optimal pattern. There are multiple potential optimal points since the frontier shows the most efficient possible combinations of the nonmarket environmental outcome and production value. How close a country is to that frontier determines the overall efficiency score, calculated as the length of $\beta/(\alpha+\beta)$ for that country, across all the dimensions in the analysis. If current performance is close to the efficiency frontier, the landscape efficiency score will be close to 1 (because α will be close to 0). These scores can also be calculated for each individual subdimension. The environmental efficiency score is defined as the distance from the current position to the maximum feasible one (length c) ($c/(a+b+c)$). This can be calculated for biodiversity (Biodiversity Efficiency Score) or carbon sequestration (Carbon Sequestration Efficiency Score), or the two jointly. An equivalent score can be calculated for economic value (Economic Efficiency Score), which compares the current value of economic production to the potential on the efficiency frontier at the same level of environmental performance. An alternative performance measure compares current performance in one dimension (length c) with that achieved without sacrificing any other dimension (length b+c), or the maximum potential that can be achieved without harming other objectives, which is called the Pareto maximum ($c/(b+c)$). This performance measure is called the Pareto Environmental or Economic Efficiency Score. These scores can be graphed in an x-y plot to show the relationship between the relative efficiency of different countries in using their land for economic or environmental benefits. These scores are graphed for Latin America and the Caribbean in figure 2.1.

Current land use maps are derived at a 10 square kilometer resolution using data from the European Space Agency (ESA 2019) coupled with modeling to estimate the economic value, biodiversity index scores, and carbon sequestration potential for each grid cell at a national level. Economic value includes income derived from agriculture, grazing, or forestry. Biodiversity combines six types of biodiversity data (potential species richness, threatened and endangered species, endemic species, rare ecoregions, forest intactness, and key biodiversity areas). Carbon storage estimates are based off the InVEST Carbon Storage and Sequestration model (Sharp et al. 2020), which is used to estimate the cumulative net amount of carbon dioxide equivalent (CO_2e) found in

box continued next page

Box 2.2

Introducing the Concept of Efficiency Frontiers *(continued)*

above-ground and below-ground biomass. The optimization used to produce the efficiency frontier incorporates the costs required to transition from one land use to another in the calculation of economic value gained. Costs of restoration are taken from the Economics of Ecosystems and Biodiversity (TEEB 2009) estimates. These range from $260/hectare (ha) for grassland restoration to $33,000/ha for inland wetlands. Pertinent to the region, lakes/rivers and tropical forests are the second-highest cost categories to restore ($4,000/ha and $3,450/ha, respectively).

Transition costs for shifts in land use patterns are estimated using the cost to clear land for agricultural or grazing use, the cost of irrigation, and the cost to restore land to a natural landcover type. Land-clearing costs are calculated from global values adjusted for regional labor costs from the International Labour Organization, while irrigation costs are regional and derived from estimates from the International Water Management Institute (Edwards 2015; ILO 2021; Inocencio et al. 2007). A full description of the modeling details can be found in appendix A of Damania et al. (2023).

Figure B2.2.1 Efficiency Frontier and Key Calculations

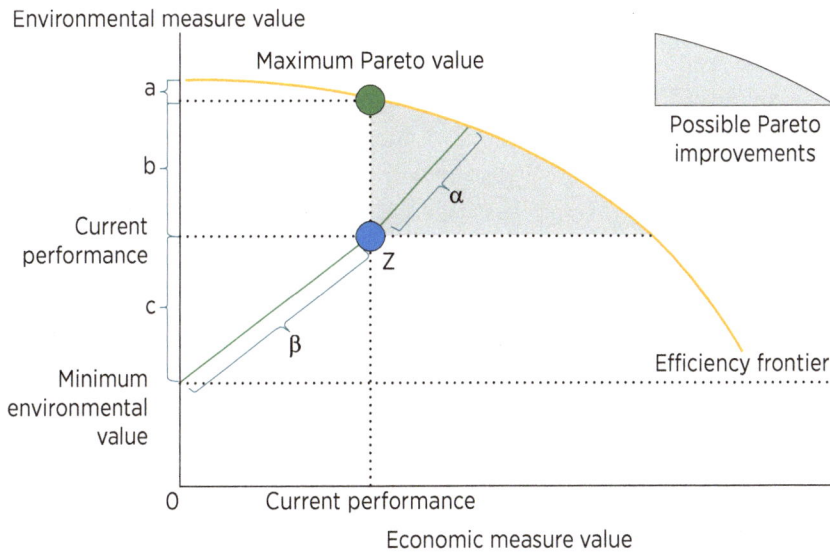

Source: Modified from Damania et al. 2023.

Latin America and the Caribbean's countries perform relatively poorly in global rankings of economic efficiency, with no country in the region scoring in the top half for economic efficiency in land use. On average, the region is 37.4 percent efficient in land use for three sectors, agriculture, grazing, and forestry. Recent productivity improvements have been observed in the region, with average agricultural productivity increasing (2.1 percent per year) well above the global mean (1.6 percent per year) between 1991 and 2015 (OECD/FAO 2019). However, these productivity gains have been driven primarily by the adoption of improved production technologies (shifting the production frontier outward) rather than by efficiency gains (reductions in the inputs needed per unit of output—moving toward the frontier) (Morris, Sebastian, and Perego 2020).

Within this overall pattern of economic inefficiency, there is significant heterogeneity in how efficiently land is used at the country level. The analysis suggests wide variation among Latin America and the Caribbean countries in how efficiently land for agriculture, grazing, and forestry is managed, echoing broader challenges to productivity in the region. Although some countries and products use highly efficient and productive technologies (for example, Peru for export-oriented agricultural products), this productivity is concentrated, and not fully characteristic of production systems across the region. Important variations persist even within regions in a single country (Morris, Sebastian, and Perego 2020; World Bank 2022). For example, agricultural systems in the sierra (mountains) and selva (forest) regions of Peru are significantly less efficient than its coastal, export-oriented systems (World Bank 2022). Figure 2.1 plots Latin America and the Caribbean countries by comparing their Pareto efficiency scores for carbon sequestration (y axis), biodiversity (color), and economic value (x axis). The countries are then grouped according to how well they perform in protecting environmental outcomes. Countries in group A have largely untransformed landscapes that score very highly on protecting environmental outcomes, although in many cases there is potential to improve economic outcomes. Countries in group B also perform well on protecting environmental outcomes, but have some room to increase their efficiency even further without harming economic outcomes. This group includes Brazil, Colombia, and Costa Rica. Countries in group C have generally experienced significant degradation and have potential for significant investment for restoration. This group includes the Dominican Republic, Mexico, and Uruguay. Finally, group D, which includes only Haiti, has significant environmental degradation and is also very far from the economic efficiency frontier.

Figure 2.1   Performance of Latin America and the Caribbean's Countries with Respect to Economic and Environmental Efficiency

Pareto environmental efficiency score [% of max Pareto environmental value]

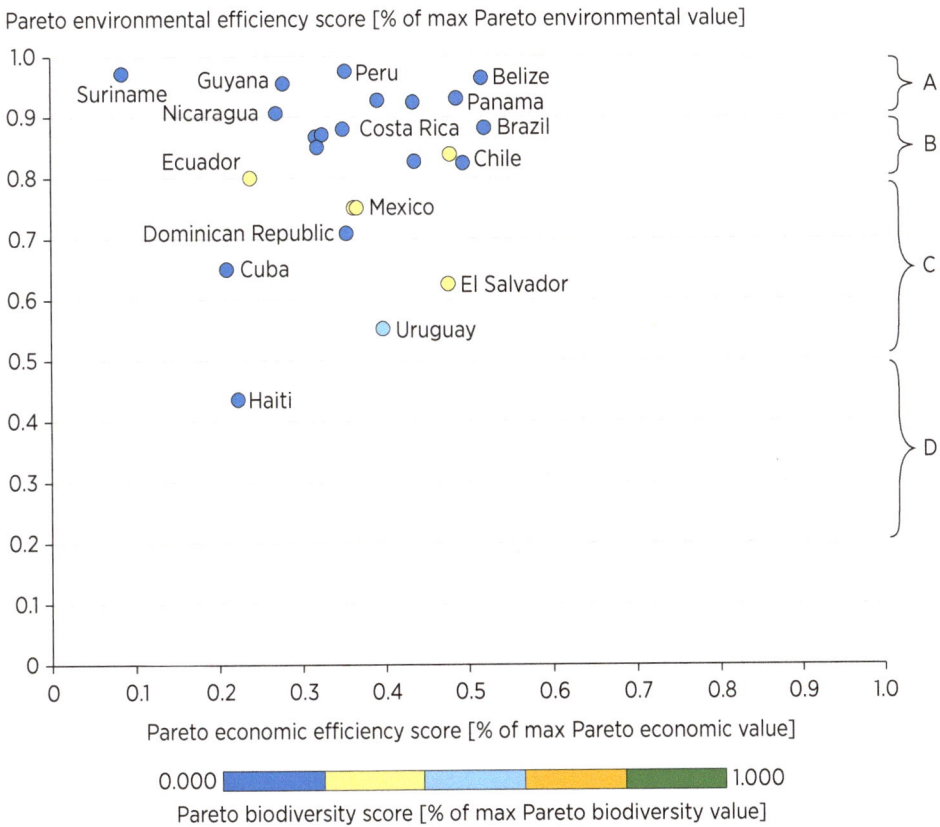

Source: World Bank calculations based on score provided for Damania et al. 2023.

Note: Group A = Suriname, Nicaragua, Guyana, Peru, Guatemala, Bolivia, Panama, and Belize. Group B = Ecuador, Venezuela, Colombia, Honduras, Costa Rica, Jamaica, Argentina, Chile, and Brazil. Group C = Cuba, Dominican Republic, Paraguay, Mexico, Uruguay, and El Salvador. Group D: Haiti.

The clear message that emerges from the analysis is that Latin America and the Caribbean has significant potential to improve economic outcomes from land-based economic activities without harming environmental objectives. Better allocation and management of land, water, and other inputs could increase the region's annual income from agriculture, grazing, and forestry by approximately $94 billion without a net loss of forests and natural habitats.

Also, the study finds that the region could potentially sequester 25 billion additional tons of carbon dioxide equivalent (CO_2e) per year (valued at approximately $1 trillion) without harming economic production. Globally, more efficient use of land could sequester an additional 78 billion tons of CO_2e with no adverse economic impacts (Damania et al. 2023).[12] The analysis finds that Latin America and the Caribbean could provide 32 percent of the potential gains. Valued using a shadow price of carbon of $40 per ton,[13] this would mean that up to $3 trillion could be mobilized from maximizing carbon sequestration opportunities.[14] It is important to note that the estimated monetary value of additional stored carbon serves only as an illustration and should not be interpreted as potential revenues from a carbon credit market. While $40 per ton is at the low end of estimates of the current social cost of carbon used by the World Bank, this valuation is overly optimistic relative to current prices in the market because the current price of forestry and land use credits in the region is significantly lower than $40. At a price of $7, close to market values in 2023, the potential would be estimated at only $500 billion (Ecosystem Marketplace 2023). Nevertheless, the exercise illustrates the tradeoffs. The monetary value of potential carbon sequestration in Latin America and the Caribbean through better allocation of land, if treated as revenue, exceeds the potential gains of maintaining current forest cover and maximizing economic outcomes.

Challenges to Improving Land Use in Latin America and the Caribbean through the Lens of Institutions, Investments, and Innovations

Conceptually, the disappointing performance of the region can be broken down into two parts: (a) misallocation of land resources and (b) low productivity in areas with high potential. The region could significantly improve its economic performance by simply reallocating land to its most productive uses, maximizing agricultural output in areas with high yield potential, and devoting less-productive lands to forestry, livestock activities, reforestation, or afforestation (to improve ecological performance). Improving agricultural productivity in areas of high potential will be key not only to improving economic efficiency, but also, when paired with a regulatory framework that incorporates the value of natural capital and its ecosystem services (and effective enforcement of those rules), to contributing to better environmental outcomes.

Moving toward more sustainable and efficient land use in Latin America and the Caribbean will require a combination of institutions, investment, and innovation to address both current and emerging challenges. How the region shapes the use of land and forests is the result of diverse and sometimes conflicting pressures: the effects of climate change threaten productivity, which, in turn, may impair food security and the affordability of healthy diets; the accelerating growth of carbon markets creates incentives to store carbon in soil and forests; changes in consumer preferences and behavior incentivize the adoption of greener production technologies; and agricultural innovation drives increased productivity in agriculture. Managing these risks and delicate tradeoffs requires creative and collaborative responses from farmers, governments, the private sector, and the international community.

Strong institutions would protect natural capital and benefit the region

Weak land rights, including carbon rights, pose a barrier to the transformation that must take place for Latin America and the Caribbean to capitalize on opportunities in land use in a greening world. Challenges include institutional weaknesses in cadastral databases, land rights allocations, parcel-based data, and systems for territorial planning. Lack of clear land tenure in the region has been associated with weaker enforcement of regulations for land use, reduced access to credit, and lower investment in land for productive use (Hanusch 2023). Insecure land tenure can have significant consequences for people, driving poverty and food insecurity (Tseng et al. 2020). Areas with undesignated land tenure in the Amazon (almost 30 percent of the land area) continue to be deforestation hot spots. Between 2013 and 2020, up to 40 percent of forest loss in the Amazon occurred on land with unclear land tenure. Lack of strictly enforced cutoff dates for regularization claims means that individuals can still use occupation as a basis for claiming a right to title land in the undesignated portions of the Amazon (Brito et al. 2021). Moreover, land is transferred from public to private ownership at prices far below market levels (Hanusch 2023). For example, in the state of Mato Grosso in Brazil, the private cost of land is over $R9,000 per hectare (ha), at least six times higher than the cost for titling undesignated land through public programs (Brito et al. 2021; Hanusch 2023). Implementation of land use and territorial planning represents another challenge to improving land use efficiency in the region. Although countries have made progress in developing strategies, implementation continues to lag. An additional challenge is that, in general, ecosystem services are not explicitly included in the standards regulating the environmental and social evaluation of projects in the region, although countries have begun to incorporate them in the analysis of costs and benefits of various policy options.

High rates of deforestation put existing natural capital at risk. Overall, Latin America and the Caribbean accounts for 8 percent of global emissions and almost 25 percent of the greenhouse gas (GHG) emissions from land-use change globally (Blackman et al. 2017; Blackman and Veit 2018). In 2021, 46 percent of emissions in the region were from agriculture, forestry, and land use change (26 percent from agriculture and 20 percent from forestry and land use change).[15] Although deforestation rates have slowed, they are still high. Between 1990 and 2020, forest cover in the region declined from 53 to 46 percent, representing a loss of 138 million ha of forested land (ECLAC 2021). The Amazon basin is at risk of transitioning from a net sink for GHGs to a net source (Harris et al. 2021).

Although the Amazon stores as much carbon as the Congo Basin, emissions from land use change and deforestation are twice as high, resulting in net carbon sequestration of only 0.1 $GtCO_2e$ per year, far below the potential if these emissions were reduced (Harris et al. 2021). Yet there are still countries with significant areas of forest cover. At the high end, the Bahamas, Guyana, Peru, and Suriname still have natural land cover over 70 percent of their land, representing a significant opportunity to preserve existing primary forest. At the opposite end of the spectrum, El Salvador, Mexico, and Uruguay retain less than 16 percent; in these countries, the core challenge is restoration and preventing further degradation.[16]

Deforestation in the region is driven by a combination of land speculation, cattle pasture expansion, forest conversion for subsistence and commercial crops, and clearing for mining (De Sy et al. 2015). Conversion of land for livestock accounts for 70 percent of forest loss in South America and 54 percent in Central America, while cropland expansion led to 22 percent of deforestation in South America and 39 percent in Central America (FAO 2021). Land grabbing and speculation are key contributors to this process, particularly in the transition of forest to pasture. Speculators will establish pastureland after deforestation to make legal claims on the land easier to substantiate, allowing the speculator to transfer the land to private ownership and then sell it for profit when private market prices rise (Borras et al. 2011). In the Caribbean, 44 percent of deforestation was driven by land conversion for urban infrastructure, 29 percent for livestock grazing, and 27 percent for dam construction and water course alterations.

Historically low or inconsistent enforcement of environmental laws and regulations has increased deforestation challenges. A large proportion of deforestation is driven by illegal activities. In Brazil, almost all deforestation is likely to be illegal, due primarily to often weak enforcement of existing laws. Between 2005 and 2018, fines, civil actions, and embargoes are estimated to have affected less than 1 percent of the Amazon's illegal deforestation (MapBiomas Alerta 2020). In Central America, illegal drug trafficking may account for 15–40 percent of national forest loss in Guatemala, Honduras, and Nicaragua (Sesnie et al. 2017). Moreover, the illegal timber trade makes up almost half the earnings of illegal environmental crime at the global level, representing up to $152 billion in value each year (INTERPOL 2022; Patrick, Butsic, and Potts 2023).

Investments to increase productivity, while large, can deliver significant benefits

Making land use more efficient carries direct and indirect costs that require significant investments and supportive public policies. First, moving from one land use pattern to another incurs direct transition costs of implementation (such as labor and capital costs for land clearing, planting, tilling, and installing or removing irrigation). Second, there are indirect opportunity costs due to the value of the land that is forgone, given that it could be used for other purposes.

Figure 2.2 provides an estimate of the impacts and costs of managing land use to maximize carbon storage in the region over the near term while maintaining current production levels.[17] The chart presents the implicit carbon prices, and the percentage and absolute change in CO_2e storage, that could be gained in the near term—estimated to be a period of five years—from a transition to maximizing carbon storage. The horizontal axis shows the absolute increase in

Figure 2.2 Comparison of Absolute and Percentage Change in CO_2e Storage and Implicit Carbon Price in the Near Term

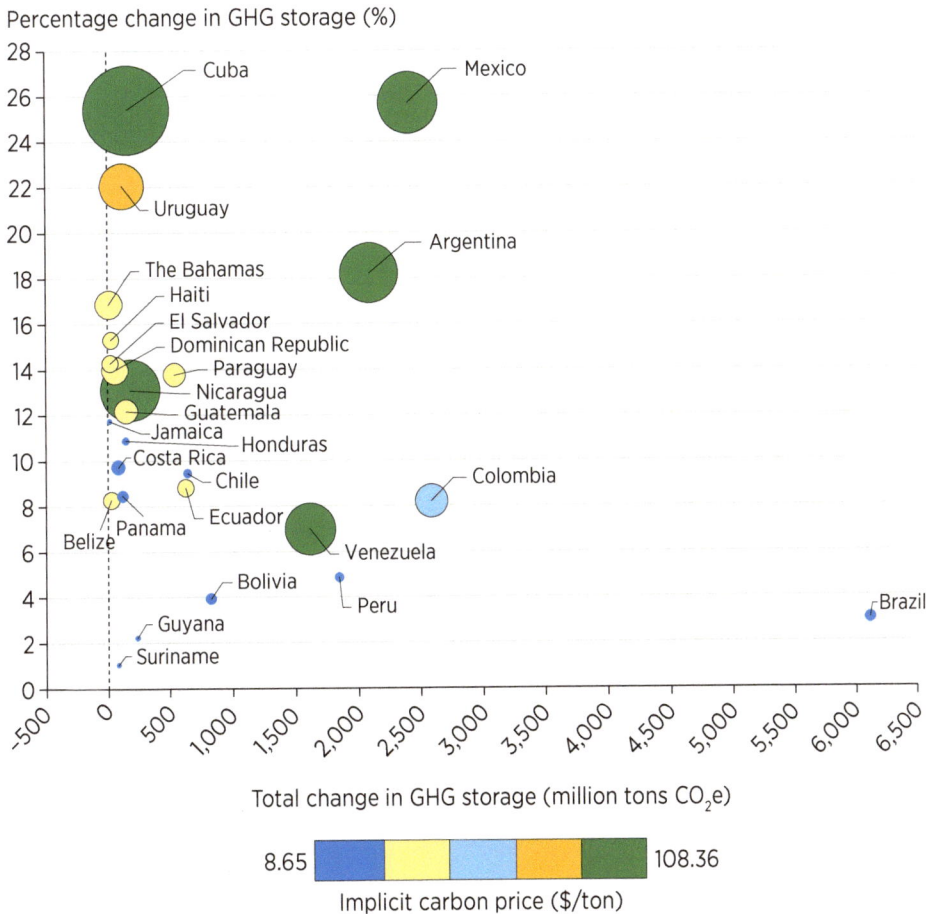

Source: World Bank calculations from World Bank 2025b.

Note: Values are derived from the first step of the transition, on a carbon storage maximizing pathway. CO_2e = carbon dioxide equivalent; GHG = greenhouse gas.

GHG storage potential, and the vertical axis shows the percentage change in storage potential for each country. The color and size of the marks show the associated implicit carbon price for the transition, a measure that captures both the financial and economic opportunity costs of the transition. The graph identifies two clear opportunities and one challenge for land use transitions in the near future. The first opportunity for large amounts of GHG storage is in Brazil, which has the largest potential for additional carbon sequestration in the region at a relatively low implicit carbon price. The second opportunity for transformation in the region lies in the large number of countries with low implicit carbon prices and relatively high percentage changes in carbon sequestration and other environmental benefits. This includes countries such as Chile, Ecuador, Paraguay, and Peru. While transformations in these countries have less impact on the absolute provision of environmental services in the region, the transition is significant in domestic terms. Figure 2.2 also identifies a challenge for the region, as many of the countries that have the most significant carbon storage potential after Brazil—such as Argentina, Colombia, and Mexico—require relatively high implicit carbon prices to enable the transition, due to either high financial costs for the transition, high economic opportunity costs, or a combination of both.

Direct financial transition costs for land use in Latin America and the Caribbean are higher on average, and more variable, than in other regions of the world. Median total transition costs for the region (for Pareto solutions across the full transition time horizon) are $1,697/sq km, the highest in the world, and the standard deviation is $1,193/sq km. This compares to a global median of $546/sq km and a standard deviation of $1,185/sq km. These high costs are due to the need for both agricultural intensification and landscape protection and restoration in the region, particularly since much of the restoration is occurring in tropical areas where active restoration costs can be quite high (Brancalion et al. 2019). Despite these high costs, the analysis suggests that the long-term benefits outweigh them. In fact, the positive economic benefits of land transformation are greater than transition costs (net economic value is always positive) across all countries (World Bank 2025b). Other research has shown that the region ranks highly in cost-effective opportunities for carbon sequestration overall (Grafton et al. 2021).

It is also important to note that the transitional costs of reallocating land uses will be borne disproportionately by specific areas in the region. In fact, analysis for this report discussed in box 3.1 (chapter 3) finds a positive and statistically significant correlation between those locations and proxy measures of both relative poverty (through relative multidimensional deprivation) and smallholder farming (proxied by dominant field size). Enabling a transition toward a more efficient allocation of land will clearly require well-targeted government support and investments, particularly to support vulnerable and poor populations.

In addition, investments in information systems to enable more efficient land use will be required. Unfortunately, Latin America and the Caribbean is not investing enough in the agricultural technologies that can significantly improve productivity, or in the technologies that allow authorities to more effectively monitor and enforce regulations across the region. Digital access, for example, which can enable adoption of both agricultural and forest monitoring technologies, lags significantly in rural areas: 63 percent of the region's rural population lacks adequate access to digital technology due to technical, cost, or knowledge barriers, compared to 29 percent of the urban population (Ziegler et al. 2020). Additionally, smart agriculture management technology adoption and entrepreneurship in many countries lag behind other regions of the world, leading to a lack of information systems that meet farmers' needs (Loukos and Arathoon 2021; Puntel et al. 2022). An important caveat is that several countries in Latin America and the Caribbean—Argentina, Brazil, and Uruguay, in particular—have high levels of adoption of agricultural information systems and technology, especially in mapping, remote sensing, and mobile apps that can improve information and market access (Puntel et al. 2022). Satellite technologies are increasingly being adopted for forest conservation and management, resulting in cost savings relative to other methods. Indigenous communities are also adopting these technologies for deforestation monitoring, which is transforming conservation practices (González and Kröger 2023).

Catching up on research and development (R&D) investments and adopting innovative technologies could significantly increase productivity

The analysis suggests that intensification, and therefore adoption of innovation technologies, will be required to support a transition to more efficient land allocation in Latin America and the Caribbean. The report finds that intensification plays an important role in increasing agricultural production and productivity.[18] In a GHG sequestration maximizing scenario, 48 percent of current agricultural lands adopt intensification and best management practices. In this scenario, although about 5 percent of regional forestlands are converted to crop agriculture, tree cover overall increases in the region, resulting in net reforestation. With the additional adoption of best management practices, agricultural lands also retain more tree cover than under current management practices. Intensification is even more important in scenarios seeking to maximize economic production, in which 65 percent of agricultural lands intensify and adopt best management practices. In this scenario, some net loss of forest cover occurs (about 10 percent), although GHG sequestration in the region remains the same by increasing forest lands with high GHG sequestration potential.

Intensification may be challenging because total factor productivity (TFP) growth has slowed significantly since 2010. Between 1990 and 2010, TFP growth provided the majority of output gains, but this declined precipitously (by 66 percent) after 2010, leaving input intensification as the core driver of continued growth at a regional level. Several factors explain the decline—namely, resource degradation and climate change, drought, economic downturns, and low levels of technology diffusion and adoption by small family farmers (Ballesteros 2022; Klein Goldewijk et al. 2017; Taylor and Rising 2021). Climate change and land degradation play especially critical roles. The region has experienced a 26 percent decline in total productivity since 1961 due to climate change impacts (Ortiz-Bobea et al. 2021). Land degradation, affecting 22 percent of the land area in the region, has also driven productivity declines or required increasing inputs to maintain yields.[19] As crop production in other regions, particularly North America, has declined, South America's production has become increasingly important for satisfying global demand for agricultural products. Since 1985, South America has experienced the greatest production increases in soybean, sugarcane, nonconiferous wood products, and beef globally, and the second-largest increases in corn (Zalles et al. 2021).

The uptick of innovations to increase efficiency of land use and agriculture in Latin America and the Caribbean has been slow and fragmented. Regionally, agriculture productivity growth has been higher than the global average (2.1 percent per year from 1991 to 2015), but lower than that of Northeast Asia, the fastest growing region, according to the Organisation for Economic Co-operation and Development (OECD). Moreover, this productivity growth has been distributed unevenly, with the Caribbean subregion having one of the world's slowest productivity growth rates (1 percent per year) (Agnew and Hendery 2023; GAP Initiative 2023; OECD/FAO 2019). The proportion of growth attributable to TFP varies by country and by product. In Argentina, for example, 75 percent of agricultural production growth is attributable to TFP growth (Morgan, Fuglie, and Saini 2023), while in Mexico, Andean countries, and Central America and the Caribbean, input intensification drove the majority of gains.

Furthermore, the structure of agricultural support in Latin America and the Caribbean varies widely and can lead to inefficiencies in productivity and reduced consumer well-being. The total agricultural support in the region is low as a percentage of total GDP relative to the United States and the European Union (EU-28). However, both the level of general support (for example, research and knowledge transfer, marketing, inspection, infrastructure, and the like) as a percentage of total support payments for agriculture and the level of market price support for producers (which can distort farmer incentives) as a share of total support payments for producers are higher on average (Egas and De Salvo 2018). The use of market price supports, which can distort farmer decision-making, has increased since the COVID-19 (coronavirus) pandemic, reaching 15 percent of producer support in 2021. Meanwhile, general services support, which is nondistorting, has declined from a high of 75 percent of total support in 2014, to 50 percent by 2021.[20] Primarily, support in agricultural R&D is driven by government and multilateral development bank expenditures, while private R&D is a key driver of innovation in just a few countries (Nin-Pratt et al. 2023).

Policy makers should be aware that the direction of agricultural innovation can have a variety of effects on land use and deforestation. Global evidence suggests that technology-driven intensification that allows for greater productivity on the same unit of land can reduce pressures for land expansion, while intensification based on the substitution of inputs, or adoption of higher-value crop mixes, can tend to worsen land expansion-driven deforestation pressures (Byerlee, Stevenson, and Villoria 2014). The context of land protection also matters. In areas that have weak land use protection and enforcement, productivity increases are more likely to lead to land expansion. Conversely, in areas where land governance and urbanization are stronger, this effect is weakened, and increases in productivity are less likely to drive expansion of agricultural land. Identifying high-risk areas and mitigating these risks is a critical component to ensuring that productivity gains do not exacerbate deforestation (Hanusch 2023).

Agricultural and land use policies and practices play a key role in reducing both deforestation and emissions and in supporting regional prosperity and health. Stopping deforestation and increasing agriculture production is not a zero-sum game. In fact, Latin America and the Caribbean is one of the few global regions that still contains non-forest, arable land that could be sustainably converted to agriculture (Morris, Sebastian, and Perego 2020; United Nations Convention to Combat Desertification 2019). It should be noted that not all agricultural land expansion directly contributes to deforestation. Moreover, cropland expansion, frequently from pastureland, is often a low-cost strategy preceding intensification and increased agricultural productivity (which is a key strategy for reducing deforestation pressures). Redesigning agricultural and land use systems through new institutions and incentives, innovation, and investments can contribute both to agriculture's essential role in supporting health, resilience, and prosperity and to reducing deforestation and GHG emissions.

Innovation in tracking and tracing products, combined with improved monitoring of deforestation, can help ensure continued access to existing markets while opening the doors to new markets. As the world moves toward greener preferences, innovation in tracking and tracing agricultural products will be important to ensure continued access to existing markets. Efforts in tracking and tracing can help countries in the region distinguish their products in the market, creating premiums if combined with efforts for reduced deforestation, improved sustainability, and greater inclusion. Table 2.1 summarizes suggested key actions in the land use and forest sector.

Table 2.1   Key Actions Needed in the Land Use and Forest Sector

Institutions	Investments	Innovation
Protect clearly defined property rights through strong environmental frameworks, up-to-date, multipurpose cadastral databases, and integrated property registry systems.	Increase market access by expanding digital and physical connectivity, while maintaining environmental sustainability and avoiding destruction of natural capital. Invest in digital and transport infrastructure, and in efficient logistics.	Facilitate the adoption of more sustainable production practices by investing in agricultural extension services that integrate long-term management of natural capital.
Align incentives with environmental and development goals by repurposing agricultural subsidies to support adoption of new technologies and sustainable production practices and provide public goods for the sector. Integrate PES with other complementary policies (for example, tax reform, credit access, and revenue recycling) to support land use for environmental goals and protect the livelihoods of vulnerable and Indigenous communities.	Improve enforcement of rules to protect people and the planet through improved MRV systems.

Develop a green NQI to capture green premiums, maintain access, and potentially increase market share in export markets. | Invest in R&D to solve local problems and increase the sustainability and productivity of the agricultural sector. Implement pilot R&D projects, develop research voucher programs, and develop a network of agricultural technology centers targeting interventions according to the sophistication of the producers. |
| Build local capacity for service provision and enforcement of rules to protect people and the planet. | | Innovate in policy design within a learning framework. Experiment with the design of PES schemes, for example, with metrics to evaluate the effectiveness of the program. |

Source: Original table for this publication.

Notes: MRV = monitoring, reporting, and verification; NQI = national quality infrastructure; PES = payment for ecosystem services; R&D = research and development.

Minerals to Support the Energy Transition: Upgrading Existing Production Processes

Box 2.3 presents an overview of the challenges to institutions, investments, and innovations of upgrading the mining industry in the region.

Box 2.3

Key Bottlenecks for Transforming and Upgrading the Mining Industry for the Energy Transition

Upgrading current production systems in the critical minerals industry will be necessary to expand the economic-environmental production possibilities frontier, improve efficiency in production processes, and ensure continued access to international markets. Currently, emissions in the sector are still high, environmental footprints are large, and social risks run deep.

• *Institutions*: Despite existing environmental and social frameworks, negative impacts on the environment and communities persist. The region has one of the world's highest levels of socioenvironmental conflicts related to mining activities.

• *Investments*: Limited investment in public goods, such as an updated geological knowledge base, has reduced incentives for exploration, limiting the expansion of future production. Excessive delays in obtaining necessary permits and certifications may delay the supply response to the surge in the demand for energy transition minerals. Lagging investments in connective infrastructure may undermine production expansion plans.

• *Innovation*: Despite some successful examples of local innovation, an underdeveloped innovative cluster of supplier firms limits the growth potential of a greener mining industry.

The World Needs the Region's Energy Transition Minerals

Minerals have a key role to play in supporting the transition toward a greener world, so demand is expected to increase as clean energy technologies take hold. Clean energy technologies and the expansion of electricity distribution systems require minerals (mainly lithium, copper, graphite, cobalt, nickel, and REE). Demand for copper is projected to increase greatly in the next 10–15 years, increasing fastest under the net zero emissions (NZE) scenario until 2035 (figure 2.3, panel a). However, after 2035, growth is expected to level off and demand eventually to slowly decline. The main driver of demand for copper is electricity networks, where copper usage peaks in 2040 and then declines. With the international community supporting a move toward NZE, expansion of copper production in the medium term will be crucial. Similarly, lithium demand is expected to rise very rapidly until 2035, and more moderately in the following decade; its increase also depends on the degree of decarbonization. Since

Figure 2.3 Copper and Lithium Demand Growth: Historical and Projected Scenarios

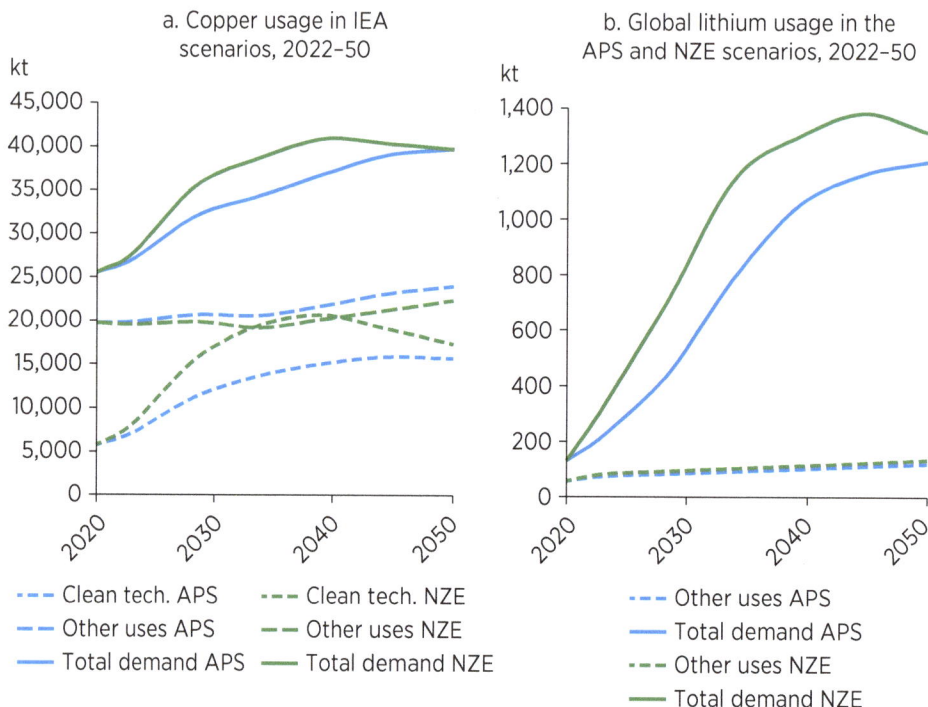

a. Copper usage in IEA scenarios, 2022–50

b. Global lithium usage in the APS and NZE scenarios, 2022–50

--- Clean tech. APS   --- Clean tech. NZE
-- Other uses APS   -- Other uses NZE
— Total demand APS   — Total demand NZE

--- Other uses APS
— Total demand APS
--- Other uses NZE
— Total demand NZE

Sources: IEA 2023a and International Copper Study Group 2022.

Note: APS = announced pledges scenario; kt = kiloton; NZE = net zero emissions.

lithium demand starts from a very low level, the absolute increase in supply needed to meet the jump in demand is much smaller than in the case of copper. In the announced pledges scenario (APS), the rate of increase over the whole period from 2022 to 2050 is 9.3 percent, and around 15 percent until 2035 (figure 2.3, panel b). Lithium demand virtually explodes in the NZE scenario, increasing at an average annual rate of 8.6 percent from 2022 to 2050, and posting an average annual growth rate of more than 18 percent until 2035. Batteries for EVs dominate the demand.

The availability and affordability of these important minerals are a concern. Demand projections point to a large growth in critical minerals' consumption that far exceeds the rate at which new primary and secondary sources are currently being developed; this gap could delay the global transition to a low-carbon economy. The world will only be able to meet the goal of NZE by 2050 if massive new mineral supplies come online in a timely way.

Latin America and the Caribbean's natural richness in such minerals puts it at the center of opportunities under these changing winds. Although there is a high concentration worldwide of countries and companies that have mining resources and processing facilities, few countries can completely meet their needs for the minerals that are critical to the energy transition from domestic sources. Chile is the main copper producer with 24 percent of the world's total production. For lithium, the main producer is Australia, with around 50 percent of mining output (Chile follows in second place with 30 percent), and China accounts for 60–70 percent of lithium processing (IEA 2023b). For Latin America and the Caribbean, copper and lithium are the most consequential of the six critical minerals mentioned earlier, given their abundance in the region. Of the 13 countries with the largest copper reserves (USGS 2023), three are in Latin America and the Caribbean (Chile, Mexico, and Peru), and they account for 36 percent of world reserves. Other countries in the region also have copper resources, although less documented: Argentina, Brazil, Ecuador, and Panama. Of the eight countries that have large amounts of lithium (USGS 2023), again, three are in Latin America and the Caribbean (Argentina, Brazil, and Chile), accounting for 47 percent of world reserves (figure 2.4). Other Latin America and the Caribbean countries, such as Bolivia, Mexico, and Peru, also have important lithium resources, but their commercial viability remains a challenge.

Figure 2.4 Latin America and the Caribbean's Share of Production and Reserves for Six Minerals Critical to the Energy Transition

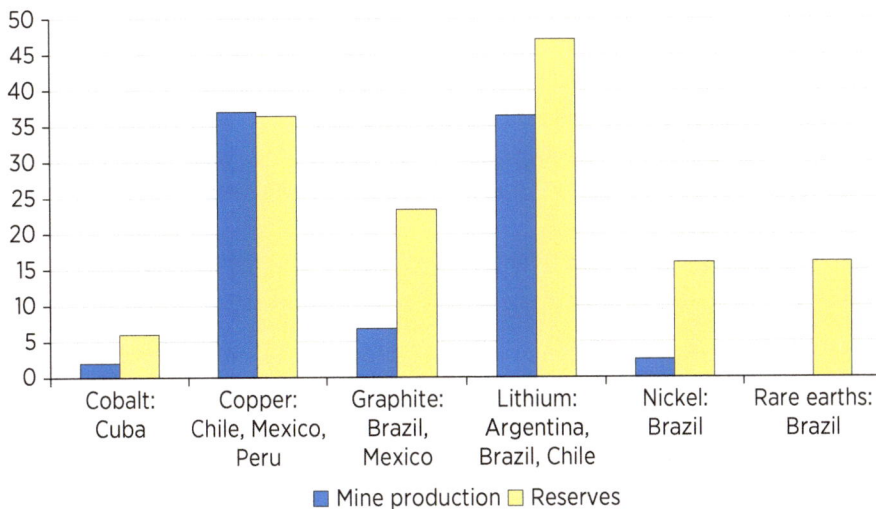

Source: USGS 2023.

Note: Only includes those countries for which the United States Geological Survey (USGS) provides figures. Note that this understates the Latin American and Caribbean region's mine production and future potential.

The global transition toward low carbon economies opens opportunities for the region to export the necessary ETMs and potentially develop downstream products such as batteries. These two paths are not mutually exclusive but are, in principle, independent of each other. Although the share of raw materials in the total cost of EV batteries has increased, this does not necessarily mean that it is profitable to locate battery production close to mines. In fact, most battery plants are in countries with large markets for batteries. However, there are several possible points of entry for Latin America and the Caribbean countries in clean energy supply chains. The best point of entry depends on many factors, of which access to raw materials is only one. The bottom line for the region, however, is that it should be actively evaluating options to leverage its natural resource endowments to achieve a higher rate of economic growth by participating in global value chains, even if the exact nature of that participation is still being determined.

Bottlenecks Exist in Institutions, Investments, and Innovation

To make the most of the green transition, existing processes will need to be updated to respond to changes in demand and preferences. Upgrading current production systems in the ETMs industry will be necessary to expand the EE-PPF and ensure continued access to international markets. With world demand shifting toward products with lower carbon content, existing production processes will have to be upgraded to ensure that Latin America and the Caribbean's products continue to be competitive in international markets. Although the need for updates applies to all industrial processes in the region, the mining industry (a well-established sector) provides a good example because it is also expected to experience increased demand from other green sectors that are expected to grow in the coming years. However, several existing bottlenecks may pose challenges, which are discussed in the following sections.

Strengthened institutions will be necessary to avoid the potentially large environmental and social costs of increased production

A lack of strong regulatory frameworks that protect the environment could aggravate the negative externalities from mining activities. Negative impacts on land and the consequent effects on local flora and fauna may be concerns when expanded production in the sector is considered. In copper and lithium mines, such effects may appear in industrial mining areas, camp sites, waste dumps, and tailings ponds. The annual amount of newly disturbed land per million metric tons (MMT) of copper ore extracted is in the 2–4.5 ha/million metric tons of copper ore (MtCu) range.[21] Surface mining can directly damage surface soil and vegetation, whereas underground mining may contribute to the collapse of land

and subsequently deteriorate surface land and vegetation. Many mining locations, such as in the Andes, are characterized by rugged geographies that limit the land area available for the safe disposal of tailings.[22] Lithium extraction can also affect land use in Latin America and the Caribbean and worldwide. Recent work suggests that lithium operations on the Atacama Salt Flat in Northern Chile's Antofagasta region have already caused significant negative impacts on the surrounding (already scarce) vegetation and wildlife (Gutiérrez et al. 2022). Water pollution may also be a concern when considering the expansion of critical mineral extraction and production. Doubling copper supply may significantly increase competition for water, since 33 percent of the world's reserves are in countries where water risk is high.[23] More than 100 lithium projects have been identified in over 32 basins in the region, which makes issues around the water footprint of these projects potentially important and suggests the need to work now to improve coordination between mining activities and water management.

In addition, the need to expand production must be weighed against increased GHG emissions. Today, GHG emissions in copper and lithium value chains are still high. The mining production process comprises three stages—mining, refining, and processing—and the attendant GHG emissions for each stage vary by mineral. For copper, GHG emissions come mainly from mining rather than processing and are principally linked to energy use. On average, 83 percent of copper-related emissions occur during mining and refining for use as an input for manufactured goods (such as wires). Seventy percent of those emissions (of the 83 percent total) are generated by mining sites, while 23 percent come from the smelting and refining stages of production. The remaining 7 percent is due to transport and the end-of-life treatment of final products (ICA 2023). The largest proportion of GHGs emitted by copper producers (46 percent) are Scope 2 emissions (indirect emissions associated with the purchase of electricity, steam, heat, and cooling), while Scope 1 emissions (direct emissions from owned or controlled sources) represent 23 percent of GHG emissions by the industry (ICA 2023). For lithium, in contrast, GHG emissions stem mainly from processing.[24] Mining from brines like those in Latin America and the Caribbean results in lower CO_2e emissions than from hard rock,[25] which could constitute a competitive advantage for several countries in the region. A recent study by Universidad Católica de Chile and Ductuc, a consulting firm, estimated that lithium emissions in Australia might be three to six times higher than those in Chile.[26]

Without institutional protection and strong enforcement mechanisms, the expansion or intensification of mining activities could pose several risks to local communities. The development of sustainable mining offers an opportunity to generate revenues that allow for greater investment in infrastructure and community benefits (OECD 2022). While direct employment generation is limited, indirect job multipliers for the local economy are often large. Moreover, spending by mine workers can induce additional economic opportunities. Estimates for the Antofagasta region in Chile suggest that one additional employment position in a large mine can lead to the creation of between 3.1 and 5.7 additional jobs (ICMM 2017).[27] Despite mining's positive effects on employment and wages,[28] negative externalities from the expansion or intensification of mining activities may exacerbate existing socioenvironmental conflicts and accentuate gender inequality. Such conflicts may arise due to the burden that additional activities place on local communities, the often limited participation of these communities in decision-making, the partial availability and accessibility of information, and the weaknesses in mechanisms for benefit sharing with such communities (Mahiques, Galuccio, and Freytes 2022).

Latin America and the Caribbean has one of the world's highest levels of socioenvironmental conflicts related to mining activities (León, Muñoz, and Sánchez 2020). These conflicts often result in production delays for product portfolios in the short and medium terms (IEA 2022a; Jones, Acuña, and Rodríguez 2021; Watkins et al. 2017). Argentina, Chile, Mexico, and Peru top the list in terms of the number of conflicts.[29] Community rejection of mining often stems from concerns about environmental and social (E&S) impact, disputes over land use, disagreements over benefits for local communities including employment expectations, and lack of supervision (Brannstrom, Seghezzo, and Gorayeb 2022; Mahiques, Galuccio, and Freytes 2022; Pragier 2019; Wagner and Walter 2020). In Bolivia, for example, a high-profile project in the Uyuni Salt Flats was cancelled in 2019 because of protests by local communities.[30] In Argentina, disagreements over lithium mining have increased in recent years, with conflicts with local communities identified in more than half of the lithium projects surveyed by the Argentine Chamber of Mining Companies (Wagner and Walter 2020).

In addition, institutions are needed to ensure macroeconomic stability related to the increase in mineral exports. Although successful examples in the region provide confidence that resources can be managed in a way that protects environmental, fiscal, and macroeconomic stability, previous experiences in Latin America and the Caribbean clearly indicate that natural resource revenues are much more volatile than other revenues. In fact, countries in the region rely more on volatile commodity revenues for their tax base than high-income commodity producers do (Sinnott, Nash, and de la Torre 2010). For copper and lithium, volatility remains a concern given the high uncertainty surrounding future demand and supply. In addition, higher dependency on commodities for fiscal revenues and under-saving of windfalls have contributed to procyclical expenditures in the region.

Coordination failures and lack of policy and institutional support have undermined value chain development

Some countries in Latin America and the Caribbean are defining policies and institutional frameworks to support downstream value addition. Value addition in the region has been limited for various reasons, such as problems with (a) access to low-cost energy, without which refining is unprofitable; (b) access to technology and innovation initiatives; (c) access to finance in competitive terms and conditions; and (d) protective trade regulatory measures, such as high import tariffs in some metal export markets. However, ongoing energy transition is opening the way for more downstream integration in the region. Foreign companies are increasingly investing in downstream industries. For example, in August 2023, China's BYD, one of the largest EV manufacturers in the world, announced an investment of $290 million to build a lithium cathode factory in northern Chile. The company has also announced plans to comprehensively integrate its EV supply chain in Brazil, including processing, battery production, and automotive manufacturing. In Mexico, China's CATL (a battery company) plans to invest in an EV battery plant to supply US-based automakers. In Argentina, some projects aim to secure the supply of lithium to specific producers, such as Toyota in Sales de Jujuy, and other small-scale initiatives aim to develop battery components and EVs (Obaya 2021).

It is important to note that ETM value chains are highly concentrated and are increasingly becoming the target of industrial policies in advanced nations. Both the United States and the EU have enacted rules to increase production, refining, processing, and recycling of critical minerals within their territories. However, geopolitical tensions have risen, and mistrust between major powers has heightened concerns about the risks of countries exploiting for political purposes their control over resources or processing capacity. Since mineral resources are available only in a few constituencies, and three countries process more than half of the global output of several key ETMs, the extreme concentration of global supply creates a significant dependency for the rest of the world (IEA 2022b). Such concerns have prompted several countries to enact legislative measures that protect and help develop local value chains. In the United States, the Inflation Reduction Act (IRA) provides $394 billion in energy and climate funding mainly through tax credits to catalyze private investments in these sectors. Many of the incentives are contingent on meeting domestic procurement requirements. For example, to unlock the full EV consumer credit, a portion of critical minerals in the battery must have been recycled in North America or been extracted or processed in a country that has a free trade agreement with the US. The battery must also have been manufactured or assembled in North America (McKinsey & Company 2022). Turning to the EU, the European Critical Raw Materials Act is designed to significantly increase the production, refining, processing, and recycling of critical raw materials in Europe.[31] Other countries, including Australia, Canada, China, Japan, and the United Kingdom (UK), also are following this example.[32] Some of these countries have entered agreements with critical mineral-producing Latin America and the Caribbean countries. Argentina is in discussions with the United States for an exception to the free trade agreement tariff requirement of the IRA (Bloomberg 2023), while Chile and the EU have signed a memorandum of understanding to, among other initiatives, develop value-added lithium in Chile (European Commission 2023).

High energy costs and limited domestic demand hamper downstream value chain development. Several challenges along the value chain currently mean that most activity in the region is limited to extraction. Most mining operations in the region export copper concentrates; less than half of mined copper is smelted and refined before export. This is particularly the case in Chile and Peru. For example, Chile's mining accounts for 24 percent of the world's copper production, but only 8 percent of the world's output of refined copper. High energy costs mean that further processing would not be profitable in many production sites. For lithium, while there is some interest across the region in expanding the downstream value chain, most companies are currently focused on extraction.

Limited local demand for refined copper restricts opportunities to expand value-added activities. The small size of the manufacturing sector in the region poses an additional barrier to diversification of the value chain. Most countries with a high intensity of copper use are middle-income countries with large manufacturing export sectors.[33] Mexico, with its important manufacturing industry, is the only Latin America and the Caribbean country that approaches the levels of demand seen in countries such as the Republic of Korea. Brazil and Chile are at the same level of domestic demand as undiversified commodity exporters such as Indonesia or rich countries with services-dominated economies such as Japan. In Brazil, domestic demand—for example through the production of semi-manufactured products that can be used in industries such as automobile production—has justified the establishment of copper smelters and refineries. However, the industry's growth has been limited by state taxes that raise the internal cost of copper and thus encourage importing copper concentrate from other Latin America and the Caribbean countries that benefit from tariff reductions due to international trade agreements (BNamericas 2022; Mejía and Aliakbari 2024).

Upstream development of value chains has also been weak. The region has underperformed in developing a productive cluster of knowledge-intensive service supplier firms for large multinational companies. The region has failed to replicate the success in the creation of these knowledge-intensive clusters of other mining-intensive countries such as Australia and Canada, or oil-extractive countries such as Norway. Despite a long history in mining, which accounts for a significant share of GDP, in many Latin America and the Caribbean countries the development of productive backward linkages remains suboptimal (Olvera and Iizuka 2020). Although mining has generally been considered an enclave sector with few opportunities for productive linkages, the literature has shown that it was an important base for industrialization and economic development in Australia, Canada, Finland, Sweden, and the United States (de Ferranti et al. 2002; Wright and Czelusta 2004).

Ramped up investments in information and complementary public goods and services will be needed to grow the sector

Governments that have been successful in attracting investment and achieving long-term mining growth owe part of their success to a robust geological knowledge base. Available geological data is critical to generating new exploration projects and increasing the likelihood of commercially viable mines being built. Developing a broad geological knowledge base may be costly, but it improves the likelihood of successful exploration and increases the attractiveness of a country to exploration companies. Countries that provide knowledge in the form of accurate and detailed geological maps and other geoscientific data— such as results of geochemical surveys, geophysical measurements, and drill cores—improve their attractiveness to investors, particularly if the data are made available online. Requiring exploration companies to provide reports, samples, and other information once they have completed their work in a particular area, as well as archiving the data and making them available, provides subsequent explorers with highly useful information.

Limited investment in the geological knowledge base may have led to low exploration. Most of the deposits discovered in the region that recently came online or inform the current investment pipeline were made over 20 years ago. For copper, less than 1 percent of copper added since 1990 originates in discoveries made in the past five years (S&P Global 2022). Geological information is key to decreasing the costs of exploration, and it is not always made available systematically in Latin America and the Caribbean, except in some countries, such as Argentina, Brazil, Chile, Colombia, and Mexico. Further, current geological surveys often do not include minerals associated with the green transition such as lithium. Brazil and Chile are notable exceptions, with Chile providing open-source geological data through its geological service SERNAGEOMIN, and Brazil creating a critical minerals division under the geology department DIPEME (Bernal, Husar, and Bracht 2023).

Transparent and efficient legal regimes, including timely authorization procedures, are also essential for new exploration investment. Despite Latin America and the Caribbean's significant critical minerals endowment, sector investments remain below the region's production potential. Integrated permitting systems (mining, environment, land, water, and the like), with online access and streamlined and predictable procedures based on clear criteria and applied in a transparent manner, need to be created across the region to facilitate the supply response of ETMs without compromising their environmental and social sustainability.

Further, current policies render the region relatively unattractive for private sector investment. A recent ranking across 62 jurisdictions puts most countries in Latin America and the Caribbean in the lower half in terms of investment attractiveness. The ranking is created using information collected through interviews of executives at mining and extraction companies on their perceptions of the attractiveness and ease of doing business in those 62 jurisdictions. When focusing on policy perception, Latin America and the Caribbean countries consistently rank low on investment attractiveness, flagging a serious constraint for the development of the sector (Mejía and Aliakbari 2024). Table 2.2 shows the rankings of some Latin America and the Caribbean countries (those providing sufficient responses to be included in the survey).

Complementary infrastructure investment needed to support increased production has also been lagging. Mining, mineral processing, and downstream value addition are capital- and energy-intensive activities that require significant transport, energy, water, and logistics infrastructure. Investing in green and shared infrastructure—such as renewables, water, rail, and port facilities—can improve efficiency and reduce costs for all companies and create economic opportunities in nearby communities. Green infrastructure can help reduce the carbon footprint of mineral processing and downstream value addition industries, protecting their carbon-competitiveness.

Lagging investments in connective infrastructure and maintenance of existing networks may pose challenges to the growth of the sector. Recent work for Argentina focusing on lithium in the northwestern region suggests that road density is the lowest among all regions in the country, with only 30.2 percent being asphalted. Estimates suggest that transport costs in the provinces of Salta and Jujuy, rich in minerals, are 50 percent higher than costs in neighboring regions. While there are some plans to improve railway connectivity, most of the lines connecting the areas in Salta and Jujuy that are rich in lithium are either in bad condition or unnavigable. In addition, energy demand is also expected to

Table 2.2   Ranking of Latin America and the Caribbean Jurisdictions in the Fraser Institute Survey of Mining Companies

		Ranking on investment attractiveness index	Ranking on policy perception index
Argentina	San Juan	19	23
	Santa Cruz	32	40
	Jujuy	39	39
	Salta	45	36
	Catamarca	49	35
Guyana		22	32
Brazil		25	29
Ecuador		27	45
Peru		34	49
Chile		35	38
Colombia		36	50
Mexico*		37	44
Bolivia		52	43

Source: Mejía and Aliakbari 2024. The closer the index to 100, the better the performance.
Note: * Recent policy changes are likely to lead to a lower rank for Mexico.

increase fourfold by 2030 in these regions. With energy currently generated by gas, investments will be required to transition to cleaner energy sources (World Bank 2023).

Some countries in Latin America and the Caribbean are articulating infrastructure development strategies based on economic corridors in mining regions. The aim is to move from mining enclaves to interregional, multipurpose corridors through an increased collaboration between mining companies and between the industry and the state, adopting a multisector approach to invest in economic corridors in mining regions for territorial development. The development of infrastructure based on economic corridors could also leverage important opportunities for suppliers in mining regions, increasing their productive potential and, in turn, reducing social tensions. Box 2.4 discusses development in Peru's Southern Road Corridor. Participative land-use planning and territorial development is key to ensuring that the development needs of indigenous people and local communities are addressed through multifaceted support.

Box 2.4

A Comprehensive Territorial Development Program in Peru's Southern Road Corridor

In southern Peru, there is a route of approximately 500 kilometers along which the ore of the Constancia and Antapaccay mines in Cusco and Las Bambas de Apurímac is transported by truck: the so-called Southern Road Corridor. Owing to the social conflicts that have occurred in the area of influence of this corridor, which have resulted in prolonged closures of the route, the government appointed a high commissioner to seek a final solution for the safe transportation of mining products, with the participation of all relevant companies and communities. The program contemplates multisector interventions to (a) improve the current road and invest in possible alternatives such as rail or a mineral pipeline; (b) close gaps in priority services, such as water and sanitation, electricity, telecommunications, and transportation; and (c) promote productive development and diversification in strategic activities in the territory, such as agribusiness, livestock, tourism, and renewable energy.

Increased innovation—limited to date—would support sustainability and future competitiveness

Latin America and the Caribbean's mining sector has increased its use of clean energy. In general, energy consumption of global mining activities is estimated to be 6.2 percent of total global energy consumption (Holmberg et al. 2017). At the same time, GHG emissions of the metals and mining industry account for approximately 4 to 7 percent of worldwide GHG emissions. Renewable energy in the copper industry is not new in Latin America and the Caribbean. There is widespread use of solar, wind, and thermal energy in Chile´s mining sector. As of 2022, 61.5 percent of the electricity consumption in copper mining in Chile comes from renewable sources, including hydropower, and 70.9 percent is expected for 2027.[34] Moreover, of the 10 cases of worldwide use of renewables in copper mining reported by the Responsible Mining Initiative as of 2019,[35] six are in Chile and two are in Australia.[36,37] Most copper mines that use renewables in Chile do so under private purchase agreement (PPA) schemes and are connected to the grid. This process differs from Australia's, where projects are often off-grid and financed through PPAs or by internal investment.

Despite successful experiences, overall penetration of RE remains low in the copper sector.[38] Barriers to the adoption of RE include concerns about its intermittency since mines operate 24/7, high switching costs from fossil fuels to alternative energy sources, and regulatory limitations concerning self-generation. However, these challenges can be alleviated, in part, by combining with biogas or energy storage, or both (Vergara-Zambrano and Diaz-Alvarado 2022). Since large-scale lithium mining is relatively recent, progress in the use of RE is at the initial stage, both in Latin America and the Caribbean and in the rest of the world, and continued adoption will be required. For lithium, RE is used in a few cases in Australia and Latin America and the Caribbean. Several companies are planning to use solar energy for lithium mining in the provinces of Salta and Jujuy in Argentina, for example.

More innovation to cut water use and care for its quality in mining is being developed, but more is needed to minimize risks. There are two main options for brine exploitation: through solar evaporation ponds (the traditional one in the Southern Cone) or the more recent direct lithium extraction (DLE) method (Vera et al. 2023), which is currently being adopted in Latin America and the Caribbean (box 2.5), including in several projects in Argentina (Goldman Sachs 2023).

Lithium Traditional Solar Evaporation Ponds versus Direct Extraction Methods

In traditional brine pond extraction, lithium brine is pumped to the surface and sent to evaporation ponds, where it remains for 9 to 18 months until most of the water has been removed through solar evaporation. Once the brine in an evaporation pond has reached a given lithium concentration, it is pumped to a lithium recovery facility for extraction using a series of treatments. The main advantage of this type of process is that it consumes relatively little energy and few chemicals. The disadvantages are that, if water in the area is limited, it can compete with other uses (Baudino et al. 2022) (half a million liters or 500 tons of water evaporated are needed to recover a ton of lithium carbonate).[a] In addition, waste accumulates from remaining impurities at each pond, and since concentration of the product is low, a large volume of brine is required for production (table B2.5.1). In the newer process, direct lithium

box continued next page

Box 2.5

Lithium Traditional Solar Evaporation Ponds Versus Direct Extraction Methods *(continued)*

extraction (DLE) technologies extract lithium from brine using filters, membranes, and other equipment, and the "used" brine can be reinjected into the basin aquifers. As shown in table B2.5.1, the main advantages of DLE technology seem to be that it is faster, does not depend on weather, uses less water, and is more efficient since it has a higher lithium recovery rate per volume of brine. However, this method also has some risks: it is a relatively new process whose consequences are still not completely understood, and it also requires a high capital expenditure.

Table B2.5.1 Advantages and Disadvantages of Alternative Lithium Methodologies

Technology	Pros	Cons
Solar evaporation ponds	Low energy and materials use	• Intensive in water use • Remaining salts with impurities generate waste
Direct lithium extraction	• Process lasts only days, not many months • Lower water use. Most water is recycled, not evaporated • Uses absorbents to separate calcium, magnesium, and other impurities, reducing waste • Does not depend on weather	• Still a new technology • Higher technical complexity. There are many DLE methods

Source: Original table for this publication.

a. This is particularly important since scarce water is lost in the process of evaporation.

Source: Goldman Sachs 2023.

There are several institutions and mechanisms for green certification, which can help producers earn green premiums or gain better access to markets. Copper demand growth is expected to outpace supply through 2030, so prices will be driven by overall demand, and copper purchasers will likely focus on accessing copper regardless of its carbon intensity. This could lead to little or no green premium. However, the copper market is expected to be balanced or oversupplied by 2030, leading to marginal premiums for green copper. Private companies are already offering green copper, as are Sweden's Boliden and Austria's Montanwerke-Brixlegg, but they are still getting a low green premium (Onstad 2021; Perry 2022). Similarly, as battery and EV manufacturers set decarbonization targets, demand for low-emission lithium hydroxide may grow, so some forecasts predict a price premium of approximately 4 to 5 percent over the commodity lithium price for that type of lithium compound. Sourcing guidelines, such as those of the London Metal Exchange,[39] lead to a price penalty for suppliers that do not meet requirements, which is a much more important factor than green premiums.

Labeling has also been used as an alternative in the copper industry, for example through the "Copper Mark," which covers one-fifth of global production (Copper Mark 2022). Several lithium battery producers also have net zero targets, including five important battery producers in China (Tycorun 2022). Other examples are the Initiative for Responsible Mining Assurance,[40] which provides third-party audits at the mining level; lithium companies SQM and Albemarle in Chile and Livent in Argentina are members (CEPAL 2023).

Although some local firms have developed important innovations for the industry, they are not the result of rich linkages between suppliers and mining firms. Large mining companies have not built formal long-term linkages or committed to joint innovation with local suppliers, with the exception of companies in Chile and, to a lesser extent, Brazil and Peru (Molina 2018; Stubrin 2018). Local innovation seems to be infrequent and carried out by only a few firms. When production challenges arise, mining firms tend to rely on their established foreign suppliers. There is increasing consensus that the radical innovations needed to significantly improve productivity, profitability, and environmental performance will require a cooperative approach throughout highly connected innovation ecosystems that include mining firms, suppliers, governments, industry associations, academia, and incubators (Olvera 2022).

Such an ecosystem appears to be underdeveloped in the region, despite the importance of mining in the GDP and export baskets of some countries. Large mining companies' preference for working with established suppliers is a major barrier for local firms. Mining firms have long-standing relationships with their suppliers—which have built up their reputational capital, in turn generating trust—and the firms' employees have been trained in the suppliers' technologies, reinforcing technological lock-in (Stubrin 2018). Table 2.3 lists key actions the mining sector needs.

Table 2.3   Key Actions Needed in the Mining Sector

Institutions	Investments	Innovation
Develop a comprehensive strategy to reduce the sector's E&S impact. Establish strong governance and E&S frameworks based on transparency and information sharing. Develop a consistent incentive structure that rewards firms for reducing negative E&S impacts.	Improve efficiency and competitiveness of exports by investing in transport, digital, and logistics infrastructure. Explore opportunities to co-develop RES and provide enabling infrastructure (transmission lines).	Increase support for innovation by creating dedicated public research institutes and technology extension services. Ensure innovators have access to facilities for piloting and prototyping.
Improve coordination between mining firms, governments, and supplier firms through sectoral councils and business associations that improve collaboration and foster high-quality links between actors.	Develop and implement a comprehensive, technology-driven geological information strategy to unlock exploration investments and enhance long-term resource development. Increase productivity of exploration by easing and facilitating exploration projects while investing in new geological infrastructure by adopting new technologies and making information public.	Nurture critical minerals-related value chains to support the expansion of knowledge-based and technology-intensive products.
Enhance intergovernmental coordination to promote the integration of mining, industrial, and environmental policies; cross-border trade; legislation; and oversight across Latin America and the Caribbean countries.	Build efficient and transparent "one-stop-shops" for online integrated permitting (mining, environmental, land, water, and the like) to expedite investments without compromising their E&S sustainability.	Foster high-quality links between mining firms and innovative supplier firms through cluster development policies.
Build local capacity for service provision and infrastructure execution.	Develop a green NQI for mining products to capture green premiums and ensure continued market access.	

Source: Original table for this publication.

Note: E&S = environmental and social; NQI = national quality infrastructure; RES = renewable energy sources.

Leveraging Green Energy to Support New Markets: Green Hydrogen

Box 2.6 presents an overview of the challenges to institutions, investments, and innovations in developing a GH_2 industry in Latin America and the Caribbean.

Box 2.6

Key Bottlenecks to Developing Green Hydrogen Markets

As a new market, green hydrogen (GH_2) production in Latin America and the Caribbean is negligible, yet energy market practitioners have highlighted the region's huge potential. Geography, abundance of renewable energy sources, and the weighted average cost of capital can contribute to or undermine Latin America and the Caribbean countries' comparative advantage in this emerging market.

• *Institutions*: An underdeveloped regulatory framework and limited efforts to build alignment on standards and certifications at the regional and international level deepen investor risk and may add unnecessary costs.

• *Investments*: Large-scale investments in renewable energy would be needed to ramp up GH_2 production, while still supporting the decarbonization of the power grid. Investments in retrofitting existing infrastructure could deliver reduced costs and strengthen comparative advantage.

• *Innovation*: The region still has catching up to do on GH_2 research and development, although some emerging leaders are investing in innovation and building alliances between the private sector and researchers.

Latin America and the Caribbean: A Potential Green Energy Powerhouse

In addition to the region's rich arable lands, there may be no more fertile ground in the green economy than a clean electricity matrix. In this regard, Latin America and the Caribbean starts from an advantageous position, with over 60 percent of its electricity generation coming from renewable energy sources (RES), including hydropower, solar, wind, geothermal, biomass, and others. While hydropower resources are already relatively more exploited and their reliability may falter with the deepening of climate change impacts, they are a great resource for the region because they are able to provide both baseload power and flexible reserves. Moreover, Latin America and the Caribbean has already made significant progress in ensuring access to electricity, with rates above 98 percent in most countries, meaning that additional capacity can be mostly directed toward demand from the productive sector.

The region, therefore, has significant scope to strategically leverage this advantageous natural capital. On the one hand, as mentioned previously, Latin America and the Caribbean can attract energy-intensive industries from around the world to relocate to the region, where firms can significantly reduce their carbon emissions by making use of the renewable electricity. Importantly, while access to abundant, reliable, and affordable RE may be a significant attraction, it is only one element of many that influence the location decisions of firms. A stable and enabling business environment, access to good infrastructure and efficient logistics, and a steady supply of effective and skilled workers are other key aspects that need to be aligned for firms to consider relocation.

On the other hand, Latin America and the Caribbean can also leverage its abundant RES by directing its innovation efforts toward new uses or products that are electricity intensive. One clear avenue is advancing innovations that replace the use of fossil fuels as an energy source with new production methods or products that use electricity instead. This study focuses on one such application, GH_2, which is produced using RE and can be used as a fuel source in many other industries.

GH_2 is a good example of a new market emerging in a decarbonizing world. The global move toward decarbonization has highlighted the need to prioritize an increased share of RE in the energy mix of all countries, and GH_2 can help accelerate this transition. GH_2 is hydrogen (H_2) that is produced by means of electrolysis using electricity generated from RES (see box 2.7 for a description of the colors of H_2). As such, GH_2 has the potential to decarbonize economies and increase energy security and resilience. Decarbonization with GH_2 could follow two channels: (a) eliminating GHG emissions from the H_2 production process and (b) substituting fossil fuels as an energy carrier in economic activities.

Currently, H_2 is primarily used in industrial processes to produce other goods (ammonia, for example), but its consumption is expected to increase across various sectors, primarily as an energy carrier. For example, in industry, new applications are particularly important in steelmaking and other industrial subsectors where H_2 can substitute for fossil fuels in high-temperature processes. In the power sector, H_2 can provide flexible power generation, off-grid power supply, and large-scale energy storage. In transport, fuel cell EVs (FCEVs) are growing rapidly in car and bus segments, but there is much promise for a greater role in energy-intensive transport such as trucks, trains, ships, and planes. Whereas in road transport, battery EVs are more efficient and more developed than H_2 FCEVs, declining costs for H_2 FCEVs will make them attractive for long-distance transport. Beyond its potential for decarbonization, a GH_2 economy could provide an opportunity for low-carbon economic development. GH_2 can also strengthen resilience to shocks by improving power grid reliability, reducing import dependence, diversifying energy sources, and allowing storage, all of which could contribute to mitigating fuel price volatility.

Box 2.7

The Colors of Hydrogen

Color labels have become a convention to distinguish end-product hydrogen (H_2), with the categories based primarily on the feedstock or method used for H_2 production. The main colors are summarized in table B.2.7.1.

Table B2.7.1   Colors of Hydrogen

Color	Fuel	Process	Product	CO_2 footprint	Global production
Black/brown	Coal	Gasification	$H_2 + CO_2$	High	27%
Gray	Natural gas	Steam reforming	$H_2 + CO_2$	High	69% (includes as by-product of oil)
Blue	Natural gas	Steam reforming	$H_2 + CO_2$ with CCS	Low	1%
Green	Renewables	Electrolysis	$H_2 + O_2$	Low	1%

Source: Original table for this publication.

Note: CCS = carbon capture and storage; CO_2 = carbon dioxide; H_2 = hydrogen; O_2 = oxygen.

Despite the simple appeal of color schemes, they obscure the great variation that exists in the greenhouse gas emissions intensity of H_2 production. Emissions from the H_2 value chain occur at production (direct emissions, typically carbon dioxide; CO_2) or in upstream and midstream segments such as the extraction, storage, and transport of natural gas, which can release CO_2 and methane. Production of H_2 through electrolysis does not release emissions at the production stage, but depending on the electricity generation fuel mix, it could release CO_2 emissions upstream and midstream. Green hydrogen (GH_2) is produced through electrolysis using renewable energy and thus is created without greenhouse gas emissions.[a]

Carbon capture and sequestration technologies mitigate direct emissions during H_2 production that uses fossil fuels, but not upstream and midstream emissions. Hydrogen production from unabated natural gas releases 10–14 kilograms of carbon dioxide per kilogram of hydrogen

box continued next page

Box 2.7

The Colors of Hydrogen *(continued)*

(kg/CO_2 eq/kg H_2), of which upstream and midstream emissions are responsible for 1–5 kg/CO_2 eq/kg H_2. Emissions intensity is reduced to around 5–8 kg CO_2 eq/kg H_2 by retrofitting existing assets with carbon capture and storage (CCS) and to 0.6–6.0 kg CO_2 eq/kg H_2 using more advanced CCS technologies, though midstream and upstream emissions remain around 0.7–5.0 kg CO_2 eq/kg H_2. The variation in H_2 emissions intensity requires regulation and certification systems to facilitate monitoring and exchange where emissions reduction is an objective. The term "clean hydrogen" is often used to refer to H_2 production processes with no or very limited CO_2 emissions. Green hydrogen is considered the "purest" form of clean hydrogen because it is produced entirely from renewable energy sources.

Source: IEA 2023d.

a. Life-cycle analysis of emissions would take a step further in looking at the emissions that were created when manufacturing the electrolyzers, for example.

Quantifying comparative advantage in GH$_2$ supply

Today, GH_2 production in Latin America and the Caribbean is negligible, yet energy market practitioners have highlighted the region's enormous potential. The relative size of H_2 supply and demand flows within Latin America and the Caribbean matches the global situation, with most supply produced with natural gas, and demand stemming from the production sectors for ammonia, methanol, and steel. Ninety percent of H_2 in the region is produced using natural gas and emits some 353 million tons (Mt) CO_2 per year (IEA 2021b). Annual demand for H_2 in Latin America and the Caribbean is currently 4 Mt, which represents about 5 percent of global demand, and the H_2 is used mainly to produce ammonia, methanol, and steel. At present, only a few GH_2 pilot projects and small-scale facilities are in operation. However, there is great optimism for the potential of GH_2 in Latin America and the Caribbean, both as a means to decarbonize domestic economies as well as a source of export revenue. This optimism is based primarily on the abundance of excellent RES across the region. But RE resource abundance is only one factor necessary to developing a thriving GH_2 economy.

Three relatively time-invariant factors have the potential either to advance or undermine the comparative advantage of Latin America and the Caribbean countries in leveraging GH_2 as an opportunity: the abundance of RES, geography, and the weighted average cost of capital (WACC). International comparative advantage is the ability to produce a good or service at a lower opportunity cost than another country. Comparative advantages are built on systematic differences in the factors that affect the costs and opportunity costs of GH_2 production. For the development of GH_2, the most systematic—or time invariant—factors are geography (as a determinant of transport costs and proximity to global markets) and resource abundance. Less permanent, but changing only very slowly, are factors typically related to the state of the economy. Of these, the WACC is one of the key determinants of cost competitiveness in GH_2 production. The following discussion dives more deeply into each of these three factors.

The abundance of RES in the region can provide an opportunity to lower costs and hence strengthen international competitiveness. The cost of zero-carbon electricity can account for as much as 75 percent of the total cost of producing H_2 through water electrolysis. Obtaining zero-carbon electricity to produce GH_2 typically involves either collocating RE-generating capacity (wind, solar photovoltaic, hydropower, or geothermal) with an electrolyzer, or connecting an electrolyzer to a high-voltage grid and purchasing clean electricity through PPAs. The production of H_2 with electrolyzers will require vast amounts of power. For example, producing all of today's dedicated H_2 output would result in an electricity demand exceeding annual electricity generation in the EU (IEA 2019). This suggests that regions with favorable RES will have a comparative advantage in the production of GH_2.

Access to solar and wind power generation capacity, in particular, is a powerful enabler of a clean H_2 transition. Solar and wind power have received the most attention as enablers of a transition to clean H_2. There are a number of reasons for this: (a) solar and wind power account for a larger share of the RE transformation in future decarbonization projects because of their global prevalence and rapidly declining costs compared to fossil fuels and RE, such as geothermal or biomass; (b) solar and wind are variable RES, which may pose fewer challenges as an input to the production of H_2 than they do for the generation of electricity, where gridsupply-and-demand balance must be maintained in real-time; and (c) hydropower resources are already relatively more exploited and dedicated to electricity generation, given that they are able to provide both baseload power and flexible reserves.

Latin America and the Caribbean has excellent solar and wind energy resources, with Mexico standing out in terms of potential to generate H_2. In terms of potential solar energy output, Latin America and the Caribbean is second only to Africa (figure 2.5).[41] Using four different photovoltaic (PV) classes, depending on capacity factors,[42] figure 2.5 shows technical H_2 production potential for

Figure 2.5 Production Potential for Green Hydrogen

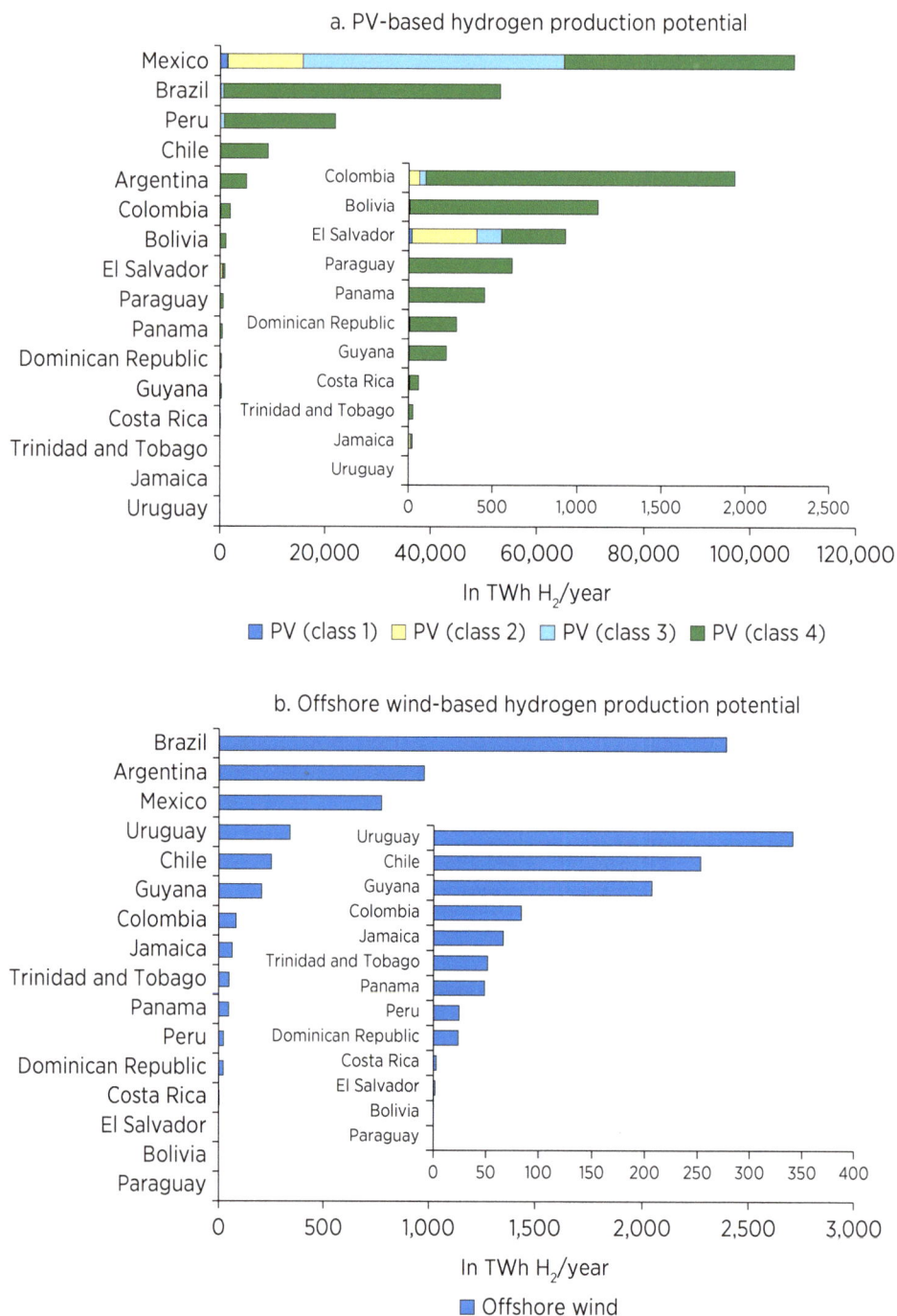

a. PV-based hydrogen production potential

In TWh H$_2$/year

■ PV (class 1) □ PV (class 2) ■ PV (class 3) ■ PV (class 4)

b. Offshore wind-based hydrogen production potential

In TWh H$_2$/year

■ Offshore wind

Source: Original figure for this publication based on World Bank 2025a, building on Moritz, Schönfisch, and Schulte 2025.

Note: CF = capacity factor; PV = photovoltaic; TWh H$_2$/yr = terawatt-hour hydrogen per year.

selected countries. Results indicate that output potential correlates strongly with country size. Mexico exhibits the highest PV potential, with around 110,000 terawatt-hours (TWh) annual technical H_2 production potential based on PV (one TWh is equivalent to about 33 Mt H_2). Argentina, Brazil, Chile, and Peru are also among the countries with large PV potential but weaker solar irradiation (meaning lower capacity factors). As depicted in figure 2.5, panel b, wind energy is less uniformly distributed than solar energy (panel a) and, within Latin America and the Caribbean, it is concentrated in the Southern Cone, with the highest densities in Argentina. Southern Chile, all coastlines, the northern tip of Venezuela, and Caribbean countries also have above-average wind power densities within the region. Argentina exhibits the highest onshore wind potential, with around 8,000 TWh of annual technical H_2 production potential onshore and nearly 1,000 TWh annual production offshore thanks to its steady winds. Brazil, owing to its large size, has the second-highest potential, located primarily along its coastlines given that capacity factors are lower in the equatorial area. Chile and Colombia possess high-quality potential due to high wind speeds along certain coasts.

By affecting transportation mode and costs within and between continents, geography can influence trade patterns. Demand for clean H_2—both domestic and international—is necessary for GH_2 to become competitive with traditional energy sources. However, at the nascent technology stages, production and demand centers are geographically dispersed, so transportation costs are an important factor in identifying a viable market. Given that Europe and East Asia are expected to be the largest global net importers of H_2, geography puts the Latin America and the Caribbean region at an initial disadvantage relative to other high potential GH_2 exporters such as North Africa and Australia. However, countries in strategic locations with developed logistics infrastructure and deep-sea harbors (Panama, for example) have opportunities for an easier transition to exporting H_2. Within Latin America and the Caribbean, large countries that are meeting domestic demand would face only marginal additional costs in supplying smaller neighboring countries. This suggests that resolving coordination issues across the region could unlock large gains.

Analysis conducted for this report estimates the supply costs of Latin America and the Caribbean economies to three international markets: Berlin, New York, and Tokyo. Generally, costs related to distance account for a relatively small share of total supply costs for a given mode of transportation. For example, the total GH_2 supply costs to Japan are only slightly higher than supply costs to Germany, even though the shipping distance is three times farther. Rather, key drivers of costs are the mode of transportation and the desired product at destination. For the supply of GH_2 across oceans, key costs include liquification and regasification (in the case of shipping as liquid H_2) or conversion and reconversion (in the case of shipping as ammonia). Between these two options, shipping as liquid H_2 was found to be cheaper in all cases. Where pipelines exist and can be repurposed, such as between Mexico and the United States, this mode of supply for GH_2 is the cheapest. The costs are illustrated for five Latin America and the Caribbean economies in supplying Germany (figure 2.6). If the desired product at the destination is not GH_2 but an H_2 derivative, the relative competitiveness changes substantially. For example, exporting ammonia from the region has received a lot of attention because without the ammonia cracking costs (costs of converting ammonia back to H_2), Latin America and the Caribbean overseas exports are more competitive than local ammonia suppliers.

The WACC is another key component of the cost of producing H_2 that can affect the sector's competitiveness in Latin America and the Caribbean. The WACC varies across nations, firms, and projects, and has a significant impact on the cost of GH_2 production and hence on a country's GH_2 development. For example, a recent study showed that a threefold reduction in the WACC (from 15 percent to 5 percent), holding other factors constant, would reduce the estimated levelized cost of hydrogen production (LCOH) by up to 45 percent (ESMAP et al. 2024). As a measure of the average rate of return that must be achieved to access debt and

Figure 2.6 Levelized Costs of Hydrogen Supply to Germany

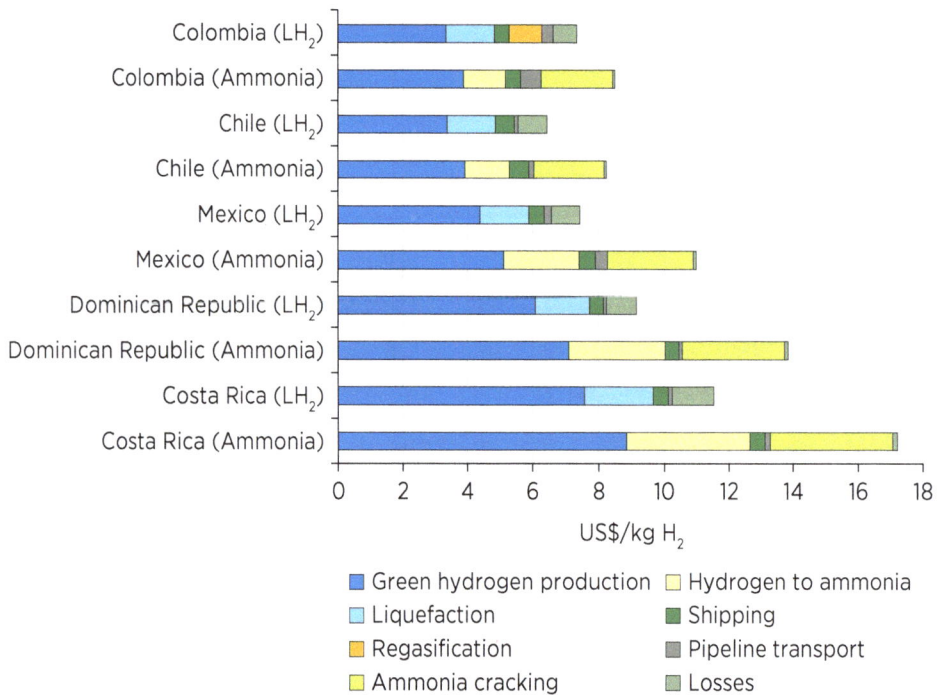

Source: Original figure for this publication based on World Bank 2025a.

Note: kg H_2 = kilograms hydrogen; LH_2 = liquid hydrogen.

equity financing, the WACC reflects all the factors that affect an investor's opportunity cost of capital.[43] Across countries, systematic differences in country-specific risk can lead to systematic differences in the WACC that can either hasten or hinder the pace of H_2 development. Such risks include those that arise from the specific market context for clean H_2 but also from broader political and macroeconomic risks. As a proxy for data from clean H_2 projects specifically (which is minimally available), the data on the WACC for RE indicate that among regions, Latin America and the Caribbean faces the second-highest costs of capital. The estimated WACC for RE is 4.4 percent in Europe, 5.4 percent in North America, 5.6 percent in Asia-Pacific, 6.9 percent in Latin America, and 8.2 percent in the Middle East and Africa (ESMAP et al. 2024).

Compiling data on RES and the WACC, together with costs of both RE and electrolyzer facilities, this study estimates country- and RES class-specific LCOH. The LCOH is calculated on the basis of the labor and capital costs to build and operate newly constructed facilities where RE is generated solely for the electrolyzers that split water into H_2 and oxygen. By ranking a country's LCOH for each of eight RES classes (four solar, three onshore wind, and one offshore wind), a country's GH$_2$ supply curve can be constructed. Although the RES potential is a technical measure, saying nothing about the economic or market viability of producing GH$_2$ with those resources, it is reasonable to assume that, on average, the lowest-cost production possibilities will be exploited first. For this reason, a weighted average LCOH is calculated for the first 50 TWh of GH$_2$ production in the supply curve.[44]

Combining all RES options, the lowest-cost GH$_2$ supply in Latin America and Caribbean countries ranges from $3.30/kg to $8.10/kg. Chile and Colombia achieve an LCOH lower than $4/kg using onshore wind. However, the production potential is limited and LCOH rises quickly with increasing volume. In Brazil, onshore wind is also the lowest cost supply option but is significantly higher at $4.70/kg, on par with Peru generating GH$_2$ through solar PV. The Dominican Republic and Guyana achieve LCOH in the range of $5.40–6.10/kg, followed by the southern countries of Argentina, Paraguay, and Uruguay. Smaller Central American and Caribbean countries with limited RES potential, such as, Costa Rica, El Salvador, Jamaica, and Trinidad and Tobago, have supply costs in excess of $7/kg. Bolivia, El Salvador, and especially Argentina's production costs are inflated substantially by a high WACC (figure 2.7).

Figure 2.7 Weighted Average LCOH for GH$_2$ across All RES Classes

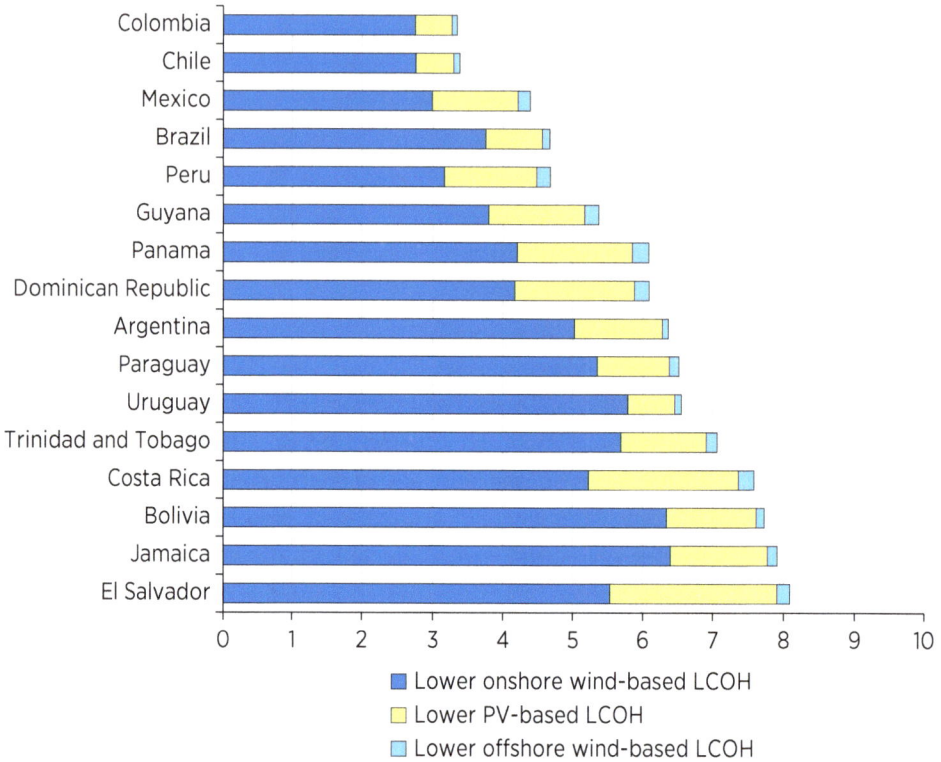

Source: Original figure for this publication based on World Bank 2025a.

Note: GH$_2$ = green hydrogen; LCOH = levelized cost of hydrogen; OPEX = operating expense; PV = photovoltaic; RES = renewable energy source.

Considering the significant current uncertainty regarding most of the LCOH components, a sensitivity analysis is useful to understand how LCOH may change under various scenarios. Analysis for this report included a sensitivity assessment of LCOH, considering variation in PV investments costs, onshore and offshore wind investment costs, electrolyzer investment costs, and the WACC.[45] The LCOH was found to be most sensitive to RES investment costs and the WACC.[46] The sensitivity of the LCOH to electrolyzer costs is relatively low as they constitute a smaller share of the costs compared to new RE facilities.[47] Using these estimated cost sensitivities, countries can assess (a) where it makes sense to drive down costs at both national (for example, competitive RE procurement) and project-specific (for example, risk mitigation instruments to lower project WACC) levels and (b) where GH$_2$ production can be competitive, depending on project-specific RES and WACC characteristics.

The path from potential to reality: High uncertainty and high costs surround the GH$_2$ market

To further refine the assessment of Latin America and the Caribbean's H$_2$ opportunity, this report developed a scorecard for the GH$_2$-enabling environment and applied it to 12 representative Latin America and the Caribbean countries. The scorecard first aims to assess the level of market potential in a country by rating each country in two dimensions: resource availability and domestic demand. Then the scorecard identifies potential bottlenecks and policy action areas that can foster or hinder the development of each country's potential by rating every country along three dimensions: institutions and regulatory framework, enabling infrastructure, and innovation and development of an H$_2$ ecosystem.

Box 2.8 provides a detailed description of the scorecard. The scorecard presents 33 indicators along six key pillars to evaluate the enabling environment for GH$_2$ in the listed countries. Each indicator received a score scaled from one to five, with one representing the lowest and five the highest score.[48] The 12 countries evaluated with the scorecard were selected for being representative of the region in terms of their economies, geographical features, populations, and resources, among other factors.[49]

Box 2.8

A Scorecard for the Green Hydrogen–Enabling Environment

A framework was developed to assess the potential, and hence possible competitive advantages, of various Latin America and Caribbean countries and identify possible bottlenecks with regard to the development of their green hydrogen (GH$_2$) economies. Two dimensions capture the potential of each country, and four dimensions assess progress in policy areas that can foster or hinder the development of the GH$_2$ market:

Potential

- **Resource availability:** This variable assesses renewable energy sources (RES) potential, water availability, electricity access, and the integration of renewables within a country's energy matrix. High-quality RES and the availability of water reduce the potential costs of GH$_2$ and its derivatives, while a large share of renewable energy (RE) in the grid and high electricity access rates decrease the opportunity costs (both in terms of

box continued next page

Box 2.8

A Scorecard for the Green Hydrogen–Enabling Environment (*continued*)

decarbonization of grid power and the availability of increased electricity access) associated with using RE for hydrogen (H_2) production instead of feeding it into the grid.

- **Domestic demand:** This variable evaluates a country's current—and potential—domestic demand for GH_2 and derivatives. It assesses a country's current H_2 consumption and identifies the potential for increased future local demand in sectors such as ammonia production, steel, methanol, refining, transportation, bunkering, and electricity generation. Countries with current or potential local demand can more efficiently develop a GH_2 ecosystem, as they face less friction in GH_2 demand creation. Introducing a product into an established market is simpler than creating this market from scratch.

Policy Action Areas

- **Institutional stability and financing:** This variable primarily evaluates aspects related to a country's political stability, as well as its macroeconomic and financial conditions (economic growth, average interest rates, and existence of subsidies for H_2 project development, among others). This variable is crucial for understanding the general conditions that potential investors consider when deciding to invest in projects within a particular country, and how these factors can play a role in a project's weighted average cost of capital. Investors will prefer stable economies with low financial risk, especially when investing in early-stage and capital-intensive technologies.

- **Regulatory and policy framework:** This variable evaluates a country's progress in establishing an appropriate regulatory framework and fiscal incentives for the development of a clean H_2 economy. A robust and well-defined regulatory and policy framework is necessary to create a stable environment for investment, decrease risk for investors, ensure alignment between sustainability goals and the H_2 ecosystem, and promote technology competitiveness through incentives and tax reductions.

- **Enabling infrastructure:** This variable evaluates a country's infrastructure in terms of its potential use in the clean H_2 economy. Examples include port facilities, gas pipelines, power grids, and industrial hubs that could

box continued next page

A Scorecard for the Green Hydrogen–Enabling Environment (*continued*)

evolve into centers for clean H_2 consumption and production in the future. Leveraging existing infrastructure for H_2 project development can significantly reduce initial investments, promote quick deployment of projects, and generally facilitate the link between H_2 supply and demand.

- **Innovation and H_2 ecosystem:** This final variable assesses a country's progress in structuring a clean H_2 economy. It includes indicators such as project announcements or developments related to H_2, commitments of funds for H_2 research and development, the existence of associations or industry groups focused on H_2, and agreements with potential importing countries, among other factors. A more advanced H_2 sector provides a country with a head start relative to nations in earlier stages of ecosystem development.

The framework yielded scores for each country (figure 2.8), from which four typologies were drawn: emerging leaders, next wave players, industrial integrators, and early explorers. Emerging leaders are countries that have already recognized that they have inherent, stable competitive advantages for participation in the H_2 market, including high-quality RES, developed infrastructure or large potential internal demand, stability, and favorable access to finance, and they have capitalized on these advantages by supporting the development of a regulatory framework and a local ecosystem for H_2 in recent years.

Latin America and the Caribbean's emerging leader countries are Chile, Colombia, Brazil, and Uruguay. Chile offers the most supportive ecosystem in the region by capitalizing on its world-class RES. It is therefore no surprise that it was also one of the first countries to seek further assistance from World Bank in developing GH_2 (box 2.9). Colombia developed its H_2-friendly regulatory framework early and designed it to take full advantage of the country's excellent geographical location, existing oil and gas (O&G) capabilities and infrastructure, and abundant natural resources. Uruguay boasts a robust H_2 ecosystem thanks to its highly renewable grid (91 percent share of RE) and history of rapid RE technology implementation, supported by innovative regulatory approaches. Brazil has rapidly capitalized on its huge industrial sector and favorable location for exports to Europe by promoting the development of regulation both on the national and local levels.

Figure 2.8 Scorecard Assessments

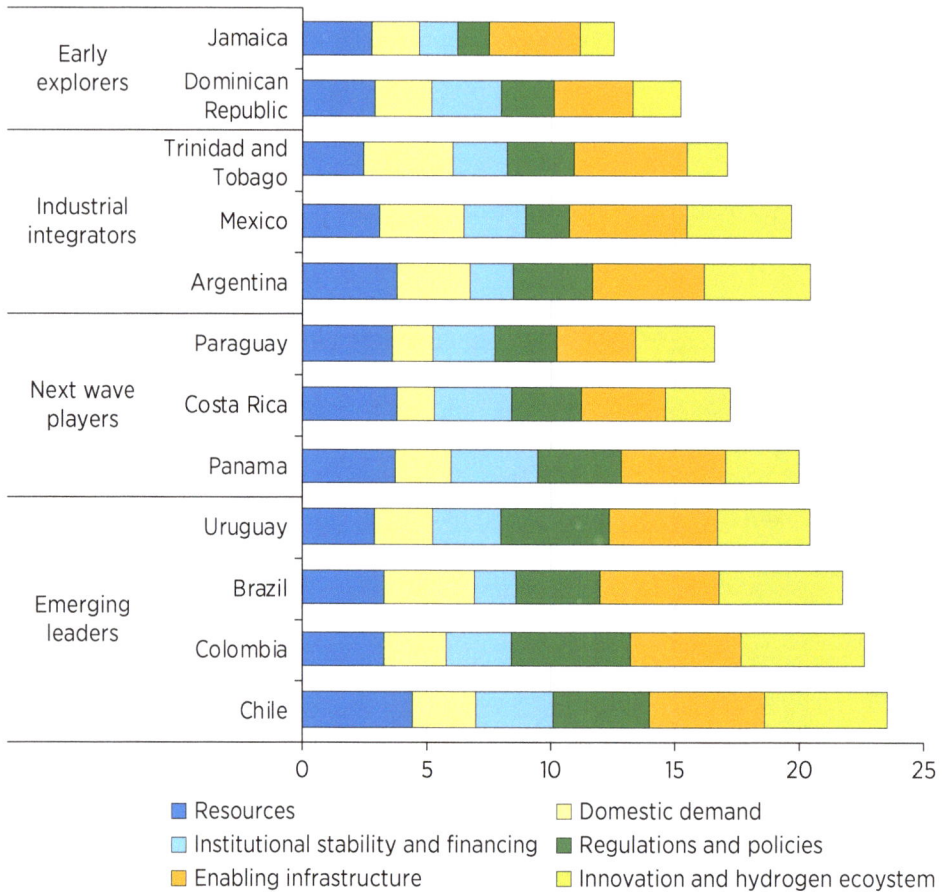

Source: Original figure for this publication based on World Bank 2025a.

World Bank Support for Green Hydrogen In Chile

The World Bank's current engagement with the government of Chile has resulted in $150 million being allotted to green hydrogen (GH_2) projects to support green, resilient, and inclusive economic development in line with the administration's goals to spur long-term, sustainable growth while supporting a net zero transition by 2050.[50] Among the first countries worldwide to deregulate its electricity market, Chile is now a pioneer in Latin America and the Caribbean of integrating GH_2 into its national decarbonization strategy. Although rich in natural renewable resources,

box continued next page

Box 2.9

World Bank Support for Green Hydrogen in Chile *(continued)*

Chile continues to rely heavily on imported energy in both its electricity system and hard-to-abate industries. An economy-wide net zero transition will require a suite of sustainable solutions, but GH_2 is well-suited to fill several roles as a versatile energy carrier, ranging from heavy industry and transportation to long-term energy storage.

This project will work through the public sector (with the decentralized public service agency CORFO as an intermediary) to implement two critical components necessary to attract further investment and adoption of GH_2: (a) a financing mechanism providing investment subloans and risk mitigation instruments and (b) capacity building and project management. Additional key outcomes of this effort are boosting Chile's GH_2-enabling environment, stimulating domestic demand, diversifying exports, and providing a development framework to other countries in Latin America and the Caribbean and globally.

Next wave players are Paraguay, Panama, and Costa Rica. Countries in this typology have also identified their inherent competitive advantages including high quality RES, but the advantages are not as immediately exploitable as they are for emerging leaders, in part because of the absence of significant domestic demand for H_2. As a result, these countries have been slower to support an H_2 ecosystem that would capitalize on the significant enablers that they do possess. The competitive advantage of Paraguay, for example, lies in the fact that it has an electrical grid that is almost fully hydropowered, with an opportunity to provide low-cost baseload electricity for GH_2 production. Meanwhile, Panama's maritime infrastructure is highly developed, and a positive financial environment has recently enabled the country to begin developing its H_2 ecosystem. Finally, Costa Rica has capitalized on its highly sustainable grid to get an early start on its H_2 ecosystem, although development has been slower than expected.

Industrial integrators include Mexico, Argentina, and Trinidad and Tobago. These countries have highly developed industrial sectors and could easily leverage existing H_2 demand to increase their competitive advantage and further develop their H_2 ecosystems. That said, these countries are lagging in terms of their institutional stability and the development of a regulatory framework. As a result, they have relatively underdeveloped H_2 ecosystems that are necessary to capitalize on their competitive advantages. Mexico, with its abundant RES, proximity to the United States, and one of the largest industrial sectors in Latin America and the Caribbean, has moved backward on RE policies (and definitely made no progress on H_2 regulation) with a recent focus on nationalized O&G support. Argentina, with a historically large industrial and O&G sector, and despite initial advances in the development of a regulatory framework as well as some pilot experiences, is now stalled in terms of an H_2 ecosystem because of its negative macroeconomic and financial situation. Finally, Trinidad and Tobago has not managed to tap the potential of the H_2 sector despite being Latin America and the Caribbean's largest ammonia producer and boasting the region's largest methanol and ammonia production capacities.

Early explorers include the Dominican Republic and Jamaica. These countries do not have a clear view of their inherent competitive advantages yet. They are only starting to explore whether there is a relevant role for H_2 in their economies— and, if so, what that could look like. These countries are in the very early stages of development of their H_2 ecosystems.

Aligning the enabling environment with GH_2 ambitions

Decarbonization goals include an important role for GH_2, and barriers to the development of this nascent technology must be addressed to be on track to meet them. While the role of H_2 in the global energy mix is expected to increase significantly in coming years, there is substantial uncertainty as to the scale of the increase. That uncertainty stems from the technology's early developmental stage and the difficulty in predicting future demand, which will depend on global progress toward decarbonizing economies. On average, decarbonization models estimate that H_2's share of final energy demand will increase from the current negligible levels to 1 percent in 2030 and then to an average of 10 percent across models by 2050.[51] Current estimates for production by 2030 fall short of projected needs by more than four times. If all projects currently in the pipeline are realized, by 2030 global production of GH_2 is projected to be 16–24 Mt. But under the NZE, GH_2 production in 2030 needs to be at least 80 Mt (IEA 2021a).

The high production cost of GH_2 is still a key barrier. GH_2 is still significantly more expensive than gray and blue H_2. In 2023 the global production cost for gray H_2 was \$0.98–\$2.93/kg. Blue H_2 costs were estimated at \$1.80–\$4.70/kg and GH_2 \$4.50–\$12.00/kg. However, GH_2 production costs are expected to come down substantially in the short run thanks to economies of scale and supportive policies. When comparing newly built gray H_2 plants to those for GH_2, a recent study found that GH_2 outcompetes gray H_2 by 2030 in eight of the 28 major markets modeled. In Brazil, newly built GH_2 plants are forecast to even outcompete gray H_2 from existing facilities (Bhashyam 2023).

Governments have an important role to play in stimulating GH_2 markets by creating institutions, accelerating investments, and spurring innovation. As current production prices remain high, potential producers and consumers may be wary of committing to the use of a new technology—particularly if there are high switching costs. The nascent nature of the technology and other inefficiencies in energy sectors also pose the risk of market failures.[52] Governments have the ability to shape the GH_2-enabling environment to create comparative advantages. Such measures entail creating the conditions for the market to function by developing the appropriate institutions that reduce costs and risks that lead to underinvestment in GH_2 (from a societal perspective) by the private sector. Market failures can also provide a rationale for the government to take a more active role in supporting investments in GH_2 projects as well as R&D. These recommendations are summarized in box 2.10.

Box 2.10

ESMAP Hydrogen Lighthouse Initiative

To accelerate the deployment of clean hydrogen (H_2), the World Bank launched a 10 gigawatt (GW) Hydrogen Lighthouse Initiative (HLI) as part of its Energy Sector Management Assistance Program (ESMAP). Launched at COP28 in Dubai, HLI was developed by the World Bank in collaboration with partner financing institutions to expand clean H_2 production capacity in emerging markets and developing countries. The aim is to demonstrate the viability of clean H_2 production by overcoming barriers to adoption, such as high costs and financial risks, and create scalable models that can be replicated elsewhere.

HLI focuses on developing clean H_2 projects, ranging in size from 100 megawatts to 1 GW, which collectively would increase global H_2 electrolysis capacity tenfold. This would prove that clean H_2 can play a vital role in reducing emissions in sectors like steel production and long-haul transportation, which are difficult to decarbonize.

Among the biggest barriers to clean H_2's growth are its high production and financing costs, particularly in developing countries. To reduce these costs and de-risk projects, thereby stimulating investment and the development of clean H_2 infrastructure, ESMAP is designing financing mechanisms that remove uncertainties around future buyers, pricing, and regulatory conditions. Particularly focused on lowering financial risks, ESMAP is working with its partners to make clean H_2 projects more commercially viable to enable broader adoption. In fiscal year 2024, World Bank approved $1.6 billion in funding for renewable H_2 loans, in addition to $1.65 billion approved in fiscal year 2023, bringing the total loan amount for H_2 activities to $3.25 billion.

Creating Institutions That Reduce Market Risk and Stimulate Private Sector Investment

Lack of regulatory and policy frameworks undermines incentives for market development. Although a country may possess a "natural" comparative advantage in GH_2 production thanks to permanent characteristics such as resource availability and geography, there are other dimensions in the GH_2-enabling environment where governments can make progress. In the short run and at little expense, governments can reduce investor risk by creating "regulatory certainty" through the development of a regulatory and policy framework for the market. There are, for example, information asymmetry problems to be addressed as most countries lack institutionalized mechanisms to track the production and consumption of any shade of H_2 and identify its characteristics (origin and life-cycle missions, for example) (IRENA 2022). Standards and certification are lacking, especially for establishing internationally compatible certification and guarantees of origin for exporters. The scorecard results clearly show wide dispersion in the region. Countries such as Chile, Colombia, and Uruguay have significantly advanced their policy and regulatory frameworks while the rest of the region has moderate to low development.

Regional coordination on regulatory frameworks to facilitate cross-border trade could help markets achieve scale. In the absence of regional coordination, some countries are pushing ahead with regulation on standards and certification with associated risks. For example, Argentina and Brazil, which participate in the International Organization for Standardization (ISO) H_2 technical committee on H_2 technologies (ISO TC 197), published their own safety standards for H_2. Adherence to international standards—such as those for safety (ISO 15916), fuel quality (ISO 14687), and electrolyzers (ISO 22734)—may be preferable. Unilateral developments must be treated with care, especially when the intention is to trade, as uncertainty about the compatibility of regulatory regimes of developers and importing countries could lead to increased transaction costs or even to the exclusion from contractual agreements. Given that standards are still very much being created and evolving, Latin America and the Caribbean countries have an opportunity to partake in their development and early adoption.

Long-term policies to lower the costs of capital can have an important effect on the viability of GH_2 projects. Background analysis for this report revealed that both the cost of renewable electricity and the WACC have an equal impact (percentage-wise) on the LCOH. Therefore, institutional stability reflected in macroeconomic and political conditions are key variables that affect the WACC and therefore the financing conditions for projects. Investors will prefer stable economies with low financial risk, especially when investing in early-stage and capital-intensive technologies. Cases such as Argentina highlight the benefits of reducing investor risk in Latin America and the Caribbean, but this happens slowly. Countries seeking to advance GH_2 should provide targeted support to reduce GH_2 investor risk at a project level. Here, again, lessons can be learned from RE risk migration.

Strategic Investments Can Further the Region's Comparative Advantage

Investing in RE development is a low-regret strategy that can further Latin America and the Caribbean's comparative advantage in resource availability. As a decarbonization strategy, investing in GH_2 without compromising the decarbonization of the grid will require a massive and rapid scale-up of renewable power. A renewables revolution is already under way, but the prospect of a GH_2 economy adds further impetus to overcoming the challenges to RE scale-up itself. Although the quality of renewable resources for power generation may be relatively slow to change over time, it does vary tremendously within countries. This variability should be fully exploited through systematic mapping, planning, and targeted investing. Areas where investments in renewable power for GH_2 may make most sense are those where the opportunity cost of such power is limited because of fully decarbonized grids, no unmet demand for grid power, or specific geographical features (remote mines not connected to transmission lines).

Large upfront investments in infrastructure connecting market actors may be needed to resolve coordination failures and generate positive externalities associated with network economies. Infrastructure for transport, storage, and conversion of GH_2 may be needed to connect producers with domestic consumers and export markets. A good place to start is the repurposing of existing infrastructure for transporting and storing H_2. Retrofitted pipelines are the most cost-effective means of H_2 transport. For example, existing natural gas transmission pipelines can be repurposed to carry H_2. Wherever possible, they would provide significant competitive advantages to suppliers. Several countries in the region score well in this dimension as they are traditional O&G producers and have well-developed energy infrastructure that could potentially be repurposed. Pipeline transport from Latin America and the Caribbean to other regions is currently limited to the connection between Mexico and the United States, but for GH_2 supply within the region, O&G-producing countries are well placed because they can leverage: (a) established energy export infrastructure (ports, pipelines, and storage facilities); (b) a skilled workforce familiar with producing, converting, and handling energy fuels and gases; and (c) existing energy trade relations.

Supporting Innovation for GH$_2$ Customized to Country Strengths and Needs

Improving GH$_2$ technology is a complex innovation endeavor that requires sophisticated capabilities from firms and well-designed policies to support firms' R&D efforts. Policy makers may consider engaging the region's industrial sectors in which new applications of GH$_2$ may be particularly important, including steelmaking or other industrial subsectors with high-temperature production processes. With H$_2$ providing a competitive opportunity as fuel for long-haul road transport, large countries with robust truck fleets could also leverage internal demand to strengthen the supply of H$_2$ and thus increase the sustainability of value chains for exported goods (IEA 2021b). As costs come down, the number of applications in which GH$_2$ is competitive as an energy carrier will increase. Each country has the ability to exploit GH$_2$ to its advantage, and early identification and support through R&D of such applications should be encouraged.

While regional innovation in the sector is still lagging, emerging leaders such as Brazil, Chile, and Colombia are investing in R&D initiatives with a focus on the energy transition and H$_2$. It is important to develop a dense H$_2$ ecosystem, with mechanisms for coordination and information exchanges between the various actors in the market (suppliers, consumers, and potential consumers), academia, and government regulators. Brazil's National Program of Hydrogen (PNH$_2$ for its name in Portuguese) has articulated a specific objective aimed at bolstering R&D funding for H$_2$-related initiatives. In Colombia, a collaboration between the energy ministry and Ecopetrol to address energy transition issues supports the development of clean H$_2$ projects; a first funding proposal of $1 million has already been awarded (IEA 2023c). In addition, there has been an alliance between academia and the private sector in Colombia since 2022 focused on R&D in renewable gases including H$_2$ (Universidad del Norte 2022). In Chile, the Production Development Corporation (CORFO), which supports entrepreneurship, innovation, and competitiveness, has allocated resources for an innovation project to design and build GH$_2$ mining vehicles, with wider implications for the transport sector (CORFO 2020). Such efforts are important because they help define and guide the country-specific way in which GH$_2$ can add value to the economy. Table 2.4 lists key actions to accelerate the market for GH$_2$.

Table 2.4 **Key Actions Needed to Lay the Foundations for a Successful GH$_2$ Sector**

Institutions	Investments	Innovation
Enable market development by establishing basic rules for market functioning, such as safety and quality standards as well as E&S frameworks.	Reduce transaction costs by investing in transport, storage, and conversion facilities.	Increase support for innovation in GH$_2$ by creating dedicated public research institutes and technology extension services. If capabilities exist, further support innovation with different instruments such as R&D tax incentives, grants, and matching grants for R&D.
Foster market development and economies of scale by establishing regional regulatory frameworks that enable cross-border trade.	Foster market development and economies of scale by developing regional infrastructure for trade in GH$_2$.	
Reduce informational asymmetries by developing and adopting internationally recognized standards.		Accelerate technology development by promoting frequent interaction between developers, users, governments, and researchers.
Improve coordination between producers, government, and users through business associations and sectoral councils that foster frequent high-quality interactions that can help improve nascent technologies.		Improve policy effectiveness by designing regulatory frameworks with government learning in mind.

Source: Original table for this report.

Note: E&S = environmental and social; GH$_2$ = green hydrogen; R&D = research and development.

Notes

1. World Bank calculations from World Bank Group Open Data: Latin America and the Caribbean Forest Area. Accessed February 2024.
2. According to World Bank Group Open Data, the renewable internal freshwater resources for Latin America and the Caribbean is the highest in any region, with 21,337 cubic meters per capita compared to a world average of 5,500. See World Bank Group, Renewable Internal Freshwater per Capita (cubic meters) (dataset), https://data.worldbank.org/indicator/ER.H2O.INTR.PC?_sm_au_=iVV5HJRSW06s 2QTq&view=map.
3. The Environmental Performance Index combines seven indicators: terrestrial biome protection (weighted for the national and global rarity of biomes), marine protected areas, Protected Areas Representativeness Index, Species Habitat Index, Species Protection Index, and Biodiversity Habitat Index). The 2022 index shows that 65 percent of the countries in the region are above the world average. See Environmental Performance Index, Biodiversity and Habitat (dataset), https://epi.yale.edu/epi-results/2020/component/bdh.
4. FAOSTAT Agricultural Production Data 2021 and Agricultural and Food Trade by Value 2021 https://www.fao.org/faostat/en/.
5. Global Solar Atlas v2.11.2 (2024). This free, web-based application was developed and is operated by the company Solargis s.r.o. on behalf of World Bank Group, using Solargis data, with funding provided by the Energy Sector Management Assistance Program (ESMAP). See https://globalsolaratlas.info/map.
6. Data from Global Wind Atlas (2025), https://globalwindatlas.info/en.
7. According to the UN Environment Programme World Conservation Monitoring Centre, https://www.biodiversitya-z.org/content/megadiverse-countries.
8. World Bank calculation based on data from FAO (2020).
9. Ecosystem services are defined as the direct and indirect goods or services provided by a natural system to humans. Examples include water purification, water cycle regulation, flood risk protection, pollination, food production, medicine, recreation, therapeutic, spiritual, or religious uses, soil formation, and habitat formation, to name just a few.
10. Payments for ecosystem services programs have a long history in Latin America, which initiated the world's first national payment for ecosystem services (PES) program in Costa Rica in 1997. The number and value of PES has grown significantly over the past two decades. Currently, there are over 550 active programs around the globe worth $36–$42 billion in annual transactions. At least 57 of these funds have been set up in Latin America as of 2018, with another study estimating at least 72 funds by 2020. Both estimates are likely incomplete as there is no consolidated registry of PES programs.
11. The cost of a healthy diet in Latin America and the Caribbean is the highest in the world, and food and nutrition security indicators have declined following COVID-19 and the Russian Federation's invasion of Ukraine. The Caribbean is particularly affected; prevalence of undernourishment in the subregion affected more than 16 percent of the population in 2022, the third-highest level across global subregions behind Middle and Eastern Africa. In 2022, 37.5 percent of the region's population reported being moderately or severely food insecure, with indicators worsening in Central America (34.5 percent of population) and the Caribbean (60 percent of population) between 2021 and 2022. See FAO (Food and Agriculture Organization of the United Nations), Suite of Food and Security Indicators (database), FAOSTAT, 2023, https://data360.worldbank.org/en/dataset/FAO_FS.

12. In most countries, more efficient land use frees up agriculture and forestry land for transition back into natural landscapes. Agriculture-to-natural landscapes is the predominant shift, but in some countries, secondary forest, agroforestry, and commercial forestry are significant land uses that have displaced primary forest and natural landscapes. On average, 15 percent of the land in Latin America and the Caribbean is classified as forestry (which includes secondary forests, agroforestry, and other mosaic land uses), but in some countries, such as El Salvador and Jamaica, over 50 percent of the land mass is categorized as forestry. To assess quality of the assessment, these results were compared to the most recent forest resource assessment of Jamaica. A 2013 report from the Forestry Department reports approximately 65 percent of land is classified as forest, with 70 percent of that classified as secondary, disturbed, or plantation forest. [See Forestry Department, "Jamaica's Land Use Cover Assessment: A Comparative Assessment of Forest Change between 1998 and 2013" (Forest Resource Information Management Branch—GIS Unit, Forest Science and Technology Services Division, Kingston, Jamaica, 2013), https://www.forestry.gov.jm/resourcedocs/LUCA_FINAL2013.pdf.] This report's estimates suggest 73 percent of land is forested or natural land cover with 77 percent of that classified as secondary forest. These differences may be the product of the different base years for the two estimates and differences in classification of various land cover types. (The Forest Reclamation Approach is a bottom-up assessment, while this report uses a top-down, satellite-based approach.) These differences may also be influenced by the difficulty of identifying various types of land use using satellite data. In El Salvador, 60 percent of land area is classified as forestry and 15 percent as natural landscapes. By contrast the global tropical forest cover database estimates that 20 percent of the landscape is more than 90 percent forested, with 62 percent of the landmass classified as between 10 and 90 percent forest cover mixed with other land cover types. A final 16 percent is less than 10 percent forested. As a result, a significant share of the tree cover in the country lies outside of forests. This mixed mosaic of land use can be difficult to classify from satellite data, and estimates of tree cover that rely on narrow definitions of "forest" may undercount cover leading to discrepancies in classification between different methods. See Brandt et al. (2023) and Sloan and Sayer (2015).

13. The High-Level Commission on Carbon Prices suggests that a price of at least $40–$80 by 2020 and $50–$100 by 2030 is needed to achieve the Paris climate goals (High-Level Commission on Carbon Prices 2017). This report uses $40 as a conservative estimate of shadow carbon prices.

14. This represents the raw value of the carbon sequestered. Actual revenue generated could be significantly lower depending on the scheme utilized.

15. Climate Watch (website), World Resources Institute, 2022, www.climatewatchdata.org.

16. World Bank calculations.

17. Until now, this analysis has focused on the total potential gains from transitioning to more efficient land use. However, the scale of the transformation is such that those gains will not be realized for decades. To give a near-term picture of the potential, the following analysis focuses on the initial time step of the transition, which the team treats as though it occurs over a five-year time horizon. For some countries this may be ambitious and a 10-year timeframe might be a more reasonable near-term timeframe. In the report, whenever this near-term timeframe is being considered, it will be noted as being the near term. If not so noted, the analysis is referring to the full transition.

18. The modeling developed for this report quantifies the share of agricultural land moving toward intensification and adoption of best management practices. Intensification was modeled by optimizing the application of irrigation, depending on the sustainability of water for irrigation and increasing fertilizer required to

close 21 yield gaps for rainfed or irrigated production, respectively. Agricultural best management practices were represented by increasing the presence of natural buffers, restoring riparian buffers and reducing the fertilizer application rate. Damania, Esteban Balseca et al. (2023).

19. United Nations Convention to Combat Desertification, Sustainable Development Goal (SDG) Indicator 15.3.1, https://data.unccd.int/land-degradation?grouping=SDG &region=JZryW9G.

20. Data from Agrimonitor, Agricultural Policies Monitoring System, https://agrimonitor .iadb.org/en.

21. Estimated impacts using remote-sensing images (see for example Zhang, Hu, and Lu 2021 for a mine in China).

22. Copper tailings are the solid waste material (with water and chemicals) left during the purification of copper from the copper ores, and tailings ponds are engineered dams used for safe storage to avoid leaching of harmful chemicals and pollutants that result from the mining and beneficiation processes into groundwater that may contaminate drinking water supplies. Thomas, Damare, and Gupta (2013).

23. Water risk is based on "water scarcity," which refers to the physical abundance or lack of freshwater resources that can significantly affect businesses (IFC 2023).

24. Carbon emissions of the production of all the lithium value chain (from raw material up to batteries) go from 42 to 140 kilograms (kg) CO_2e per kilowatt-hour (kWh). Specific estimates for China, where approximately 70 percent of the world's batteries are produced, show that their production carbon footprint is 91.21 kg CO_2e/kWh, in which the cathode production process— 47.15 kg CO_2e/kWh—and the battery assembly process—28.11 kg CO_2e/kWh—are the main sources of emissions (Chen et al. 2022).

25. There are two main ways to extract lithium: from brine (by pumping lithium-rich brine from underground aquifers into evaporation ponds, using the sun to evaporate the water, and then processing the concentrated content to extract lithium) or from hard-rock mining (extracting lithium from mineral ores found in pegmatite deposits). Countries with salt flats, such as Argentina, Bolivia, Chile, and China, extract lithium from brine; others, such as Australia, do so from hard rock.

26. The Atacama Salt Flat carbon footprint for lithium carbonate is 4.022 kg CO_2e/ton (t), and for Salar de Oroz in Argentina it is 6.650 kg CO_2e/t, whereas for Australia, those numbers go from 15.690 to 24.200 kg CO_2e/t.

27. The total indirect and induced employment effect varies from one mine to another. In areas where the difference between mine workers' wages and the average income is larger, the number of jobs created may be considerably higher, as in the case of a mine in Ghana where between 10 and 20 jobs were created per mine project (Cordes, Östensson, and Toledano 2016).

28. In Argentina, wages are almost double the national average wage (Ali, Khan, and Pecht 2022).

29. According to the Observatory of Mining Conflicts in Latin America (Observatorio de Conflictos Mineros de América Latina, OCMAL), https://www.ocmal.org.

30. This example pertains to the agreement between the state-owned entity Yacimientos del Litio Bolivianos (YLB) and the German company ACI Systems, which envisaged the production of 40,000 tons of lithium each year for 70 years and the creation of 10,000 direct or indirect local jobs.

31. This regulation sets benchmarks for domestic capacities along the strategic raw material supply chain and sets targets for diversifying the EU's supply by 2030 (European Commission 2023). The targets are as follows: at least 10 percent of the EU's annual consumption for extraction; at least 40 percent of the EU's annual consumption for processing; and at least 15 percent of the EU's annual consumption for recycling must come from the within the EU itself. Additionally, not more than 65 percent of the EU's annual consumption of each strategic raw material at any relevant stage of processing can come from a single third country.

32. Blog post by Zongyuan Zoe Liu, Council on Foreign Relations (2023). See Liu (2023).
33. Copper use is measured at the stage of producing of semi-manufactured products such as wire. The production of such products is dominated by Asian countries. See World Bank 2025a for comparison with other regions.
34. GlobalData, Total GHG Emissions of Major Metals and Mining Companies Worldwide by Market Capitalization in 2021 (dataset), July 2022, https://www.globaldata.com /data-insights/mining/total-ghg-emissions-of-major-metals-and-mining -companies-worldwide-by-market-capitalization-2090964/.
35. Comisión Chilena del Cobre, Informe de Tendencias del Mercado del Cobre, Proyecciones 2024-2025, https://www.cochilco.cl/web/informe-de-tendencias-del-mercado-del -cobre-proyecciones-2024-2025-2/.
36. RMI (Responsible Minerals Initiative), https://www.responsiblemineralsinitiative.org/.
37. Other copper mines in Chile that have increased the use of renewables are Chuquicamata mine by Codelco, Escondida and Spence mine from BHP, and Zaldivar mine belonging to Antofagasta (ICA 2023).
38. For more details see Igogo et al. (2021).
39. London Metal Exchange, https://www.lme.com/en/about?sc_camp=8B7AEB5E26784 CA4F20FFDECD42BF35C.
40. Initiative for Responsible Mining Assurance, https://responsiblemining.net/.
41. Global Solar Atlas, https://globalsolaratlas.info/map.
42. The RES feed-ins have an hourly resolution for electricity from PV. The capacity factor reflects the ratio of annual electricity feed-in to the installed capacity.
43. The WACC has a standard formula that is calculated by multiplying the cost of each capital source (debt and equity) by its relevant weight in terms of market value, then adding the results together to determine the total. Because of that, it includes risk premiums and corporate taxes.
44. The choice of where to cut off supply for weighted average LCOH calculations depends on a trade-off: on the one hand, a low cutoff results in an overly optimistic LCOH, in which the country is assumed to exclusively be able to use its lowest GH_2 production cost RES. On the other hand, a high cutoff results in a volume of GH_2 that would unrealistically find a market in the near future. For comparison purposes, 50 TWH/year represents 1.5 million tons GH_2 or about 40 to 50 percent of Germany's projected hydrogen demand by 2030 (BMWK 2023).
45. For a detailed description of the variation in parameters used for the sensitivity analysis see World Bank 2025a.
46. A 1 percent increase in RES investment costs leads to an LCOH increase of 0.55–0.62 percent for solar, 0.64–0.69 percent for onshore wind, and 0.71–0.77 percent for offshore wind. A 1 percent increase in the WACC leads to an increase in the LCOH of 0.68–0.71 percent.
47. A 1 percent increase in electrolyzer investment costs increases the LCOH by only 0.07–0.22 percent, depending on the country.
48. A complete list of the indicators can be found in World Bank 2025a.
49. The 12 countries are Argentina, Brazil, Chile, Colombia, Costa Rica, Dominican Republic, Jamaica, Mexico, Panama, Paraguay, Trinidad and Tobago, and Uruguay.
50. For more information on the Green Hydrogen Facility to Support Green, Resilient, and Inclusive Economic Development Project for Chile, see https://projects .worldbank.org/en/projects-operations/project-detail/P177533.
51. There is considerable variation in this estimate, however, with the lowest forecast for 2050 being 2 percent and the highest, 26 percent.
52. Market failures include incomplete markets with limited options to hedge risks due to incomplete insurance and capital markets and imperfect markets marked by network externalities and a lack of economies of scale. These GH_2 market-specific failures are compounded by those in the overall energy market, including negative externalities resulting from the underpricing of carbon emissions and subsidies for fossil fuels (Mulder, Perey, and Moraga 2019).

References

Agnew, J. and S. Hendery. 2023. *2023 Global Agricultural Productivity Report: Every Farmer, Every Tool*, edited by T. Thompson. Blacksburg: Virginia Tech College of Agriculture and Life Sciences.

Ali, H., H. A. Khan, and M. Pecht. 2022. "Preprocessing of Spent Lithium-Ion Batteries for Recycling: Need, Methods, and Trends." *Renewable and Sustainable Energy Reviews* 168: 112809.

Ballesteros, M. 2022. "AgTech in Latin America: Small-Scale Solutions in a Large-Scale Transformation." *Economist Impact*, August 12, 2022. https://impact.economist.com /perspectives/technology-innovation/agtech-latin-america-small-scale-solutions -large-scale-transformation.

Barbier, E. B., and J. P. Hochard. 2018. "Land Degradation and Poverty." *Nature Sustainability* 1: 623–31. https://doi.org/10.1038/s41893-018-0155-4.

Baudino, L., C. Santos, C. F. Pirri, F. La Mantia, and A. Lamberti. 2022. "Recent Advances in the Lithium Recovery from Water Resources: From Passive to Electrochemical Methods." *Advanced Science* 9 (27): 2201380.

Bernal, A., J. Husar, and J. Bracht. 2023. "Latin America's Opportunity in Critical Minerals for the Clean Energy Transition." International Energy Agency, April 7, 2023. https://www .iea.org/commentaries/ latin-america-s-opportunity-in-critical-minerals-for-the-clean-energy-transition.

Bhashyam, A. 2023. "2023 Hydrogen Levelized Cost Update: Green Beats Gray." Bloomberg New Energy Finance, July 25, 2023.

Blackman, A., L. Corral, E. S. Lima, and G. P. Asner. 2017. "Titling Indigenous Communities Protects Forests in the Peruvian Amazon." *Proceedings of the National Academy of Sciences* 114 (16): 4123–28.

Blackman, A., and P. Veit. 2018. "Titled Amazon Indigenous Communities Cut Forest Carbon Emissions." *Ecological Economics* 153: 56–67.

Bloomberg. 2023. "Emerging Lithium Supplier Argentina Says It's Close to US Deal under IRA." May 23, 2023. https://www.bloomberg.com/news/articles/2023-05-23/emerging -lithium-supplier-argentina-says-it-s-close-to-us-deal-under-ira?embedded -checkout=true.

BNamericas. 2022. "Why Brazil Fails to Develop a Copper Value Chain." January 23, 2022. https://www.bnamericas.com/en/interviews/why-brazil-fails-to-develop-a-copper -value-chain.

Bhashyam, A. 2023. "2023 Hydrogen Levelized Cost Update: Green Beats Gray." Bloomberg New Energy Finance, July 25, 2023.

BMWK (German Federal Ministry for Economic Affairs and Climate Action). 2023. "National Hydrogen Strategy Update: NHS 2023." Federal Ministry of Economic Affairs and Climate Action, Berlin. https://www.bmwk.de/Redaktion/EN/Publikationen/Energie /national-hydrogen-strategy-update.pdf?__blob=publicationFile&v=2.

Borras, S. M. Jr., J. C. Franco, C. Kay, and M. Spoor. 2011. "Land Grabbing in Latin America and the Caribbean Viewed from Broader International Perspectives." Paper presented at the Latin America and Caribbean seminar, "Dinámicas en el mercado de la tierra en América Latina y el Caribe," FAO Regional Office, Santiago, Chile, November 14–15. https://www.tandfonline.com/doi/full/10.1080/03066150.2012.679931.

Brancalion, P. H. S., P. Meli, J. R. C. Tymus et al. 2019. "What Makes Ecosystem Restoration Expensive? A Systematic Cost Assessment of Projects in Brazil." *Biological Conservation* 240: 108274.

Brandt, J., J. Ertel, J. Spore, and F. Stolle. 2023. "Wall-to-Wall Mapping of Tree Extent in the Tropics with Sentinel-1 and Sentinel-2." *Remote Sensing of Environment* 292: 113574.

Brannstrom, C., Lucas Seghezzo, & Adryane Gorayeb. (2022). ¿ Descarbonización con justicia? Conceptos y enfoques. *Descarbonización En América Del Sur: Conexiones Entre Brasil y Argentina*, 236–253.

Brito, B., J. Almeida, P. Gomes, and R. Salomão. 2021. *10 Essential Facts about Land Tenure Regularization in the Brazilian Amazon*. Bèlem, Pará, Brazil: Imazon. https://imazon.org .br/en/publicacoes/10-essential-facts-about-land-tenure-regularization-in-the -brazilian-amazon/

Byerlee, D., J. R. Stevenson, and N. B. Villoria. 2014. "Does Intensification Slow Crop Land Expansion or Encourage Deforestation?" *Global Food Security* 3 (2): 92–98.

CEPAL (La Comisión Económica para América Latina). 2023. "Extracción e industrialización del litio: Oportunidades y desafíos para América Latina y el Caribe." CEPAL, Santiago.

Chen, Q., X. Lai, H. Gu et al. 2022. "Investigating Carbon Footprint and Carbon Reduction Potential Using a Cradle-to-Cradle LCA Approach on Lithium-Ion Batteries for Electric Vehicles in China." *Journal of Cleaner Production* 369: 133342.

Copper Mark, The. 2022. "The Copper Mark Reaches Coverage of 20% of Global Mined Production and Secures over 40 Participants." The Copper Mark website, August 30, 2022. https://coppermark.org/the-copper-mark-reaches-coverage-of-20-of-global -mined-production-and-secures-over-40-participants/.

Cordes, K. Y., O. Östensson, and P. Toledano. 2016. *Employment from Mining and Agricultural Investments: How Much Myth, How Much Reality?* New York: Columbia Center on Sustainable Investment, Columbia University. https://scholarship.law.columbia .edu/sustainable_investment_staffpubs/88/.

CORFO. 2020. "Corfo Will Support New Project to Boost the Massive Use of Green Hydrogen in Mining." News release, July 29, 2020. https://www.corfo.cl/sites /Satellite?c=C_NoticiaNacional&cid=1476726420760&d=Touch&pagename=CorfoPo rtalPublico%2FC_NoticiaNacional%2FcorfoDetalleNoticiaNacionalWeb.

Damania, R., Esteban Balseca, C. de Fontaubert et al. 2023. *Detox Development: Repurposing Environmentally Harmful Subsidies*. Washington, DC: World Bank. https:// www.worldbank.org/en/topic/climatechange/publication/detox-development.

Damania, R., S. Polasky, M. Ruckelshaus et al. 2023. *Nature's Frontiers: Achieving Sustainability, Efficiency, and Prosperity with Natural Capital*. Environment and Sustainable Development Series. Washington, DC: World Bank.

de Ferranti, D., G. E. Perry, D. Lederman, and W. F. Maloney. 2002. *From Natural Resources to the Knowledge Economy: Trade and Job Quality*. Washington, DC: World Bank.

De Sy, V., M. Herold, F. Achard et al. 2015. "Land Use Patterns and Related Carbon Losses Following Deforestation in South America." *Environmental Research Letters* 10 (12): 124004.

ECLAC (Economic Commission for Latin America and the Caribbean). 2021. *Forest Loss in Latin America and the Caribbean from 1990 to 2020: The Statistical Evidence*. ECLAC Statistical Briefings no. 2, July 2021. https://repositorio.cepal.org/server/api /core/bitstreams/3840dd1c-ed48-4c0c-a0b9-a3461f3cd3f6/content.

Ecosystem Marketplace. 2023. *Paying for Quality: State of the Voluntary Carbon Markets 2023*. Washington, DC: Forest Trends Association. https://www.forest-trends.org /pressroom/report-voluntary-carbon-markets-demand-in-2023-is-concentrating -around-pricier-high-integrity-credits/.

Edwards, W. 2015. "Estimating Farm Machinery Costs. *AG Decision Maker,* file A3-29, PM 710, May 2015. Iowa State University Extension and Outreach. https://www.extension .iastate.edu/agdm/crops/pdf/a3-29.pdf.

Egas, J. J., and C. P. De Salvo. 2018. *Agricultural Support Policies in Latin America and the Caribbean: 2018 Review*. Washington, DC: Inter-American Development Bank. https:// publications.iadb.org/en/publications/english/viewer/Agricultural-Support-Policies -in-Latin-America-and-the-Caribbean-2018-Review.pdf.

ESA (European Space Agency). 2019. "ESA Climate Change Initiative" (dashboard). https://openknowledge.worldbank.org/entities/publication/4217c71d-6cbc-46b6-942c-3e4651900d29.

ESMAP (Energy Sector Management Assistance Program), OECD (Organisation for Economic Co-operation and Development), Global Infrastructure Facility, and Hydrogen Council. 2024. "Scaling Hydrogen Financing for Development." ESMAP Paper, World Bank, Washington, DC. http://hdl.handle.net/10986/41125.

European Commission. 2023. "Global Gateway: EU and Chile Strengthen Cooperation on Sustainable Critical Raw Materials Supply Chains." Press release, July 17, 2023. https://ec.europa.eu/commission/presscorner/detail/en/IP_23_3897.

FAO (Food and Agriculture Organization of the United Nations). 2020. *Global Forest Resources Assessment 2020: Main Report*. Rome: Food and Agriculture Organization of the United Nations.

FAO (Food and Agriculture Organization of the United Nations). 2021. "Part 2—Trade and Nutrition: Identifying the Linkages" in *The State of Agricultural Commodity Markets 2024—Trade and Nutrition: Policy Coherence for Healthy Diets*. Rome: Food and Agriculture Organization of the United Nations. https://openknowledge.fao.org/server/api/core/bitstreams/7ca7c051-6ad2-4595-820b-c373fdb365f1/content/state-of-agricultural-commodity-markets/2024/pattern-evolution-food-trade.html.

FAO (Food and Agriculture Organization of the United Nations). 2023. "Land Use Statistics and Indicators 2000–2021: Global, Regional and Country Trends." FAOSTAT Analytical Brief 71, Food and Agriculture Organization of the United Nations, Rome.

GAP Initiative 2023. Regional Spotlight: Latin America and the Caribbean." GAP Initiative at Virginia Tech University. https://globalagriculturalproductivity.org/2023-gap-report/latin-america-and-the-caribbean/.

Goldman Sachs. 2023. *Global Metals and Mining: Direct Lithium Extraction—A Potential Game Changing Technology*. Goldman Sachs, April 27, 2023. https://www.goldmansachs.com/insights/goldman-sachs-research/direct-lithium-extraction.

González, N. C., and M. Kröger. 2023. "The Adoption of Earth-Observation Technologies for Deforestation Monitoring by Indigenous People: Evidence from the Amazon." *Globalizations* 20 (3): 415–31.

Grafton, R. Q., H. Long Chu, H. Nelson, and G. Bonnis. 2021. "A Global Analysis of the Cost-Efficiency of Forest Carbon Sequestration." OECD Environment Working Paper 185, Organisation for Economic Co-operation and Development, Paris.

Gutiérrez, J. S., J. N. Moore, J. P. Donnelly, C. Dorador, J. G. Navedo, and N. R. Senner. 2022. "Climate Change and Lithium Mining Influence Flamingo Abundance in the Lithium Triangle." *Proceedings of the Royal Society B* 289 (1970): 2021–2388.

Hanusch, M., ed. 2023. *A Balancing Act for Brazil's Amazonian States: An Economic Memorandum*. Washington, DC: World Bank. https://openknowledge.worldbank.org/entities/publication/26dc1f44-f50e-4a71-b4b6-b5dc143f5dfb.

Harris, N. L., D. A. Gibbs, A. Baccini et al. 2021. "Global Maps of Twenty-First Century Forest Carbon Fluxes." *Nature Climate Change* 11 (3): 234–40.

High-Level Commission on Carbon Prices. 2017. *Report of the High-Level Commission on Carbon Prices*. Washington, DC: World Bank.

Holmberg, K., P. Kivikyto-Reponen, P. Harkisaari, K. Valtonen, and A. Erdemir. 2017. "Global Energy Consumption Due to Friction and Wear in the Mining Industry." *Tribology International* 115: 116–39.

ICA (International Copper Association). 2023. *Copper: The Pathway to Net Zero*. McLean, VA: ICA. https://internationalcopper.org/wp-content/uploads/2023/03/ICA-GlobalDecar-202301-English-Final-singlepgs.pdf.

ICMM (International Council on Mining and Metals) 2017. *Role of Mining in National Economies*. 3rd edition. https://www.icmm.com/website/publications/pdfs/social-performance/2016/research_romine-3.pdf

IEA (International Energy Agency). 2019. *The Future of Hydrogen: Seizing Today's Opportunities*. Paris: IEA. https://www.iea.org/reports/the-future-of-hydrogen.

IEA (International Energy Agency). 2021a. *Global Hydrogen Review 2021*. Paris: IEA. https://www.iea.org/reports/global-hydrogen-review-2021.

IEA (International Energy Agency). 2021b. *Hydrogen in Latin America: From Near-Term Opportunities to Large-Scale Deployment*. Paris: IEA. https://www.iea.org/reports/hydrogen-in-latin-america.

IEA (International Energy Agency). 2022a. "Law No 928: Law of the National Strategic Public Company for Bolivian Lithium Deposits—YLB." International Energy Agency, November 1, 2022. https://www.iea.org/policies/16654-law-no-928-law-of-the-national-strategic-public-company-for-bolivian-lithium-deposits-ylb.

IEA (International Energy Agency). 2022b. *The Role of Critical Minerals in Clean Energy Transitions*. World Energy Outlook Special Report. Paris: IEA. https://www.iea.org/reports/the-role-of-critical-minerals-in-clean-energy-transitions.

IEA (International Energy Agency). 2023a. "Critical Minerals Demand Dataset." International Energy Agency. https://www.iea.org/data-and-statistics/data-product/critical-minerals-dataset.

IEA (International Energy Agency). 2023b. *Energy Technology Perspectives 2023*. Paris: IEA. https://www.iea.org/reports/energy-technology-perspectives-2023.

IEA (International Energy Agency). 2023c. "Overview: Costa Rica." Part of *Latin America Energy Outlook 2023*.Paris: IEA. https://www.iea.org/reports/costa-rica-energy-profile.

IEA (International Energy Agency). 2023d. *Towards Hydrogen Definitions Based on Their Emissions Intensity*. Paris: IEA. https://www.iea.org/reports/towards-hydrogen-definitions-based-on-their-emissions-intensity.

IFC (International Finance Corporation). 2023. "Net Zero Roadmap to 2050: For Copper and Nickel Mining Value Chains." IFC, Washington, DC. https://commdev.org/wp-content/uploads/pdf/publications/IFC_NZR4M_Final_Roadmap_C-suite_FINAL.pdf.

Igogo, T., J. Awuah-Offei, A. Newman, T. Lowder, and J. Engel-Cox. 2021. "Integrating Renewable Energy into Mining Operations: Opportunities, Challenges, and Enabling Approaches." *Applied Energy* 300: 117375.

ILO (International Labor Organization). 2021. ILOSTAT: Statutory Nominal Gross Monthly Minimum Wage. https://ilostat.ilo.org/topics/wages/.

Inocencio, A., M. Kikuchi, M. Tonosaki et al. 2007. "Costs and Performance of Irrigation Projects: A Comparison of Sub-Saharan Africa and Other Developing Regions." IWMI Research Report 109, International Water Management Institute, Colombo, Sri Lanka.

International Copper Study Group. 2022. *The World Copper Factbook*. Lisbon, Portugal: International Copper Study Group. Last accessed September 12, 2023. https://icsg.org/copper-factbook/.

INTERPOL. 2022. "Illegal Logging in Latin America and Caribbean Inflicting Irreversible Damage." INTERPOL. https://www.interpol.int/en/News-and-Events/News/2022/Illegal-logging-in-Latin-America-and-Caribbean-inflicting-irreversible-damage-INTERPOL.

IRENA (International Renewable Energy Agency). 2022. *Geopolitics of the Energy Transformation: The Hydrogen Factor*. Abu Dhabi: International Renewable Energy Agency.

Jones, B., F. Acuña, and V. Rodríguez. 2021. *Cambios en la demanda de minerales: Análisis de los mercados del cobre y el litio, y sus implicaciones para los países de la región andina*. Documentos de Proyectos (LC/TS.2021/89). Santiago: Comisión Económica para América Latina y el Caribe (CEPAL).

Klein Goldewijk, K., A. Beusen, J. Doelman, and E. Stehfest. 2017. "Anthropogenic Land Use Estimates for the Holocene—HYDE 3.2." *Earth System Science Data* 9 (2): 927–53.

Kremen, C. 2015. "Reframing the Land-Sparing/Land-Sharing Debate for Biodiversity Conservation." *Annals of the New York Academy of Sciences* 1355 (1): 52–76. https://doi.org/10.1111/nyas.12845.

León, M., C. Muñoz, and J. Sánchez, eds. 2020. *La gobernanza del litio y el cobre en los países andinos.* Documentos de Proyectos (LC/TS.2020/124). Santiago: Comisión Económica para América Latina y el Caribe (CEPAL).

Liu, Z. Z. 2023. "How to Secure Critical Minerals for Clean Energy without Alienating China." Council on Foreign Relations Renewing America Initiative (blog), May 25, 2023. https://www.cfr.org/blog/how-secure-critical-minerals-clean-energy-without-alienating-china.

López Marmolejo, A., C. Eggers Prieto, and M. Ruiz-Arranz, eds. 2023. *Opportunities for Boosting Output, Employment and Value Chains: Economic Report on Central America, Mexico, Panama and the Dominican Republic.* Washington, DC: Inter-American Development Bank.

Loukos, P., and L. Arathoon. 2021. *Landscaping the Agritech Ecosystem for Smallholder Farmers in Latin America and the Caribbean.* Washington, DC: Inter-American Development Bank.

Mahiques, M. V. A., M. Galuccio, and C. Freytes. 2022. *Gobernanza socioambiental de la minería de litio: Instituciones, acceso a la información y participación pública en Argentina.* Buenos Aires: Fundar. https://fund.ar/wp-content/uploads/2022/10/Fundar_Gobernanza_Socioamb_MineriaLitio.pdf.

MapBiomas Alerta. 2020. *Annual Deforestation Report 2019.* Brazil. https://alerta.mapbiomas.org/wp-content/uploads/sites/17/2024/03/RAD2020_MapBiomasAlerta_FINAL.pdf.

McKinsey & Company. 2022. "The Inflation Reduction Act: Here's What's in It." McKinsey & Co. https://www.mckinsey.com/industries/public-sector/our-insights/the-inflation-reduction-act-heres-whats-in-it.

Mejía, J. and E. Aliakbari. 2024. "Annual Survey of Mining Companies, 2023." Fraser Institute, May 14, 2024. https://www.fraserinstitute.org/studies/annual-survey-of-mining-companies-2023.

Molina, O. 2018. "Innovation in an Unfavorable Context: Local Mining Suppliers in Peru." *Resources Policy* 58 (C): 34–48.

Morgan, S., K. Fuglie, and E. Saini. 2023. *Crecimiento de la PTF en la Agricultura en Argentina: Inversiones en Investigación e Innovación.* GAP Initiative, Virginia Tech University.

Moritz, M., M. Schönfisch, and S. Schulte. 2023. "Estimating Global Production and Supply Costs for Green Hydrogen and Hydrogen-Based Green Energy Commodities." *International Journal of Hydrogen Energy* 48 (25): 9139–54.

Morris, M., A. R. Sebastian, and V. M. E. Perego. 2020. *Future Foodscapes: Re-Imagining Agriculture in Latin America and the Caribbean.* Washington, DC: World Bank.

Mulder, M., P. Perey, and J. L. Moraga. 2019. *Outlook for a Dutch Hydrogen Market: Economic Conditions and Scenarios.* CEER Policy Paper 5. University of Groningen, Netherlands. https://www.rug.nl/cenber/blog/ceer_policypaper_5_web.pdf.

Nin-Pratt, A., G. L. Stads, L. de los Santos et al. 2023. *Unlocking Innovation: Assessing the Role of Agricultural R&D in Latin America and the Caribbean.* Washington, DC: Inter-American Development Bank. https://publications.iadb.org/en/publications/english/viewer/Unlocking-Innovation-Assessing-the-Role-of-Agricultural-RD-in-Latin-America-and-the-Caribbean.pdf.

Obaya, M. 2021. *Una mirada estratégica sobre el triángulo del litio: Marco normativo y políticas productivas para el desarrollo de capacidades en base a recursos naturales.* Buenos Aires: Fundar. https://fund.ar/wp-content/uploads/2021/11/Fundar-Una-mirada-estrate%CC%81gica-sobre-el-tria%CC%81ngulo-del-litio.pdf.

OECD (Organisation for Economic Co-operation and Development). 2022. *Regulatory Governance in the Mining Sector in Brazil.* Paris: OECD Publishing.

OECD/FAO. 2019. *OECD-FAO Agricultural Outlook 2019–2028.* Paris: OECD Publishing. https://doi.org/10.1787/agr_outlook-2019-en.

Olvera, B. C. 2022. "Innovation in Mining: What Are the Challenges and Opportunities along the Value Chain for Latin American Suppliers? *Mineral Economics* 35 (4): 35–51.

Olvera, B. C., and M. Iizuka. 2020. "How Does Innovation Take Place in the Mining Industry?: Understanding the Logic behind Innovation in a Changing Context." MERIT Working Papers 2020-019, Maastricht University, Netherlands.

Onstad, Eric. 2021. "Boliden Launches Low-Carbon Copper." Reuters, March 19, 2021. https://www.reuters.com/article/us-copper-boliden-carbon-idUSKBN2BB1C2.

Ortiz-Bobea, A., T. R. Ault, C. M. Carrillo, R. G. Chambers, and D. B. Lobell. 2021. "Anthropogenic Climate Change Has Slowed Global Agricultural Productivity Growth." *Nature Climate Change* 11: 306–12. https://doi.org/10.1038/s41558-021-01000-1.

Patrick, E., V. Butsic, and M. D. Potts. 2023. "Using Payment for Ecosystem Services to Meet National Reforestation Commitments: Impacts of 20+ Years of Forestry Incentives in Guatemala." *Environmental Research Letters* 18 (10): 104030. https://doi.org/10.1088/1748-9326/acf602.

Perry, C. 2022. "'Green' Copper Premiums the Talk of the Town in the European Copper Market." Fastmarkets, October 6, 2022. https://www.fastmarkets.com/insights/green-copper-premiums-the-talk-of-the-town-in-european-copper-market.

Pragier, D. 2019. "Comunidades indígenas frente a la explotación de litio en sus territorios: Contextos similares, respuestas distintas." *Polis—Revista Latinoamericana* 18 (52).

Puntel, L. A., É. L. Bolfe, R. J. M. Melchiori et al. 2022. "How Digital Is Agriculture in a Subset of Countries from South America? Adoption and Limitations." *Crop and Pasture Science* 74 (6): 555–72. https://doi.org/10.1071/CP21759.

S&P Global. 2022. *The Future of Copper: Will the Looming Supply Gap Short-Circuit the Energy Transition?* New York: S&P Global. July 2022.

Sesnie, S. E., B. Tellman, D. Wrathall et al. 2017. "A Spatio-temporal Analysis of Forest Loss Related to Cocaine Trafficking in Central America." *Environmental Research Letters* 12 (5): 054015. https://iopscience.iop.org/article/10.1088/1748-9326/aa6fff/pdf.

Sharp, R., J. Douglass, S. Wolny et al. 2020. "InVEST 3.10.2.post24+ug.g99a876b.d20220317 User's Guide." Natural Capital Project, Stanford University, University of Minnesota, Nature Conservancy, and World Wildlife Fund.

Sinnott, E., J. Nash, and A. de la Torre. 2010. *Natural Resources in Latin America and the Caribbean: Beyond Booms and Busts?* Washington, DC: World Bank.

Sloan, S., and J. A. Sayer. 2015. "Forest Resources Assessment of 2015 Shows Positive Global Trends but Forest Loss and Degradation Persist in Poor Tropical Countries." *Forest Ecology and Management* 352 (7): 134–45.

Stubrin, L. 2018. "Innovation, Learning and Competence Building in the Mining Industry: The Case of Knowledge Intensive Mining Suppliers (KIMS) in Chile." *Resources Policy* 54: 167–75.

Taylor, C. A., and J. Rising. 2021. "Tipping Point Dynamics in Global Land Use." *Environmental Research Letters* 16 (12): 125012.

TEEB (The Economics of Ecosystems and Biodiversity). 2009. "TEEB Climate Issues Update." TEEB, Geneva, Switzerland. http://www.teebweb.org/media/2009/09/TEEB-Climate-Issues-Update.pdf.

Thomas, B. S., A. Damare, and R. C. Gupta. 2013. "Strength and Durability Characteristics of Copper Tailing Concrete." *Construction and Building Materials* 48: 894–900.

Tseng, T.-W. J., B. E. Robinson, M. F. Bellemare et al. 2020. "Influence of Land Tenure Interventions on Human Well-Being and Environmental Outcomes." *Nature Sustainability* 4 (3): 242–51.

Tycorun. 2022. "Top 5 Power Battery Zero Carbon Company in China." Tycorun, May 9, 2022. https://www.takomabattery.com/top-5-power-battery-zero-carbon-company-in-china/.

United Nations Convention to Combat Desertification. 2019. *Global Land Outlook, Latin America and the Caribbean Thematic Report*. Bonn: United Nations Convention to Combat Desertification.

United Nations Framework Convention on Climate Change. 2023. "Latest IPCC Science on Implications for Agriculture." December 15, 2023. https://www.cisl.cam.ac.uk/system /files/documents/IPCC_AR5__Implications_for_Agriculture__Briefing__WEB_EN.pdf.

Universidad del Norte. 2022. "Promigas anuncia alianza con 3 universidades colombianas para investigación y desarrollo en gases renovables." News portal, March 31, 2022. https://www.uninorte.edu.co/en/web/grupo-prensa/w/promigas-anuncia-alianza -con-3-universidades-colombianas-para-investigacion-y-desarrollo-en-gases -renovables?p_l_back_url=%2Fen%2Fweb%2Fgrupo-prensa%2Fresultados-noticias %3Fdelta%3D4%26start%3D180.

USGS (US Geological Survey). 2023. *Mineral Commodity Summaries*. Reston, VA: USGS. https://pubs.usgs.gov/periodicals/mcs2023/mcs2023.pdf.

Vera, M. L., W. R. Torres, C. I. Galli, A. Chagnes, and V. Flexer. 2023. "Environmental Impact of Direct Lithium Extraction from Brines." *Nature Reviews Earth and Environment* 4 (3): 149–65.

Vergara-Zambrano, K. W., and F. A. Díaz-Alvarado. 2022. "Integration of Renewable Energy into the Copper Mining Industry: A Multi-Objective Approach." *Journal of Cleaner Production* 372 (1): 133419.

Wagner, L. S., and M. Walter. 2020. *Cartografía de la conflictividad minera en Argentina (2003–2018): Un análisis desde el Atlas de Justicia Ambiental*. Buenos Aires: Ediciones CICCUS.

Watkins, G., S.-U. Mueller, H. Meller, M. C. Ramirez, T. Serebrisky, and A. Georgoulias. 2017. *Lessons from Four Decades of Infrastructure Project-Related Conflicts in Latin America and the Caribbean*. Washington, DC: Inter-American Development Bank.

World Bank. 2022. *Peru Country Climate and Development Report*. Washington, DC: World Bank.

World Bank. 2023. *Corredores Económicos Transformadores de Noroeste Argentino*. Washington, DC: World Bank. https://documents1.worldbank.org/curated/en /099100923161014616/pdf/P17940301690e70200a800002036794540c.pdf.

World Bank. 2025a. "Improving Land Use for a Prosperous, Low-Carbon Latin America." Background paper for this publication. World Bank, Washington. https://documents .worldbank.org/en/publication/documents-reports/documentdetail/09906022 5142510052.

World Bank 2025b. "Green Hydrogen in Latin America and the Caribbean." Background paper for this publication. World Bank, Washington. https://documents.worldbank .org/en/publication/documents-reports/documentdetail/099060225142533687.

Wright, G., and J. Czelusta. 2004. "Mineral Resources and Economic Development." Working Paper 209, Stanford Center for International Development, Stanford University, Stanford, CA. https://kingcenter.stanford.edu/sites/g/files/sbiybj16611/files/media /file/209wp_0.pdf.

Zalles, V., M. C. Hansen, P. V. Potapov et al. 2021. "Rapid Expansion of Human Impact on Natural Land in South America since 1985." *Science Advances* 7 (14): eabg1620. https://doi.org/10.1126/sciadv.abg1620.

Zhang, K., C. Hu, and H. Yu. 2021. "Remote Sensing Image Classification Based on Deep Learning." *Scientific Programming* (special issue). https://doi.org/10.1155/2021/6203444.

Ziegler, S., J. Arias, M. Bosio et al. 2020. *Rural Connectivity in Latin America and the Caribbean—A Bridge to Sustainable Development during a Pandemic*. San Isidro, Costa Rica: Inter-American Institute for Cooperation on Agriculture.

PART II

The Way Forward: Institutions, Investment, and Innovation

The Three I's

How can the region harness its natural assets and strengths to lay the foundations for sustainable growth? The answer lies in the ways that countries respond to—and, ideally, prepare for—ongoing, fast-paced changes in prices, regulations, preferences, and technology. As the world moves toward higher carbon prices and as preferences shift toward greener and low-carbon products, Latin America and the Caribbean countries can differentiate themselves by decarbonizing production while exporting deforestation-free goods and sustainably extracted minerals. Additionally, investing in well-functioning national innovation systems that support climate-friendly technologies and practices will provide a competitive advantage and diversify exports.

This report offers insights for overcoming the multiple challenges to leveraging dynamic, sustainable, and inclusive growth. The lessons are applicable to most of the economic opportunities provided by the transition, although each sector presents specific obstacles.

Market failures—such as asymmetric information, coordination challenges, and the management of externalities and public goods—jeopardize all sectors. It can be difficult to assess the reliability of claims that goods are sustainably produced, making consumers less likely to pay green premiums. Uncertainty about willingness to pay, the scale of demand, and the profitability of projects causes producers to underinvest. Consequently, some markets may fail to reach the scale they need to significantly reduce costs and compete with traditionally produced goods. Diffuse property rights and a lack of regulatory clarity only make underinvestment a greater problem.

The transition to a new economic development model means addressing the three I's: institutions, investment, and innovation. First, institutions: the right policy and regulatory frameworks must be built to guide and incentivize actions in key sectors while protecting people and the environment. Policy makers must have access to the information they need to make good policy decisions, as well as the capacity to implement them. To enable private sector participation and attract international investment, countries must establish clear regulations, strengthen institutions, and build capacity. To resolve failures of coordination and asymmetric information, countries should foster transparency and establish reliable information systems while also enhancing communication between public and private actors.

Second, governments must invest in infrastructure and other productive public goods. Markets are still incomplete and imperfect, and the social benefits of developing them are not likely to be incorporated into private decisions. Investments in infrastructure and public goods can help lock in private investment and lower technological, social, and political risks. Complementary public goods can also reduce information asymmetries and coordination failures by strengthening linkages between actors in a particular sector.

Finally, regarding innovation, countries should develop systems that can adopt, adapt, imitate, and invent new technologies and practices. This adaptation will support the diffusion of well-established technologies (for example, to improve agricultural productivity) and the transformation of legacy production processes (for example, in mining). Since new markets depend on sustained innovation efforts, a thriving innovation ecosystem is required to enter and benefit from them.

The following three chapters build on the challenges for the three sectoral examples identified in chapter 2 by discussing specific actions that Latin America and the Caribbean countries can take to improve the three I's. In this way, they can seize the technological and economic window of opportunity afforded by a greening world.

CHAPTER 3

Institutions

Guillermo Beylis and Nancy Lozano Gracia

The Foundations for Economic Transformation

A solid institutional setup is crucial for addressing the market failures that plague the new economy and drive the inefficient allocation of resources. The economic transition has exposed the great value of the different environmental services provided by nature, thus revealing, as well, the presence of significant externalities in many existing markets. While the benefits are clear, the technological upgrading of production processes to boost both productivity and sustainability is often hampered by failures in information markets, poor coordination between actors, and a lack of incentives. Similarly, the adoption of new technologies and the opening of new markets require not only an enabling environment to reduce risk for investors but also careful coordination between actors. These improvements are necessary to foster growth in demand and supply simultaneously while also facilitating learning and competence building, which help lower costs and spread technology.

Addressing the presence of significant externalities requires, on the one hand, establishing clear property rights and strong regulatory frameworks. Diffuse property rights are a major barrier to enabling the efficient reallocation of resources (Coase 1960), as they undermine productive investments and the effectiveness of government policies. Strong regulatory frameworks set clear rules for all, reducing risk and uncertainty and, therefore, fostering investment. On the other hand, the institutional design of supportive public policy—like taxes and subsidies—accompanied by effective enforcement of the rules and regulations will also shape the incentives of actors in these markets.

Implementing such an important technological and economic transformation requires deep coordination. Governments can help resolve coordination failures by establishing the appropriate institutions that foster communication, align incentives, and induce coordination between different actors in each market. Coordination failures can happen between private actors when it is unclear whether their counterparts will adopt new technology, causing the market to remain undeveloped. Similarly, public-private coordination failures happen if, for example, a government—lacking the necessary information—does not provide certain market-enabling public goods. Finally, at the public-public level, policies may not be coordinated between different ministries or jurisdictional levels, resulting in contradictory rules or misalignment of incentives.

Establish New Rules for a New Economy

The economic and technological transformation implied by the transition to a low-carbon economy will also require an institutional and regulatory transformation. As markets, governments, and people increasingly recognize the value of nature and ecosystem services, they are also recognizing some of the— often large—negative externalities associated with certain economic activities. As such, a new set of "rules of the game" needs to be developed that explicitly protects the value of a country's natural capital. Just as important will be the effective enforcement of such rules, as well as well-designed supportive public policies that shape incentives.

Clear property rights are a prerequisite for addressing externalities and efficiently allocating resources (Cooter 1989). Strong legal frameworks that protect well-defined property rights, environmental regulations, land use policies, and effective protection mechanisms are essential for addressing inefficiencies and incentivizing investment and growth in sustainably produced agricultural, forestry, energy, and mineral goods and services. Currently, private actors perceive risks that are preventing engagement with emerging markets, instead incentivizing maladaptive speculation. Regional rules and regulations could generate even more clarity and confidence for international partners and private actors.

Diffuse property rights—particularly in land and carbon credit markets— prevent the efficient reallocation of land that would allow Latin America and the Caribbean to capitalize on emerging opportunities. Land titling, particularly collective titling, improves forest outcomes by enabling landholders to exclude competing users while enhancing their access to government incentives for the management and preservation of forests, such as payments for environmental services (including carbon markets). Lack of clear land tenure has led to weaker enforcement of regulations, reduced access to credit, and lower investment in land for productive use (Hanusch 2023). Areas with undesignated land tenure in the Amazon (almost 30 percent of its area) continue to be deforestation hot spots; between 2013 and 2020, up to 40 percent of forest loss in the Amazon occurred on land with unclear tenure. The lack of strictly enforced cutoff dates for regularization claims enables individuals to use occupation as a basis for claiming the right to title land in undesignated areas (Brito et al. 2021). Not only can regularization of tenure alleviate poverty and food insecurity (Tseng et al. 2020), but it can also help governments ensure that the benefits from land-use projects are equitably distributed and that Indigenous peoples' concerns are adequately reflected in project design.

Improving land rights requires action to update cadastral databases and promote the granting of land titles and other territorial rights to local communities. One necessary measure is the incorporation of prior consultation and free and prior informed consent (FPIC) of Indigenous peoples in the environmental evaluation and licensing procedures for projects. A second is the incorporation of an assessment of a project's risks for and impacts on local communities in environmental and social project evaluation to help ensure effective monitoring and enforcement of rights and regulations.

In Brazil, for example, an interoperable cadastre could support the strengthening of secure property rights and help reduce incentives for deforestation. Currently, many public lands in Brazil are unregistered and without an assigned use, putting them at risk of being targeted by squatters or land grabbers, contributing to deforestation. According to the National Institute of Colonization and Agrarian Reform (INCRA 2023), the Terra Legal Program georeferenced 72 million hectares of federal public land; however, the Amazon federal public land is not yet georeferenced. The Land Management System (SIGEF of INCRA) is responsible for certifying the georeferencing of rural properties registered or regularizing the state's public lands. Not all public or private lands are registered in the property registry offices; therefore, they are outside the universe of certified properties. This deficiency could be overcome with an efficient and interoperable cadastre with geospatial data encompassing property rights, other tenure rights, and possession rights. For example, the registration of property and possession with geospatial data would make it feasible to identify the owner responsible for possible noncompliance with obligations relating to respect for environmental rules, among others.

Both Colombia and Ecuador have implemented effective policies to ensure that the benefits of markets for environmental goods and services reach local communities. Community engagement in Colombia has been essential in protecting land rights by enabling the recognition of on-field tenure typologies, particularly in municipalities with a fragility, conflict, and violence context, high tenure informality, and risks of forced eviction or property dispossession. Colombia's multipurpose cadastre policy enables the recording of legitimate land tenure rights, facilitates the establishment of alternative dispute resolution mechanisms for land-related conflicts, contributes to the clarification and recognition of legitimate land rights, and safeguards the rights of vulnerable groups such as Indigenous peoples, Afro-descendants, women, and smallholder farmers. Meanwhile, land titling for Indigenous communities in the coastal region of Ecuador appears to have had a significant positive effect in reducing deforestation; the process was also supported by local nongovernmental organizations focused on ensuring effective policy implementation (Tanner and Ratzke 2022).

Strong environmental frameworks are needed to protect standing forests and support the regeneration of degraded lands. For example, despite ongoing challenges, the Dominican Republic's forest cover has increased since the 1960s after the country introduced environmental and forest legal frameworks, enforcement of timber harvest restrictions, a robust system of protected areas (SINAP), and government-sponsored reforestation programs (World Bank Group 2023b). Across the region, there has been a push to expand protected areas, with 24 percent of the land mass and almost 19 percent of marine areas designated as protected in 2020 (Proyecto IAPA—Visión Amazónica 2020). However, more needs to be done to strengthen and expand these systems. For example, protected areas do not always align with areas of high biodiversity. Just over half of the key areas for biodiversity, as defined by the International Union for Conservation of Nature (IUCN), have protected status, leaving 44 percent vulnerable to deforestation and degradation (Proyecto IAPA—Visión Amazónica 2020). In addition to increasing the area under protection, the region could improve management practices in protected areas. Management of protected areas in the region is split between governments (57 percent), private actors (15 percent), Indigenous communities (6 percent), and shared (2 percent).[1]

Legal frameworks could incorporate ecosystem services as part of the standards for regulating the environmental and social (E&S) evaluation of projects. Across the region, it is common for a project's impact on ecosystem services to be missing from the criteria that would trigger an E&S evaluation unless it is part of a payment for ecosystem services programs. For example, in Brazil, the Forest Code incorporates payments for ecosystem services (PES) and initiatives in the Amazon region grant payments to local communities for the protection of forests. For its part, El Salvador has a regulation that recognizes different forms of environmental compensation to facilitate the development of a collection and PES system. In Peru, PES to Indigenous communities have reduced deforestation and financed local infrastructure, services, and value chains, as well as advancing cultural and forest protection (FAO and FILAC 2021). In Guatemala, incentives for the conservation and sustainable use of forestry have been created, with nearly 600,000 hectares enrolled since 1998 (Patrick, Butsic, and Potts 2023).

While PES prioritize E&S considerations, there is scope for improving their design, implementation, and enforcement. For example, to ensure the quality of E&S assessments, licenses, and monitoring processes, laws can specify minimum standards. PES should require evaluations of the risks to and impacts on ecosystems. This evaluation can prevent irreparable damage to ecosystems and help make important forest benefits explicit in the analyses used to approve (or reject) projects. Guidelines should be updated to ensure that E&S impact assessments are required for the types of projects most prone to deforestation. Strengthening the management capacity of relevant government entities and the tools available to them can support effective implementation and enforcement of regulations. Countries will also need to develop good practice guidelines and standards for E&S risk and impact assessment, which could help identify how vulnerable people might be affected as well.

A new set of rules, complemented by supportive public policy and investments, can help countries transform existing production processes and expand their frontiers of productivity and sustainability. Regulatory frameworks should clearly define the E&S impacts of production methods. Yet policy makers can go further by designing mechanisms that incentivize investment in new technologies that reduce environmental impact. Moreover, cleverly designed policies can foster local solutions, promoting learning and competence capabilities and deepening the development impact. Norway's development of its oil and gas sector serves as a guiding example for the region.

Given the increasing global demand for energy transition minerals and the well-known environmental impact of their production, the region's mining sector is an excellent candidate for the transformation of its production processes. The rapid growth of the sector, if not well managed, poses serious risks to the environment. Open pit mining can cause deforestation, resulting in carbon emissions. The water surrounding a mine can be polluted, which can harm groundwater aquifers, fish, wildlife, and farmland (not only through pollution but also because of competition between the mining and agricultural sectors when water is scarce). The specific problem of acid mine drainage—which occurs when water leaches sulfide components from waste rock or ore volumes left in a mine, contaminating groundwater—is most serious in regions with significant rainfall. Other environmental impacts include noise and dust from operations and transport. Different segments of the copper and lithium value chains are associated with several environmental impacts, including carbon emissions, land occupancy, and alterations in water flows (Moreno-Leiva et al. 2020; Paz et al. 2023). Conditions must favor building long-term E&S sustainability to develop a healthy mining industry. With this purpose, governments can set sustainability goals and objectives in areas such as water use (particularly in dry regions), waste management, carbon footprint, air pollution, and so on.

The Latin America and the Caribbean region has made significant progress in including E&S impact assessments of mining projects in legal frameworks. While normative frameworks for lithium and copper mining vary, most countries have introduced specific complementary guidelines and standards for mining activities and have even established roles for sectoral authorities in licensing processes. For example, in Argentina, E&S impact assessments for mining are mainly governed by the Mining Code at a basic level,[2] but local jurisdictional regulations complement it. In terms of best practices, Bolivia and Peru have established specific environmental standards for mining through regulations that address its different stages and have stipulated the environmental permits required.[3] Peru also has several environmental guidelines for the mining sector. Chile has published two sets of mandatory guidelines to standardize requirements, particularly regarding the information needed for E&S assessments[4]—one for mitigating the impact of lithium mining (SEA 2021) and the other for copper mining (SEA 2017). The guidelines were developed jointly with the country's Environmental Assessment Service (SEA) and the mining sector agency. They apply to both the entities responsible for conducting environmental impact studies and those responsible for evaluating their accuracy. Regional and bilateral agreements can support the exchange of good practices, experiences, technology, and capacities in sustainable management across Latin America and the Caribbean.

In the same way, policy can support the development of productive inputs—such as renewable energy (RE)—that can help decarbonize downstream industries. Because market prices may not capture all potential positive spillovers, well-designed policies can incentivize the development of RE sources. Latin America and the Caribbean's already relatively clean energy matrix and its huge potential for increasing RE generation could be a competitive advantage. The development of green industrial parks, for example, may attract energy-intensive industries to relocate to areas with abundant low-carbon energy (Hausmann 2023). Institutional mechanisms could ensure that new demand is met with additional RE rather than existing capacity.

The development of new markets and technologies will clearly require a regulatory framework to define how they will function—including basic property rights, assessing E&S impacts, and identifying the safety and quality standards necessary for commercialization. In nascent markets, there is great social value in policy experimentation and regulatory learning, so governments would benefit from designing regulatory frameworks with the explicit objective of gathering knowledge (see chapter 5). Governments can establish certain goals—that are clear, realistic, attainable, and measurable—and institute monitoring and information-gathering mechanisms to show the effectiveness of their policy frameworks. Naturally, there are large economies of scale in learning, so regionally and even globally coordinated actions would create the greatest value.

The emerging carbon credit markets are a great example of a new market with a wide variety of regulatory approaches around the world; the outcomes of these different approaches are not yet clear. Policy makers will need to balance the value of learning about policy effectiveness with providing stability and clarity to market actors. Countries adopting legal frameworks that specifically address carbon crediting—and that very clearly define property rights around carbon credits—will be at an advantage. In carbon credit markets, unclear legal rights make trade agreements risky, particularly when associated property rights are ambiguous. Clear legal rights will increase stakeholder confidence, reduce uncertainty for project developers, enable enforcement of regulations, facilitate implementation of Article 6 of the Paris Agreement and the granting of authorizations for corresponding adjustments (where applicable), and enhance E&S safeguards. Again, there are different approaches around the world for defining the legal nature of carbon credits. For instance, in Colombia, carbon credits are treated as intangible assets, whereas in Australia, they are recognized as financial instruments (Hedley and Hillis 2022). International efforts are under way to better define and harmonize the legal nature of carbon credits (UNIDROIT 2023), potentially leading to a more efficient market for carbon credits (adelphi and Gold Standard 2023; Clifford Chance 2022).

Greater clarity in legal definitions of carbon rights and the legal nature of carbon credits could provide a more stable investment environment. Who will have the right to benefit from carbon crediting activities? How will credits be treated for accounting and taxation purposes? Embedding key elements of a carbon market framework in national law—from governance arrangements to institutional responsibilities—provides for greater stability and more transparency. That, in turn, can enhance stakeholder confidence. Recent pilot projects suggest that this will be an important part of implementing Article 6 in host countries. In recent years, legislation has been adopted in countries including Colombia, Ghana, India, Indonesia, Mozambique, Uganda, Thailand, and Viet Nam. It is being prepared in Kenya, Nepal, Nigeria, and Peru (adelphi and Gold Standard 2023). Such laws are needed to address unclear carbon rights and concerns about social and environmental integrity, which can otherwise be a barrier to implementation (Clifford Chance 2022). A domestic crediting mechanism requires specific legislation that details key design features, including the clear definition of all project cycle elements (eligibility; baselines for additionality; monitoring, reporting, and verification requirements; and so on), the designation of an administrator agency, the definition of procedures for validation and verification, and the assignment of responsibility for noncompliance as well as potential liabilities (see spotlight).

The efficient design of these markets is essential to encourage widespread entrepreneurship and competition. Given the large fixed costs and risks associated with the transition, it is reasonable to expect substantial market concentration. Latin America and the Caribbean is a region that struggles with productivity growth, challenges which are due, in part, to market concentration and lack of competition (Cusolito and Maloney 2018; Motta 2004). Moreover, in many instances large firms and elites have gathered significant political power, influencing policy and dampening antitrust measures (Maloney et al. 2024). Therefore, regulations should be designed to favor general welfare and not private interests, and renewed efforts are needed to strengthen the power and independence of competition laws and agencies.

Coordinate to Accelerate the Transformation

If Latin America and the Caribbean is to transform its economy successfully, coordination between diverse stakeholders is imperative. Policy makers can play a key role by establishing appropriate institutions to foster communication, align incentives, and induce coordination between different actors. But coordination can fail for multiple reasons: when market participants are unsure whether their counterpart will invest in a new technology, when governments don't provide key complementary public goods in a market, or when inconsistencies in public policy between ministries or jurisdictions lead to regulatory uncertainty or misalignment of incentives. Too often, the outcome is an underdeveloped—or even failed—market.

A focus on enhancing coordination within the public sector can help align incentives and reduce the unintended consequences of policies, and address market inefficiencies. For example, improved integration of planning activities across ministries, sectors, and local and national governments can help reduce deforestation by clearly defining permissible land uses, providing a basis for enforcement activities in the case of violations, and targeting planned development to minimize deforestation risks. To go even further, a policy focus on agricultural intensification, coordinated with the creation of an enabling environment for land regularization (with a focus on the conservation of natural lands), could, in turn, reduce land grabbing and expansion of the agricultural frontier.

Similarly, horizontal and vertical coordination of land use policies is a critical tool for tackling deforestation. Colombia has begun to align policies across ministries, which includes creating systems for local, state, and national governments to coordinate efforts to achieve deforestation goals. Developing a holistic strategy for Nationally Determined Contributions (NDC) implementation can help identify policy inconsistency, allowing improved coordination (World Bank 2025). Examples of horizontal coordination include aligning agricultural support with environmental goals, harmonizing land taxes to disincentivize agriculture, and supporting transport planning and financing that is consistent with deforestation control objectives. Vertical alignment policies include incentives for subnational government entities to manage forests sustainably, conditioning access to credit from national development banks and fiscal transfers to incentivize decentralized performance on managing deforestation, and rewarding performance in implementing policies (for example, completion of a cadastre or the application of green infrastructure guidelines) (World Bank Group 2023a).

A regional approach can help develop Latin America and the Caribbean's expertise and capabilities faster and more efficiently, helping sectors achieve scale and save on learning and enforcement costs. In the land use and forestry sectors, for example, regional agreements can promote the exchange of good practices, experiences, technology, and capacities in sustainable forest management. Regional agreements for sustainable forest management already exist in Latin America and the Caribbean, providing successful examples that can be replicated and expanded. For example, the Dominican Republic and Costa Rica have agreed to strengthen a joint PES mechanism. Additionally, 17 Latin America and the Caribbean countries are partners in the United Nations Collaborative Program to Reduce Emissions from Deforestation and Forest Degradation in Developing Countries (UN-REDD), which also addresses aspects of social inclusion and gender equality. There are also important opportunities to leverage economies of scale in monitoring and verification mechanisms. Coordinating on monitoring, reporting, and verification (MRV) systems makes sense, given the risk of spillover effects beyond national boundaries, helping to identify and prevent the displacement of deforestation from one jurisdiction to another.

Pushing out the technological and sustainability frontier in established markets also requires coordination between governments and the private sector. Success in the new economy, as described previously, requires that governments reward firms for pushing the technological frontier toward more sustainable production. Developing new technologies, however, generally requires an effective innovation system, in which companies frequently interact among themselves and with universities and research centers. New technologies may require complementary infrastructure; for example, automation or artificial intelligence–enabled solutions need digital connectivity. Business associations or sectoral councils can promote public-private coordination.

In Latin America and the Caribbean's mining sector, institutional coordination between public and private actors (and local communities) has led to improved governance and new sustainable development strategies. Examples include the 2022 creation of the National Roundtable on Mining Open to the Community in Argentina,[5] the National Lithium Roundtable,[6] and the interprovincial treaty for the creation of the Lithium Mining Region.[7] Chile, Bolivia, and Peru have similar examples of coordination efforts.[8] At the international level, the United Nations Environment Programme (UNEP), with the support of the Group of Friends of Paragraph 47 (which includes Argentina, Brazil, Chile, and Colombia), has developed specific guidelines for both governments and mining companies (IEA 2023).

When new technologies emerge, leaving market and public actors in uncharted territory, coordination is needed to prevent markets from failing. Demand and supply must be fostered simultaneously, which requires deep coordination and communication between users and producers. Despite their information problems, governments must provide regulatory frameworks that enable markets to develop. They must also invest in effective national innovation systems (NISs) that foster frequent interaction between technology users and developers. Technology centers can help diffuse new technologies, allowing markets to reach scale and lower costs. NISs can also help public officials understand new technologies better, improve regulations, and make markets more efficient.

The green hydrogen (GH_2) market shows how national and regional coordination can help develop a new technology. The regulatory framework for GH_2 is still in its infancy. Recent surveys highlight the lack of a global market backed by clear and stable international standards as a key constraint to progress. Uncertainty around prices and weak regulations restrict commitments to long-term offtake agreements. Governments should aim to move toward border trade and prioritize regional collaboration that will create scale through institutional arrangements and coordinated infrastructure investments. The European Union (EU) currently follows a regional approach to GH_2, which includes energy infrastructure investments, state aid rules, and targets for RE in industry and transport. Such a framework would be ambitious for Latin America and the Caribbean. The EU's GH_2 regulatory framework benefits from greater cooperation, and it has recently formally defined GH_2 as a methodology for calculating life-cycle greenhouse gas (GHG) emissions for renewable fuels of nonbiological origin. Weaker regional coordination can lead to duplication and unnecessary costs. Because standards are still evolving, Latin America and the Caribbean countries should seize the chance to partake in their development.

Increase Sustainability through Meaningful Enforcement

For the region to thrive in green markets, government policies and actions must be consistent with goals set in legal frameworks. Protecting property rights and adopting environmental and social regulations are only part of the equation; monitoring and enforcement as well as the design of taxes, subsidies, and government support will, ultimately, define incentives.

Two factors most influence decisions to commit crimes: the probability of getting caught and the severity of the penalty. Governments have the most influence over the former by investing in monitoring and enforcement technologies and services. Meanwhile, legal frameworks should establish economic penalties that reflect the newfound value of a country's natural capital and ecosystem services.

Effective monitoring and enforcement define incentives. Agents will be less likely to break the rules if the probability of getting caught is high, so this piece is key to limiting negative externalities and the associated misallocation of resources. Although clearing forests may be profitable for individuals (despite risks where it is illegal), it is almost certainly socially and environmentally optimal to conserve the land as forests.

Nevertheless, historically low or inconsistent enforcement of environmental laws and regulations has deepened deforestation challenges. Illegal activities drive much of deforestation. In Brazil, almost all deforestation is likely to be illegal since authorities do not formally permit it, but enforcement of existing laws is often weak. Between 2005 and 2018, less than 1 percent of the Amazon's illegal deforestation resulted in fines, civil actions, or embargoes (MapBiomas Alerta 2020). In Central America, illegal drug trafficking may account for 15-40 percent of national forest loss in Guatemala, Honduras, and Nicaragua (Sesnie et al. 2017). Moreover, the illegal timber trade accounts for almost half the global annual earnings of environmental crime, representing up to $152 billion (INTERPOL 2022; Patrick, Butsic, and Potts 2023).

Deforestation can decline rapidly if monitoring and enforcement are consistently strong. Between 2004 and 2012, Brazil's deforestation rate fell 70 percent below the 1996–2005 average, although it later rebounded (World Bank calculations based on PRODES data;[9] Silva Junior et al. 2021). Federal budgeting and staffing of environmental enforcement agencies were drastically reduced between 2010 and 2020, with the number of enforcement agents falling from 1,311 in 2010 to 694 in 2020 (Carvalho 2020). In 2021, Brazil spent less than half the allocated budget for the Brazilian Institute of Environment and Renewable Natural Resources (IBAMA) (Spring 2022). Enforcement of deforestation regulations (as measured by the number of citations and embargoes) weakened over the same period. In 2019–20, at the federal level, only 6 percent of deforestation led to an enforcement action (citation or embargo) (Coelho-Junior et al. 2022). Enforcement at the state level was more robust, covering 25 percent of deforested areas. Recently, the Brazilian government has significantly strengthened enforcement activity: fines in 2023 were 67 percent higher than the 2019–22 average, and the area embargoed more than doubled (Maisonnave 2023). It also began seizing embargoed cattle, rather than merely issuing fines, as well as crosschecking financial data with rural registries and satellite information to identify funding flows that are supporting deforestation (Paraguassu 2023). These measures worked: between August 2022 and July 2023, Brazil lost 9,001 square kilometers of forest, the lowest rate recorded in the previous five years.[10]

Provide Incentives to Promote Green Goals

Governments can also shape incentives by designing policies that support the goals of the new economy. Subsidies and taxes can help align private and social values by requiring private actors to internalize the true costs of their actions,[11] thereby limiting negative externalities and the misallocation of resources. Creative mechanisms can be explored to reward actors who adopt or develop new technologies, particularly if they alleviate E&S challenges. Although subsidizing the cost of a new technology can accelerate its adoption, other policy tools could be as or more important, particularly early on. Establishing interactive learning and innovation institutions in new markets can signal that the government is committed in the long term to developing an emerging technology, reducing uncertainty and risk while boosting investment.

Land use and forest markets are riddled with externalities, causing serious inefficiencies. Reducing deforestation, for example, is an enormous challenge for the region. However, decoupling agricultural support from current production levels would neutralize the distortionary effect of subsidies while increasing productivity in agriculture. Decoupling would encourage agrifood producers to compete based on actual production costs, thus fostering modernization and innovation. Although risks exist, experiences from countries like New Zealand demonstrate substantial long-term benefits. Governments must gradually phase out distorting policies, linking decoupled payments to other priorities and leveraging digital technologies for targeted support. Reallocating subsidies can have an important impact on productivity: a 10 percentage-point shift in the composition of agricultural support from private to public goods, without a change in total spending, would lead to a 5 percent increase in agricultural value added per capita (Anriquez et al. 2016; Lopez, Salazar, and De Salvo 2017). In addition, knowledge and innovation support systems could move toward direct payments that do not distort farmers' choices. Importantly, since forest clearing for agriculture is the leading cause of deforestation, adjusting these incentives across global and regional value chains would be beneficial. In Latin America and the Caribbean, most countries have positive subsidies on agriculture (reducing the costs of farmer production), primarily through price supports (UNEP, FAO, and UNDP 2023). But some important subsidies are not even in producer nations: US subsidies to domestic livestock producers fuel deforestation in Latin America and the Caribbean by driving demand for soy and other feed crops (Damania et al. 2023). This interconnectedness illustrates the importance of a regional and global approach to policy reform. Subsidies should not merely be phased out but should be reallocated in a way that is less distortionary (not tied to specific crops) and that includes conditionalities for the preservation of landscapes and soil health (Damania et al. 2023).

Some Latin American and Caribbean countries have addressed deforestation challenges by establishing a consistent set of incentives. Costa Rica is an excellent example, as it is one of the few countries that has successfully reversed significant levels of deforestation. It increased its forest cover from 24 percent to over 50 percent between 1985 and 2011 by cutting subsidies for livestock, updating requirements for land titling, establishing protected areas, increasing incentives for forest protection, and enforcing deforestation regulations. This transformation began when more environmentally aware multilateral development banks withdrew funding for livestock projects (although this was available domestically until the 1990s) (Kaimowitz 1996), and legal reforms removed incentives to clear land for pasture prior to titling (Kaimowitz 1996). Also, environmental, forestry, and biodiversity laws in the mid-1990s established ecological balance as the bedrock of Costa Rican environmental policy along with a centrally managed system of protected areas and a national payment for an ecosystem services scheme funded through a tax on fossil fuels (Tafoya et al. 2020).

Incentive structures will need to vary depending on the specific systems involved. For example, in the case of land use, incentives in the Amazon favor lower-productivity extensive agriculture, which relies on large land endowments and minimal inputs from capital and labor, often driving deforestation. To resolve this, and support a shift away from extensive, expansive agricultural production, governments need to reform credit systems and land taxes while promoting revenue recycling and conservation finance (Hanusch 2023). Increasing the productivity of Brazil's non-land-intensive tradable sectors, like manufacturing, would also improve welfare and lower deforestation.

Policies to reduce incentives for extensive production may be different from those designed to develop more productive, intensive production systems. For example, efforts to restrict the supply of land through more effective enforcement could increase the relative value of more capital-intensive production on existing agricultural land. In the case of land use, productivity increases can be an important tool to support agriculture, but caution is required. Depending on the characteristics of agricultural production in a specific area, these productivity gains can either increase or decrease incentives to deforest, highlighting the importance of spatial considerations in terms of where revised incentive structures are likely to maximize benefits and minimize harm.

Adjustments to the valuation of land will also be necessary in many places to rectify discrepancies between private and public valuations. In Brazil, there is a significant discount between the private value of land and the cost of acquiring public land for private purposes, a situation which results in an implicit subsidy that strongly favors agricultural expansion over other uses. In the state of Mato Grosso, for example, private land value is almost six times greater than the cost of acquiring land from the state (Hanusch 2023). Without adjusting these costs, continued land regularization will tend to favor agricultural expansion. To rebalance incentives in favor of conservation while maintaining land regularization and tenure security as a priority, governments should bring statutory adjudication values closer to market rates, increase penalties for illegal deforestation on public land, freeze the cutoff dates for valid land regularization claims, and increase information transparency on land claims and sales and purchases of public and private land (Hanusch 2023).

In addition, making agricultural cash transfers conditional on sustainable techniques and integrating forest technical assistance into agricultural extension programs can help increase the use of sustainable forest management principles (Szott et al. 2020). Smart subsidies have been used to support technology transfer among family farmers in Argentina. The Program for Rural Development and Family Agriculture, which ran from 2013 to 2019, assisted with business plans to adopt appropriate production technologies, improved access to additional financing for technology adoption, and technical assistance for business management. Investments provided direct transfers to beneficiaries, covering a share of the expected costs. The program increased the likelihood of accessing credit by 47 percentage points and the likelihood of adopting the technology by 21 points (Schling and Pazos 2022).

The adoption of new digital MRV technologies could unlock new opportunities for carbon credit markets. Traditional MRV processes are costly and time-consuming because of manual data collection and independent third-party verification, often involving expensive on-site visits from international firms. However, automating data collection and reporting could improve accuracy, reduce costs, and shorten processing times. While not all project types and data parameters will be suitable for digital MRV, forestry projects probably are.

Focus on Inclusion to Ensure That No One Is Left Behind

The region's resource-driven model of development has often come at the expense of Indigenous communities and vulnerable populations. In addition to the economic opportunity to leapfrog ahead of developed nations in green technologies, economic institutions can be developed that are more inclusive and protective of the most vulnerable people. In fact, inclusion may even be desirable from an economic standpoint.

Analysis for this report suggests that increased land use efficiency requires complementary actions to protect the most vulnerable people. As outlined in box 3.1, the costs of maximizing carbon storage will fall disproportionately on specific areas. Moreover, there is a positive and statistically significant correlation between those locations and proxy measures of both relative poverty (through relative multidimensional deprivation) and smallholder farming (proxied by dominant field size). There is, therefore, a strong argument to be made for governments to ensure that people experiencing poverty are not unduly burdened with the costs of the transition. Well-targeted mechanisms can also provide the right incentives to encourage the most efficient land use.

The management of forests by Indigenous peoples within a stronger general framework for land rights can help reduce deforestation and support inclusion. There is a strong association between indigenous land titling and management and lower rates of deforestation (Blackman et al. 2017; Blackman and Veit 2018; Busch and Ferretti-Gallon 2023; Holland et al. 2014; Schleicher et al. 2017; Vergara-Asenjo and Potvin 2014). Indigenous peoples occupy 35 percent of the forest areas in Latin America and the Caribbean. According to the UN Food and Agriculture Organization (FAO) and FILAC (Fund for the Development of Indigenous Peoples of Latin America and the Caribbean), indigenous territories avoid deforestation equally or better than other protected areas. In this context, various strategies for the protection of indigenous forests have been implemented across the region, including recognition of territorial rights, community forest management arrangements, and PES (FAO and FILAC 2021). Peru, for example, has fostered Indigenous participation in forest monitoring and has developed initiatives to strengthen and train Indigenous organizations. The country has also integrated a focus on Indigenous populations into its National Forest and Wildlife Information System. In Argentina, legislation has established that clearing of native forests and sustainable management projects must address E&S risks and impacts on Indigenous communities.

Box 3.1

Poverty Impacts of Land Use Efficiency

Analysis for this report suggests that changes will be needed to improve efficiency in land use, thereby allowing increased production while still preserving natural capital. Understanding where these changes need to happen can shed light on *who* will bear the brunt of land use transition costs. A comparison of land use transition maps with estimates of multidimensional deprivation,[a] a proxy for poverty, and farm size based on high-resolution satellite images can provide insight into locations where the transition may disproportionately affect people experiencing poverty, smallholder farmers, and others.

This analysis relies on land use transition maps prepared under a scenario of transition toward maximum greenhouse gas (GHG) sequestration. It calculates the opportunity cost (forgone economic earnings when future land use transitions toward greater carbon sequestration) of not maximizing value. It then compares forgone values to maps of relative deprivation and farm size (map B3.1.1) (Lesiv et al. 2019).[b]

It emerged that the spatial distribution of transition costs is concentrated both in terms of administrative and opportunity costs, generating identifiable clusters of costs (the darkest areas in the two panels of map B3.1.1) that are also areas where transitioning to different land use patterns could help maximize GHG storage. Thirty percent of the land area with the highest transition costs (top 20 percent) is located in areas with the highest levels of relative deprivation (top 20 percent). Less than 10 percent is located in areas with the lowest levels of deprivation. Statistical testing with Moran's I identified statistically significant (pseudo-p <.001) positive global spatial autocorrelation between higher median poverty and both economic and financial transition costs.[c] Administrative and economic opportunity costs of the transition are particularly concentrated in southern Mexico, Central America, Colombia, the western Amazon, and northern Argentina. Field size, a proxy for smallholder agriculture, is globally positively correlated with economic transition costs (Moran's I, pseudo-p <0.001) but negatively correlated with financial costs at a global level (pseudo-p <.001). Twenty-three percent of the land area with the highest transition costs is located where small farms (>3 hectares) dominate. Less than 3 percent of the land is located where large farms dominate (>100 hectares). Financial transition costs tend to be lower in regions with smaller field sizes, but there are several statistically significant local groupings of high financial costs and small field sizes. These are in Central America, Colombia, parts of Peru, and Haiti. The economic opportunity costs of maximizing GHG storage are concentrated in areas with smallholder farming systems in southern Mexico, Central America, the Dominican Republic, Colombia, and parts of Peru and Ecuador.

box continued next page

Box 3.1

Poverty Impacts of Land Use Efficiency *(continued)*

Map B3.1.1 Impacts of the Transition on the Poor

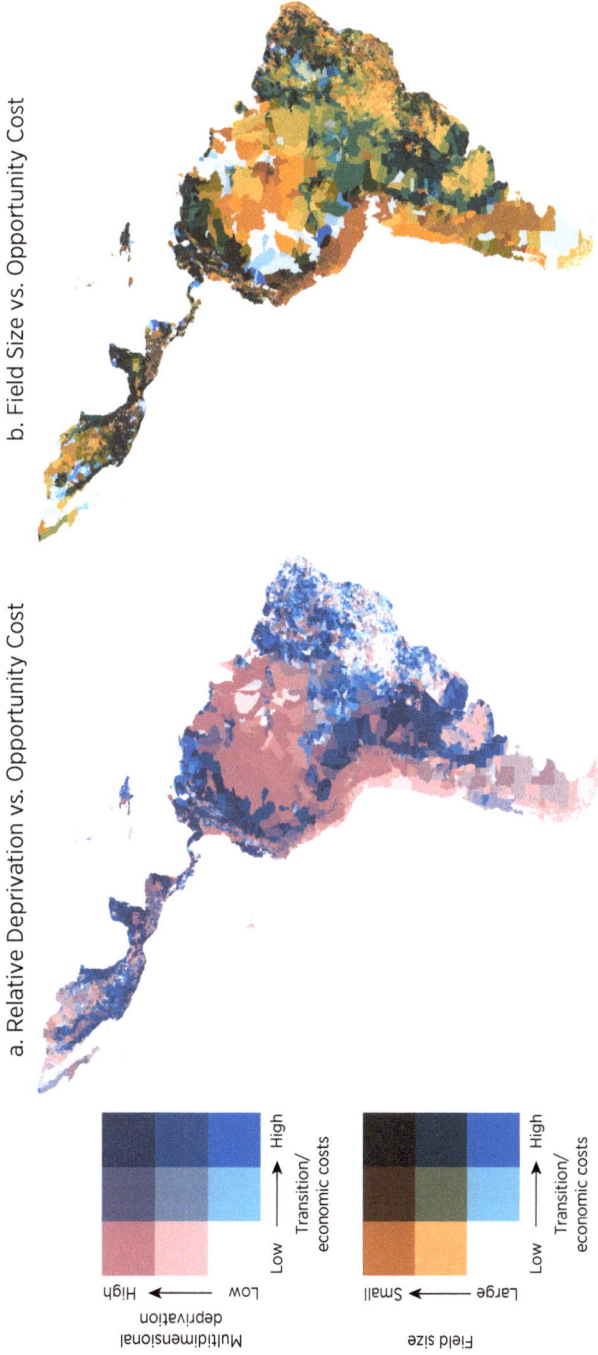

a. Relative Deprivation vs. Opportunity Cost

b. Field Size vs. Opportunity Cost

Multidimensional deprivation: High ← Low

Transition/economic costs: Low → High

Field size: Small ← Large

Transition/economic costs: Low → High

Source: World Bank elaboration.

box continued next page

Box 3.1

Poverty Impacts of Land Use Efficiency *(continued)*

a. The measure used here is the gridded relative deprivation index, which is derived from satellite and administrative data. The measure serves as a metric for relative levels of deprivation that should correlate with measures of multidimensional poverty. It relies on six subindexes: subnational Human Development Index, infant mortality, child dependency, built-up areas, nighttime lights, and the change in nighttime lights over time.

b. CIESIN (Center for International Earth Science Information Network), Columbia University, Gridded Relative Deprivation Index, 2022.

c. Moran's I is a global measure of statistical association for spatial data, varying between −1 (for perfect negative correlation) to 1 for perfect positive correlation across a given geographic area or map. There is also a related measure named Moran's I (Local) that provides information on local patterns of covariance associated with nearby spatial units within a map.

In mining, positive outcomes from strong community involvement with both the public and private sectors could be replicated elsewhere. There are good examples of participatory environmental monitoring in Argentina (box 3.2), Bolivia, and Peru.[12] These monitoring bodies can improve the identification and management of E&S risks and impacts (including environmental contamination and health and safety), as well as gender equality (Pareja, Xavier, and Daitch 2019). Participatory monitoring strengthens trust between parties and empowers local communities (Morrison-Saunders, Nykiel, and Atkins 2024). In Argentina, the Federal Mining Council (Consejo Federal de Minería) and the National Space Commission recently agreed to monitor mining activities using satellite images.

Some countries have also begun to adopt strategic policies to address gender disparity in mining employment, complemented by private and third-party initiatives. Chile, for example, convened a National Roundtable on Women and Mining[13] and published a guide to good gender practices for the sector (Ministerio de Mineria y Ministerio de la Mujer y la Equidad de Genero 2018).[14] The National Lithium Strategy set a goal of achieving at least 20 percent female participation in the industry by 2030 and 35 percent by 2050, and all companies should have policies on diversity, inclusion, and work-life balance by 2030. In Peru, the Ministry of Energy and Mines, under Ministerial Resolution No. 394/2017, created a Committee for Gender Equality and established specific programs, such as the Emerging Women Leaders Program in the Mining and Energy Sector. Argentina has developed the Strategic Plan for Argentine Mining Development 2020–2050, which seeks to promote gender-inclusive mining.

Box 3.2

Participatory Environmental Monitoring in Critical Mining Projects

In Argentina, various mining projects have participatory environmental monitoring committees. At Bajo de la Alumbrera, a copper mine in the province of Catamarca, local people and environmental organizations have set up a Community Transparency System to mitigate contamination or perceived risk, actively participating in project supervision. At the Olaroz lithium extraction project in the province of Jujuy, participatory monitoring resulted from an environmental and social impact assessment process, which is carried out every three months. Committee members also oversee project implementation (Pareja, Xavier, and Daitch 2019).

Chile also has some experience in this area. In 2016, Albemarle, a US company mining lithium in the Atacama Salt Flats, signed the Cooperation, Sustainability, and Mutual Benefit Agreement with the 18 communities that make up the Council of Atacama Peoples in the Salt Flats. The communities receive a royalty of 3.5 percent of lithium carbonate and potassium chloride sales. In 2018, a total contribution of $13.7 million was paid to the communities. The agreement includes a participatory monitoring protocol, an environmental committee, regular workshops to address governance issues, project execution, and environmental monitoring. It also calls for audits to be carried out independently by both parties.

For the private sector, there have been positive innovations in community relations policies. Chile considers the shared value concept as a form of relationship to the land, recognizing the right of communities to receive benefits for the use of public goods and to be compensated for externalities. For example, in the Atacama Salt Flats, local communities receive a royalty linked to annual lithium sales (Poveda Bonilla 2020). In Bolivia, productive links were established with community cooperatives and training opportunities were offered to high school students (Obaya 2021). Peru is also a good example of arrangements between public, private, civil society, and community actors: the government created a mining "canon" that goes to subnational governments to finance social and physical infrastructure; mining companies have implemented corporate social responsibility policies; and the legal framework requires community participation, prior consultations, and informed consent for Indigenous peoples (Erwin et al. 2022).

Sources: Pareja, Xavier, and Daitch 2019. See also Ministerio de Ambiente y Cambio Climático, Jujuy con la Gente (n.d.), and Cámara de Diputadas y Diputados (n.d.).

Efforts at the regulatory and project level must be aligned with ongoing existing agreements. The Escazú Agreement of 2018 is the first worldwide pact to incorporate specific provisions for the promotion and protection of human rights defenders in environmental matters. The first meeting of the signatories included the establishment of an ad hoc working group whose main objective was to prepare an action plan for 2024. Peru also has a protocol that seeks to guarantee the protection of human rights defenders through actions, procedures, and interinstitutional coordination measures.[15] In Chile, employing intersectoral work,[16] a Protocol for the Protection of Human Rights Defenders, the Environment, Communicators, and Legal Practitioners is being developed.

Notes

1. The remaining 20 percent of reported areas in public databases do not have declared ownership. Proyecto IAPA—Visión Amazónica (2020).
2. This code establishes that each subnational government can determine the enforcement authority it chooses for environmental protection against mining activity. Thus, four provinces chose the mining authority itself to lead the E&S impact assessment procedures. This was introduced by the Resolution #3 of 2019 of the Secretary of Government for the Environment and Sustainable Development of Argentina (Secretaria de Gobierno de Amiente y Desarrollo Sustentable; SAyDS), https://www.argentina.gob.ar/normativa/nacional/resoluci%C3%B3n-3-2019 -332258.
3. Bolivia: Supreme Decree No. 24.782/1997 establishes the Environmental Regulations for Mining Activities. Peru: Supreme Decree No. 42/2017 establishes the Regulation for Environmental Protection for Mining Exploration Activities, and Supreme Decree No. 40/2014 establishes the Regulation for Environmental Protection of Exploitation, Beneficiation, General Labor, Transportation, and Mining Storage Activities.
4. Approved under SEA Exempt Resolution No. 202199101134/2021 and SEA Exempt Resolution No. 0039/2017, respectively.
5. Resolution No. 89/2022.
6. Also, at the subnational level, the Interprovincial Treaty for the Creation of the Lithium Mining Region was signed.
7. The treaty was signed by the provinces of Catamarca, Jujuy, and Salta and approved by the provincial legislatures.
8. Decree No. 2/2023 on National Mining Policy for Chile; Ministry of Energy and Mines Resolution No. 302/2019 for Peru.
9. PRODES (Program for the Calculation of Deforestation in the Legal Amazon) is a project to monitor deforestation in the Brazilian Amazon. It is run by the National Institute for Space Research (INPE) and provides annual estimates of the rate of deforestation in the region.
10. INPE, "TerraBrasilis: Deforestation Dashboard," 2024, http://terrabrasilis.dpi.inpe.br /app/dashboard/deforestation/biomes/legal_amazon/rates. Preliminary data for January to November 2023 show deforestation rates falling even further to 4,977 sq km. See Reuters, "Deforestation in Brazilian Amazon down 64% in November, December 8, 2023, https://www.reuters.com/business/environment/deforestation -brazilian-amazon-down-64-november-2023-12-08/.
11. These are known in the economic literature as Pigouvian taxes.

12. In Argentina, some Indigenous communities developed an ad hoc protocol recognized by the National Ombudsman. "Kachi Yupi—Free, prior and informed consent process for the Indigenous Communities of the Cuenca de Salinas Grandes and Laguna de Guayatayoq," recognized by Resolution No. 25/2016 of the Ombudsman.
13. The first roundtable was held in 2018 and convened by the Ministry for Women and Gender Equity and the Ministry of Mining. The participants were mining companies and suppliers, industry, public servants, unions, and civil society organizations.
14. An example is the certification of mining companies in the Chilean voluntary standard NCh3261:2021, which establishes the requirements of a management system that seeks gender equality and work-family balance. Once certified, companies may apply for the Equality-Conciliation Seal awarded by the National Service for Women and Gender Equality, inspired by the Gender Equality Seal certification program promoted by the United Nations Development Programme since 2009. According to the Chilean Mining Skills Council (Consejo de Competencias Mineras de Chile 2020, https://consejominero.cl/mineria-en-chile/cifras-actualizadas-de-la-mineria/), recent years have shown an increase in the participation of women, with greater relevance of female leadership and increased incorporation of young women in operations.
15. Ministerial Resolution No. 159/2019.
16. A subcommission was established and is composed of the ministries of Environment, Justice and Human Rights, and Foreign Affairs; representatives of the judiciary, the National Institute for Human Rights [Instituto Nacional de Derechos Humanos], the Office of the Public Prosecutor, Office of the Public Defender, the police [carabineros], and the criminal investigations police [policía de investigaciones de Chile].

References

adelphi and Gold Standard. 2023. "Implementing Article 6: An Overview of Preparations in Selected Countries." Gold Standard, Châtelaine, Switzerland. https://www.gold standard.org/publications/implementing-article-6---an-overview-of-preparations.

Anriquez, G., W. Foster, J. Ortega, C. Falconi, and C. De Salvo. 2016. *Public Expenditures and the Performance of Latin American and Caribbean Agriculture*. Washington, DC: Inter-American Development Bank. https://publications.iadb.org/en/public -expenditures-and-performance-latin-american-and-caribbean-agriculture.

Blackman, A., L. Corral, E. S. Lima, and G. P. Asner. 2017. "Titling Indigenous Communities Protects Forests in the Peruvian Amazon." *Proceedings of the National Academy of Sciences* 114 (16): 4123–28.

Blackman, A., and P. Veit. 2018. "Titled Amazon Indigenous Communities Cut Forest Carbon Emissions." *Ecological Economics* 153: 56–67.

Brito, B., J. Almeida, P. Gomes, and R. Salomão. 2021. *10 Essential Facts about Land Tenure Regularization in the Brazilian Amazon*. Bélem, Pará, Brazil: Imazon. https://imazon.org .br/wp-content/uploads/2021/09/10-Essential-Facts-About-Land-Tenure -Regularization-in-the-Brazilian-Amazon.pdf.

Busch, J., and K. Ferretti-Gallon. 2023. "What Drives and Stops Deforestation, Reforestation, and Forest Degradation? An Updated Meta-Analysis." *Review of Environmental Economics and Policy* 17 (2): 217–50.

Cámara de Diputadas y Diputados. n.d. Accessed January 15, 2024. https://www.camara.cl/.

Carvalho, I. 2020. "From Lula to Bolsonaro: Number of Ibama Officials Falls by Up to 55%." *Brasil de Fato*, September 9, 2020. https://www.brasildefato.com.br/2020/09/09/from -lula-to-bolsonaro-number-of-ibama-officials-falls-by-up-to-55.

Clifford Chance. 2022. "Enabling the Voluntary Carbon Market in the Context of the Paris Agreement." City of London. https://www.theglobalcity.uk/PositiveWebsite/media /Research-reports/Enabling-the-voluntary-carbon-market-2022.pdf.

Coase, R. H. 1960. "The Problem of Social Cost." *Journal of Law and Economics* 3: 1–44.

Coelho-Junior, M. G., A. P. Valdiones, J. Z. Shimbo et al. 2022. "Unmasking the Impunity of Illegal Deforestation in the Brazilian Amazon: A Call for Enforcement and Accountability." *Environmental Research Letters* 17: 041001.

Cooter, R. D. 1989. "The Coase Theorem." In *Allocation, Information and Markets*, edited by J. Eatwell, M. Milgate, and P. Newman, 64–70. The New Palgrave. London: Palgrave Macmillan. https://doi.org/10.1007/978-1-349-20215-7_6.

Cusolito, A., and W. F. Maloney. 2018. *Productivity Revisited: Shifting Paradigms in Analysis and Policy*. Washington, DC: World Bank.

Damania, R., E. Balseca, C. de Fontaubert et al. 2023. *Detox Development: Repurposing Environmentally Harmful Subsidies*. Washington, DC: World Bank.

Erwin, A., Z. Ma, E. Salas O'Brien et al. 2022. "Centering Community Voices in Mining Governance." *Society & Natural Resources* 35(10): 1043–62.

FAO (Food and Agriculture Organization of the United Nations) and FILAC (Fund for the Development of Indigenous Peoples of Latin America and the Caribbean). 2021. *Forest Governance by Indigenous and Tribal Peoples. An Opportunity for Climate Action in Latin America and the Caribbean*. Santiago: FAO.

Hanusch, M., ed. 2023. *A Balancing Act for Brazil's Amazonian States: An Economic Memorandum*. Washington, DC: World Bank. https://doi.org/10.1596/978-1-4648-1909-4.

Hausmann, R. 2023. "The Case for Green Industrial Parks." *Project Syndicate*, July 13, 2023. https://www.project-syndicate.org/commentary/green-industrial-parks-could-help -accelerate-decarbonization-by-ricardo-hausmann-2023-07.

Hedley, A., and B. Hillis. 2022. "Voluntary Carbon Market Trading: Key Risks and Mitigations." Reed Smith LLP. Energy Transition, June 27, 2022. https://www .reedsmith.com/en/perspectives/energy-transition/2022/06/voluntary-carbon -market-trading-key-risks-and-mitigations.

Holland, M. B., F. de Koning, M. Morales, L. Naughton-Treves, B. E. Robinson, and L. Suárez. 2014. "Complex Tenure and Deforestation: Implications for Conservation Incentives in the Ecuadorian Amazon." *World Development* 55: 21–36.

IEA (International Energy Agency). 2023. "Critical Minerals Market Review 2023." IEA, Paris. https://www.iea.org/reports/critical-minerals-market-review-2023.

INCRA. 2023. Programa de Governança e Sustentabilidade Territorial na Amazônia e no Semiárido. "Amazônia e Semiárido + Sustentáveis." Ministério do Desenvolvimento Agrário e Agricultura Familiar. Instituto Nacional de Colonização e Reforma Agrária Brasília.

INTERPOL. 2022. "Illegal Logging in Latin America and Caribbean Inflicting Irreversible Damage." https://www.interpol.int/en/News-and-Events/News/2022/Illegal -logging-in-Latin-America-and-Caribbean-inflicting-irreversible-damage-INTERPOL.

Kaimowitz, D. 1996. *Livestock and Deforestation: Central America in the 1980s and 1990s: A Policy Perspective*. Jakarta, Indonesia: Center for International Forestry Research. http://www.bio-nica.info/biblioteca/Kaimowitz1996Livestock.pdf.

Lesiv, M., J. C. Laso Bayas, L. See, M. Duerauer et al. 2019. Estimating the Global Distribution of Field Size Using Crowdsourcing. *Global Change Biology* 25 (1): 174–86.

Lopez, C., L. Salazar, and C. De Salvo. 2017. *Agricultural Input Subsidies and Productivity: The Case of Paraguayan Farmers*. Washington, DC: Inter-American Development Bank. https://publications.iadb.org/en/agricultural-input-subsidies-and-productivity-case -paraguayan-farmers.

Maisonnave, F. 2023. "In Lula's First Six Months, Brazil Amazon Deforestation Dropped 34%, Reversing Trend under Bolsonaro." AP, July 6, 2023. https://apnews.com/article/brazil -amazon-deforestation-lula-climate-change-2fe225f71a8f484e8d365ea641acd65e.

Maloney, W. F., P. Garriga, M. Meléndez et al. 2024. "Competition: The Missing Ingredient for Growth?" Latin America and the Caribbean Economic Review (April 2024). World Bank, Washington, DC.

MapBiomas Alerta. 2020. "Annual Report on Deforestation in Brazil 2019." MapBiomas Alerta, São Paulo. https://alerta.mapbiomas.org/wp-content/uploads/sites/17 /2024/03/MBI-relatorio-desmatamento-2019-FINAL5.pdf.

Ministerio de Ambiente y Cambio Climático, Jujuy con la Gente. n.d. Accessed January 23, 2024. https://www.ambientejujuy.gob.ar/.

Ministerio de Mineria y Ministerio de la Mujer y la Equidad de Genero, Gobierno de Chile. 2018. "Mesa Nacional, Mujer y Mineria 2018–2020: Buenas Practicas de Genero para el Sector." [National Roundtable, Women and Mining 2018–2020: Gender Best Practices for the Sector]. Santiago. https://minmujeryeg.gob.cl/wp-content/uploads/2020/07 /MESA-NACIONAL-MUJER-Y-MINERIA-2018-2020.pdf.

Moreno-Leiva, S., J. Haas, T. Junne et al. 2020. "Renewable Energy in Copper Production: A Review on Systems Design and Methodological Approaches." *Journal of Cleaner Production* 246: 118978.

Morrison-Saunders, A., A. Nykiel, and N. Atkins, 2024. "Understanding the Impact of Environmental Impact Assessment Research on Policy and Practice." *Environmental Impact Assessment Review* 104: 107334. https://doi.org/10.1016/j.eiar.2023.107334.

Motta, M. 2004. *Competition Policy: Theory and Practice*. Cambridge: Cambridge University Press.

Obaya. 2021. "The Evolution of Resource Nationalism: The Case of Bolivian Lithium." *The Extractive Industries and Society* 8 (3): 100932.

Paraguassu, L. 2023. "Brazil's Lula Unveils Plan to Stop Deforestation in Amazon by 2030." Reuters, June 5, 2023. https://www.reuters.com/world/americas/brazils-lula-launches -plan-stop-deforestation-amazon-by-2030-2023-06-05/.

Pareja, C., A. Xavier, and S. Daitch. 2019. "Participatory Environmental Monitoring Committees in Mining Contexts: Lessons from Nine Case Studies in Four Latin American Countries" [Comités de Monitoreo Ambiental Participativo en Contextos Mineros: Lecciones a Partir de Nueves Estudios de Casos en Cuatro Países de Latinoamérica]. United Nations Development Programme, New York. https://www .undp.org/publications/participatory-environmental-monitoring-committees -mining-contexts.

Partnership for Market Readiness. 2021. *A Guide to Developing Domestic Carbon Crediting Mechanisms*. Washington, DC: World Bank. https://doi.org/10.1596/35271.

Patrick, E., V. Butsic, and M. D. Potts. 2023. "Using Payment for Ecosystem Services to Meet National Reforestation Commitments: Impacts of 20+ Years of Forestry Incentives in Guatemala." *Environmental Research* 18: 104030. https://doi.org/10.1088/1748-9326 /acf602.

Paz, W. F. D., M. Escosteguy, L. Seghezzo, M. Hufty, E. Kruse, and M. A. Iribarnegaray. 2023. "Lithium Mining, Water Resources, and Socio-Economic Issues in Northern Argentina: We Are Not All in the Same Boat." *Resources Policy* 81: 103288.

Poveda Bonilla, R. 2020. *Estudio de caso sobre la gobernanza del litio en Chile*. serie Recursos Naturales y Desarrollo, N° 195 (LC/TS.2020/40). Santiago: Comisión Económica para América Latina y el Caribe (CEPAL).

Proyecto IAPA—Visión Amazónica. 2020. *Informe Final de Consultoría*. Redparques.

Schleicher, J., C. A. Peres, T. Amano, W. Llactayo, and N. Leader-Williams. 2017. "Conservation Performance of Different Conservation Governance Regimes in the Peruvian Amazon." *Scientific Reports* 7 (1): 11318.

Schling, M., and N. Pazos. 2022. "The Impact of Smart Subsidies on Agricultural Production: Innovative Evidence from Argentina Using Survey and Remote Sensing Data." IDB Working Paper Series IDB-WP-01358, Inter-American Development Bank, Washington, DC.

SEA (Servicio de Evaluación Ambiental). 2017. *Guía para la descripción de proyectos de desarrollo minero de cobre y oro-plata en el SEIA*. Servicio de Evaluación Ambiental de Chile. https://sea.gob.cl/sites/default/files/imce/archivos/2017/12/19/guia_dp _desarrollo_minero_cobre_y_oro-plata.pdf.

SEA (Servicio de Evaluación Ambiental). 2021. *Guía para la descripción de proyectos de explotación de litio y otras sustancias minerales desde salares en el SEIA*. Servicio de Evaluación Ambiental de Chile. https://sea.gob.cl/sites/default/files/imce/archivos /2021/03/12/guia_litio_version_para_publicar_compressed.pdf.

Sesnie, S. E., B. Tellman, D. Wrathall et al. 2017. "A Spatio-temporal Analysis of Forest Loss Related to Cocaine Trafficking in Central America." *Environmental Research Letters* 12 (5): 054015. https://iopscience.iop.org/article/10.1088/1748-9326/aa6fff.

Silva Junior, C. H. L., A. C. M. Pessôa, N. S. Carvalho, J. B. C. Reis, L. O. Anderson, and L. E. O. C. Aragão. 2021. "The Brazilian Amazon Deforestation Rate in 2020 Is the Greatest of the Decade." *Nature Ecology and Evolution* 5: 144–5. https://doi.org/10.1038/s41559 -020-01368-x.

Spring, J. 2022. "Brazil Spent Less Than Half Its 2021 Environmental Enforcement Budget." Reuters, February 1, 2022. https://www.reuters.com/world/americas/brazil-spent -less-than-half-its-2021-environmental-enforcement-budget-2022-02-01/.

Szott, L. T., G. Obando, G. Solano, and R. Rivera. 2020. "El Salvador—Country Forest Note (vol. 2): Summary for Policymakers." World Bank Group, Washington, DC.

Tafoya, K. A., E. S. Brondizio, C. E. Johnson et al. 2020. "Effectiveness of Costa Rica's Conservation Portfolio to Lower Deforestation, Protect Primates, and Increase Community Participation." *Frontiers in Environmental Science* 8: 212.

Tanner, M., and L. Ratzke. 2022. "Deforestation, Institutions, and Property Rights: Evidence from Land Titling to Indigenous Peoples and Local Communities in Ecuador." CAF Working Paper 2022/22, Development Bank of Latin America, Caracas. https://scioteca .caf.com/handle/123456789/1995.

Tseng, T.-W. J., B. E. Robinson, M. F. Bellemare et al. 2020. "Influence of Land Tenure Interventions on Human Well-Being and Environmental Outcomes." *Nature Sustainability* 4 (3): 242–51.

UNEP (United Nations Environment Programme), FAO (Food and Agriculture Organization of the United Nations), and UNDP (United Nations Development Programme). 2023. *Rethinking Our Food Systems: A Guide for Multi-Stakeholder Collaboration*. Nairobi: UNEP, Rome: FAO, and New York: UNDP.

UNIDROIT (International Institute for the Unification of Private Law). 2023. "Item No. 7 on the Agenda: Update on Certain High-Priority Projects on the 2023–2025 Work Programme: Legal Nature of Voluntary Carbon Credits." Governing Council 102nd session, Rome. https://www.unidroit.org/wp-content/uploads/2023/05/C.D.-102-14 -Legal-nature-of-Voluntary-Carbon-Credits.pdf.

Vergara-Asenjo, G., and C. Jeanne Potvin. 2014. "Forest Protection and Tenure Status: The Key Role of Indigenous Peoples and Protected Areas in Panama." *Global Environmental Change: Human and Policy Dimensions* 28: 205–15.

World Bank. 2025. "Improving Land Use for a Prosperous, Low-Carbon Latin America." Background paper for this publication. World Bank, Washington, DC. https:// documents.worldbank.org/en/publication/documents-reports/documentdetail /099060225142510052.

World Bank Group. 2023a. *Colombia Country Climate and Development Report*. CCDR Series. Washington, DC: World Bank Group.

World Bank Group. 2023b. *Dominican Republic Country Climate and Development Report*. CCDR Series. Washington, DC: World Bank.

Leveraging AFOLU Carbon Credit Markets for Development in a New Economic Model

Mariana Conte Grand

At present, the carbon policy landscape in Latin America and the Caribbean is witnessing a remarkable level of activity. Compliance markets are taking shape in several countries, with voluntary carbon credit markets also gaining significant traction. Currently, the Latin America and the Caribbean region is the second-largest provider of carbon credits globally, with a significant portion originating from projects in the agriculture, forestry, and other land use (AFOLU) sectors (Sullivan et al. 2021).

Well-implemented forestry and land use projects can offer valuable additional co-benefits. Afforestation and forest conservation have benefits beyond avoided emissions. Often referred to as co-benefits, these advantages can include local employment, community development, and biodiversity protection. Forests also enhance resilience to the impacts of a changing climate. They do this directly through provisioning services (for example, wood, fuel, and fodder), regulating services (for example, water or soil erosion), and supporting services (for example, nutrient cycling) (Behr et al. 2015). For some carbon credit buyers, these co-benefits—particularly those related to biodiversity and community impacts—are a major motivating factor for purchasing forestry carbon credits (Goldstein 2016).

In addition to environmental benefits, a growth in carbon pricing can also deliver potential financial benefits. One of the advantages of compliance carbon pricing is that, aside from reducing emissions, it also raises government revenues. To date, however, these types of regulations have predominantly been implemented in high-income countries. There are also carbon taxes in Argentina, Chile, Colombia, Mexico, and Uruguay, as well as carbon emissions trading programs under consideration in Brazil, Chile, and Colombia.[1] The increased uptake of carbon pricing around the world offers a new income stream for governments of developing countries. Governments can and do use these additional revenues in different ways. A priority for some jurisdictions may be to mitigate any negative distributional impacts on low-income households, such as increased fuel prices. However, in practice, this objective can be challenging to implement.[2] Governments may also use revenues to finance adaptation or mitigation measures. There is already an example of this in Latin America and the Caribbean, where 80 percent of the revenues raised from Colombia's carbon tax will be targeted to coastal erosion management, water conservation, and protection of ecosystems. The remaining revenues will target the substitution of illicit-use crops.[3]

While the promise of carbon crediting in the AFOLU sector is significant, there are reasons to temper expectations. Host countries and local actors may rush into engaging with the credit market before fully understanding the implications. While carbon credit markets are not completely new markets, they are still in their infancy and, therefore, face many of the challenges discussed throughout this report, including the lack of clear market rules, a broad set of externalities that are often not priced, incomplete information, and limited coordination.

Recognizing some of the challenges posed by the AFOLU sector in carbon credit markets will be important to harness the region's comparative advantages. First, generating high-quality AFOLU carbon credits is difficult—notably because of challenges in quantification, monitoring, and permanence—which limits the types of activities that can benefit from carbon credit finance. Second, carbon credits incentivize action only if there is a reliable source of demand for them. While demand growth projections seem encouraging, demand has been primarily driven by voluntary mechanisms,[4] which have not yet been tested in a high-price environment. Third, market prices limit the range of mitigation options that can be financed through carbon crediting: current prices in carbon credit markets fall significantly short of the $30–$50 per credit average cost of forest carbon. Latin America and the Caribbean countries may, therefore, find that carbon crediting markets are more effective at financing lower-cost abatement opportunities, at least in the medium term. Fourth, engaging in sales of correspondingly adjusted credits can lead to a situation in which the country can no longer meet its Nationally Determined Contributions (NDCs).[5] Governments must, therefore, manage their engagement with carbon credit markets in a manner that is consistent with meeting their domestic targets. Fifth, it is important to note that even in optimistic growth scenarios, the scale of potential finance from carbon credits would only be a fraction of the region's total investment needs.

For Latin America and the Caribbean to establish itself as a major supplier of carbon credits in a way that is consistent with sustainable and inclusive development, a new path forward along three axes would be required: institutions, investments, and innovation.

Build Better Institutions to Leverage Benefits for the Economy, the Planet, and the People

The adoption of legal frameworks for carbon crediting markets, particularly for carbon rights in land-use projects, can ensure that opportunities in carbon credit markets are leveraged. Given the diversity of national contexts, there is no one-size-fits-all approach to an appropriate legal framework. For countries that do not foresee deep involvement in carbon crediting, it may be possible to continue with minimal or no explicit regulation of carbon credits. However, legislation could be advantageous, especially for forest and land use projects, where a lack of clarity over the rights to carbon could hinder implementation. It is also essential to ensure that national assertions of ecosystem service rights do not override or diminish the rights of Indigenous peoples and local communities (IPLCs). Another advantage of setting a clear regulatory framework for carbon credits is that where there are well-established laws on land titling—including forested land—landowners and communities can directly receive the revenues and benefits from carbon rights, ensuring the realization of co-benefits.

A stable governance and regulatory environment, with transparent rules for project approval and authorization, effective communication, and efficient administration, would support investment into carbon-crediting projects. The institutional structures and decision-making processes necessary to manage a country's participation in and engagement with carbon crediting (Missbach, Steckel, and Vogt-Schilb 2022) could include the following:

- Oversight level: a steering group exercises overall authority, making decisions, deciding policy, and facilitating coordination between ministries (Spalding-Fecher, Macias, and Guzmán Barraza 2022).

- Administrative level: the administrator handles day-to-day operational matters, dealing with stakeholder queries, collecting fees, and processing requests.

- Expert advisory level: a technical committee or advisory group provides input or technical expertise, for instance, on crediting methodologies or monitoring, reporting, and verification (MRV) procedures, when necessary.

Countries in Latin America and the Caribbean already have governance structures from the Clean Development Mechanisms, and in some cases, compliance instruments, on which they can and should build. These structures will need to be further developed to scale up crediting activity and participation in Article 6. Appropriate governance structures will vary by country, depending on existing arrangements, available resources, and the model chosen for carbon market participation. However, several common features will need to be considered. Governments must ensure that governance of carbon crediting activities is integrated within any existing governance structures and that it includes cross-ministerial coordination. In all cases, governments must consider how the administration of the system will be funded and whether a system of fees for services by the administrator is needed to ensure the program's financial sustainability or if funds would come from the government's general budget.

The case for a domestic crediting mechanism is strongest where there is significant and predictable local demand, which in practice is often driven by a compliance instrument. When such a compliance instrument is in place, the potential associated savings (for example, from reducing administrative fees and streamlining processes) may outweigh the costs of operating the mechanism. Alternatively, a regional mechanism—operating in multiple countries and collectively governed—could be considered given its potential for greater scale and sharing of administrative costs. It is always critical to adopt internationally recognized approaches to ensure the environmental integrity of carbon credits. Doing so will also increase the likelihood that such credits would be purchased by international buyers. Initiatives that aim to improve integrity in the voluntary carbon market (VCM)—such as the Integrity Council for the Voluntary Carbon Market, the Voluntary Carbon Markets Integrity Initiative, the Carbon Credit Quality Initiative, and other agencies that rate the quality of individual carbon crediting projects (for example, BeZero Carbon, Calyx Global, Sylvera)—offer benchmarks that can be considered to frame all country efforts in the direction of greater integrity.

Building human capacity across all elements of the crediting value chain is necessary, including in local and Indigenous communities. Successful carbon markets involve different actors possessing the appropriate capacities: government regulators, project developers, project operators, carbon crediting mechanisms, validation and verification bodies, retail traders, brokers, financial sector actors, engineering and geological services providers, local consultancies, third-party infrastructure providers, and end buyers. The development of local capabilities allows local companies to deliver more services, thereby reducing reliance on international firms. In some cases, countries may eventually be able to export services to other regions, as seen with validation and verification companies in India. The lack of human capacity is an important bottleneck across many elements of the crediting value chain, slowing down processes and increasing costs. There are different levels of capacity requirements. At a minimum, governments need sufficient knowledge and resources to carry out core tasks, such as developing an overall strategy, establishing regulations, and implementing daily operations. Most governments in Latin America and the Caribbean will need to enhance capacity to implement these measures. Knowledge must be shared beyond the ministry of environment, typically responsible for crediting, to other interested departments, such as ministries of finance. Further, capacity-building initiatives are crucial in order to staff and train the teams that draft and implement the regulations necessary for crediting.[6] Finally, it is also important to build capacities and understanding of carbon markets in local and Indigenous communities. This training will foster understanding and reduce implementation risks, as well as equip IPLCs with the tools to negotiate with project developers effectively.

Invest in Digital Infrastructure to Support the Efficiency of the Emerging Market

The specific infrastructure needs will depend on several factors, including whether the country operates its domestic crediting mechanism and the extent to which actors engage in trades of correspondingly adjusted credits. Key pieces of digital infrastructure include the following (TSVCM 2021):

- Register: a database that only records information on individual units, such as the location of the project and unique identification number.

- Transaction Registry: includes the basic functionality of the register but goes beyond it. It can support transfers between user accounts and be linked to other registries. Trading through an exchange offers a centralized marketplace for standardized products, offering deepened market liquidity, improved price discovery, and lower transaction costs.

There are different circumstances in which countries may choose to implement their own registry, especially where they are operating a compliance instrument.[7] However, depending on their size and level of activity in carbon markets, countries could choose to have only a register and complement it by leveraging an international transaction registry built and maintained by the United Nations Framework Convention on Climate Change. Governments will be able to open a national account in this international transaction registry, which will have all the functionality required for meeting Article 6 participation requirements. This option avoids the costs associated with operating a national transaction registry and may be particularly relevant for small countries with scarce resources. Some Latin America and the Caribbean countries could benefit from a domestic public platform for trading carbon credits, particularly if the platform would serve a compliance demand or there is sufficient supply or demand locally. The rollout of national exchanges, such as Panama's planned platform, will provide a useful example for other countries in the region to operate an exchange platform. In other countries' circumstances, when domestic transaction registries are not developed, credits will still be able to be sold via international exchanges, especially when generated through independent or international mechanisms.

Coherence between national greenhouse gas inventory and crediting activity will be important. Inventories are the basis for assessing the effectiveness of mitigation policies and tracking progress against national targets. As such, they are also relevant to carbon crediting efforts. Governments in Latin America and the Caribbean should, therefore, consider whether emission reductions from crediting activities, particularly those authorized to be used for compliance by other countries, will be captured in their inventories when considering their strategy and approach toward authorization. If the inventory is not sufficiently granular, then there is a risk that emission reductions achieved by carbon crediting projects may not be fully or correctly captured, which can decrease the possibilities for achieving a country's NDC targets. Latin America and the Caribbean countries would benefit from improving the measurement of soil carbon stocks for soil carbon sequestration, considering there is still scope for increasing credit supply in this sector (Bai and Cotrufo 2022; Smith et al. 2020).

Focus on Innovation in Project Design and Ensure High-Quality Carbon Credits

Countries should consider new project types, focusing on those that can generate high-quality carbon credits. Latin America and the Caribbean countries could benefit from innovative approaches such as direct air capture, biochar, enhanced weathering, and blue carbon, building on the region's vast renewable energy potential, agricultural production, and rich ecosystems. Technical innovation and careful analysis will be needed to address challenges related to MRV and to ensure permanence and protect biodiversity and energy security. More broadly, carbon credits may play a more lasting role, including in Latin America and the Caribbean, in supporting both nature-based and engineered removals, especially in land use systems.

Countries should capitalize on the opportunities of digital MRV and share that knowledge with regional neighbors. Knowledge-sharing activities can enable countries to leapfrog challenges their neighbors have already faced by facilitating regulatory alignment, disseminating research and findings to support decision-making, and expediting the diffusion of technological advancements and lessons learned. Advances in digital MRV—in particular, the use of data collected from satellites and drones, artificial intelligence, and machine learning models—provide a key area of innovation and opportunity in Latin America and the Caribbean. Automated data collection and reporting could improve data accuracy, reduce costs, and shorten processing times associated with MRV. A digital MRV system that relies on artificial intelligence and machine learning models can be applied to data collected from satellites and drones to identify areas of deforestation and estimate carbon stocks. Automated data collection can also enable the enforcement of liability in cases of reversals. The main advantage of this approach is the ability to monitor large tracts of land without the need for physical inspections. Beyond reducing transaction costs for crediting activities and enabling enforcement of liability in cases of reversals, such systems can be key in supporting interventions to address illegal deforestation, as in Brazil.

Notes

1. World Bank Group, Carbon Pricing Dashboard, https://carbonpricingdashboard .worldbank.org/. The new Argentinean administration has also sent a project to the Congress in that same direction.
2. Among the reasons provided by authors Missbach, Steckel, and Vogt-Schilb (2022) is the lack of generalized access to cash transfer programs. The heterogeneous impact of the carbon price across different income groups requires governments to develop new mechanisms to distribute targeted transfers.
3. Columbia, Ley 2277 (2022), http://www.secretariasenado.gov.co/senado/basedoc /ley_2277_2022.html.
4. *Voluntary carbon markets* refers to markets for carbon units (typically carbon credits) in which buyers are under no regulatory obligation to purchase such units. *Voluntary demand* refers to demand for carbon units in such markets.
5. Correspondingly, *adjusted credits* refers to credits that are adjusted to prevent double counting upon transfer. Current usage focuses on the adjustment of credits according to the requirements of Article 6.2 of the Paris Agreement. These refer to adjustments applied to carbon credits that are used for trading between different countries and are aimed at ensuring that an emission reduction is not counted as mitigation toward national pledges by two countries at the same time. However, the concept of corresponding adjustment could be extended beyond Paris Agreement commitments and state action to include voluntary markets and nonstate actors and organizations.
6. Several Latin America and the Caribbean countries have experience with capacity-building activities for compliance instruments. With support from the World Bank, Colombia developed a capacity-building strategy for its emissions trading system that was designed to ensure that information was generated and appropriately shared, trust was built, and buy-in from various stakeholder groups was secured (adelphi, "Developing a Capacity Building Strategy for the Design of the Colombian Emissions Trading Scheme," 2020, https://adelphi.de/en/projects/developing-a-capacity-building-strategy-for-the-design-of-the-colombian-emissions-trading). In Mexico, MEXICO2 has been working with subnational governments to build capacity on markets for carbon credits. The PMR (World Bank) and GIZ (Germany) have also implemented several capacity-building initiatives in Mexico, providing support on the development of communications and policy coordination strategies.
7. Those countries should first consider whether existing infrastructure can be adopted, rather than building a new registry from scratch. Doing so would save both time and money. Examples to draw on from the region include the Costa Rica National Climate Change Metrics System, which was deliberately designed to be open source so that the code could be adapted by other developing countries (World Bank 2020).

References

Bai, Y., and M. F. Cotrufo. 2022. "Grassland Soil Carbon Sequestration: Current Understanding, Challenges, and Solutions." *Science* 377 (6606): 603–8.

Behr, C., D. A. Russell, B. Locatelli, E. Pramova, and G. J. Alumai. 2015. "How Forests Enhance Resilience to Climate Change: What We Know about Forests and Adaptation." Program on Forests (PROFOR), Washington, DC. https://www.profor.info/sites/default/files /2024-05/How%20Forests%20Enhance%20Resilience%20to%20Climate%20Change %20What%20we%20know%20about%20how%20forests%20can%20contribute%20 to%20adaptation_0.pdf.

Goldstein, A. 2016. "Not So Niche: Co-benefits at the Intersection of Forest Carbon and Sustainable Development." Forest Trends Ecosystem Marketplace, Washington, DC. https://www.forest-trends.org/wp-content/uploads/imported/cobenefits-final-draft -032116-_new-back-page-pdf.pdf.

Missbach, L., J. C. Steckel, and A. Vogt-Schilb. 2022. "Cash Transfers in the Context of Carbon Pricing Reforms in Latin America and the Caribbean." IDB Working Paper Series IDB-WP-01404, Inter-American Development Bank, Washington, DC. https:// publications.iadb.org/publications/english/viewer/Cash-transfers-in-the-context-of -carbon-pricing-reforms-in-Latin-America-and-the-Caribbean.pdf.

Smith, P., J.-F. Soussana, D. Angers et al. 2020. "How to Measure, Report and Verify Soil Carbon Change to Realize the Potential of Soil Carbon Sequestration for Atmospheric Greenhouse Gas Removal." *Global Change Biology* 26 (1): 219–41.

Spalding-Fecher, R., P. Macias, and D. Guzmán Barraza. 2022. "Guidance on Governance Models for Host Country Engagement in Article 6, version 2," The Global Green Growth Institute, Seoul, Korea. https://gggi.org/wp-content/uploads/2022/12/GGGI -Article-6-Governance-Guidance-V2.0_2022_FIN_2_1.pdf.

Sullivan, K., A. Diemert, C. Cordova et al. 2021. "Status and Trends of Compliance and Voluntary Carbon Markets in Latin America." Inter-American Development Bank, Washington, DC. https://icapcarbonaction.com/en/publications/status-and-trends -compliance-and-voluntary-carbon-markets-latin-america.

TSVCM (Taskforce on Scaling Voluntary Carbon Markets). 2021. *Taskforce on Scaling Voluntary Carbon Markets Final Report*. https://www.iif.com/Portals/1/Files/TSVCM _Report.pdf.

World Bank. 2020. "Partnership for Market Readiness: Costa Rica Program—The National Climate Change Metrics System" (Spanish). Program Activity brief. World Bank, Washington, DC. http://documents.worldbank.org/curated/en/581081617602706306.

World Bank. 2024. "Carbon Credit Markets for AFOLU in LAC—Status, Challenges, and Actions Needed." Background note for *LAC in Greening World Report*. World Bank, Washington, DC.

CHAPTER 4

Investments and Public Goods

Guillermo Beylis and Nancy Lozano Gracia

The Role of Public Investment

Beyond institutions, complementary investments in infrastructure and productive public goods are also essential for the green transition to prosper. Broadly speaking, government intervention in the provision of public goods is just as important in the new economy as in economies past. Government investments in infrastructure—such as roads, logistics, and electricity—complement private investments, have high spillovers, and create more productive and competitive markets. Considering the environmental impacts of such infrastructure will be important to ensure that natural capital is safeguarded. Additionally, strategic public investments can serve as commitment devices and reduce technological and political risks, helping to crowd in private investments when markets are still forming. Information asymmetries and coordination failures can be tackled by improving connections between firms.

The region's infrastructure is deficient, even without considering the green transition. Both private and public investments will be needed to enhance opportunities in selected sectors; the risk for private investments in incomplete markets can be reduced by providing public goods required by selected industries, including in the areas in which they are expected to grow. Recent estimates suggest that Latin America and the Caribbean needs to invest $2,220.7 billion in water and sanitation; energy; transport; and telecommunications infrastructure—or about 3 percent of the region's GDP every year through 2030 (Brichetti et al. 2021). For the energy transition alone, the International Energy Agency estimates that more than $80 billion in annual investments will be required for Latin America and the Caribbean until 2050 (IEA 2020).

Harness the Power of Information to Enable Green Markets

Public access to information is fundamental. Such access can help policy makers design better policies, protect vulnerable populations, foster more research and innovation, and empower the private sector to make better investments.

Poor information is a significant obstacle for the green economy. Some consumers may prefer to pay for green or sustainable products, but consumers generally lack information about how goods are produced. Producers may respond to consumer demands for sustainable products by using input suppliers that can meet new standards. In some cases, governments step in and set new rules for international trade—such as the Carbon Border Adjustment Mechanism in the European Union and deforestation regulations in the European Union and the United States—with highly demanding information requirements.

Resolving the information problems facing the new economy will require credible and reliable certification mechanisms. Better information systems may allow producers to capture green premiums, input suppliers to gain market share and increase exports, and producers to develop new technologies and products that generate new sources of exports. Strengthening information can also lead to more effective monitoring, reporting, and verification (MRV) systems. As firms rebuild supply chains, they will need to be able to determine the "environmental quality" of goods to gain market share or higher premiums on goods produced in the region.

Therefore, a green national quality infrastructure (NQI) must be developed (see discussion in the next section). In the new economy, the sustainability of goods and services is another dimension of quality for which consumers are willing to pay. Standards are the set of technical specifications used to describe a product, service, production process, or material. Standards can reduce transaction costs and information asymmetries between sellers and buyers and can minimize uncertainties over quality (Pietrobelli and Rabellotti 2009), so obtaining certification by internationally accredited bodies will be crucial in the green economy.

Better information supports innovation and pushes the productivity and sustainability frontier outward. Establishing a baseline for resource use and the environmental impact of production can inform the development of sustainability policies. Argentina, Mexico, and Peru (among others) have committed to strengthening transparency and accountability in their extractive sectors through the implementation of the Extractive Industries Transparency Initiative (EITI) standards.[1] Argentina is creating a portal called System for Open Information for the Community on Mining Activity to provide information on the economic, environmental, and social aspects of mining activity.[2] Although Chile only signed on to the EITI initiative in 2024, it had supported a Mining Transparency Project promoted by Transparency Chile (the Chilean chapter of Transparency International), the National Mining Society (Sociedad Nacional de Minería), the Mining Council (Consejo Minero), and the Chilean Copper Commission (Comisión Chilena del Cobre).[3] The Mining Transparency Project encourages companies to apply information transparency standards while creating a platform where the public can access information on the sector (Signoria and Barlettani 2023).

Effective national innovation systems enable better planning and a more efficient use of scarce resources. Increasing the information available allows governments to develop better regulations to internalize potential externalities and develop more effective monitoring and enforcement. In land markets, cadastre-linked land registries are important tools that enable a complete overview of public and private land ownership. These cadastre-linked land registries enable secure tenure rights and improve oversight and enforcement of acceptable land uses, which are needed for a transition to more sustainable and efficient land use patterns.

Governments that have successfully attracted investment and boosted long-term mining output owe part of their success to a good geological knowledge base. Information availability is critical to fostering many exploration projects, a prerequisite for creating commercially viable mines. A good geological knowledge base improves the likelihood of successful exploration and makes a country more attractive to exploration companies, particularly new ones, although exploration close to existing deposits also benefits from geological knowledge. Countries that provide geological knowledge (in the form of high-quality geological maps and other geoscientific data, such as the results of geochemical surveys, geophysical measurements, and drill cores) are attractive—particularly if inventories (and, where possible, the information itself) are available online. Although the initial costs of geological mapping may be significant, requiring explorers to provide the reports, samples, and other information they have gathered from their work in a particular area is relatively low-cost (limited to the costs of archiving and making the materials available). These types of data are highly useful to subsequent explorers.

Build a Green National Quality Infrastructure to Support Greener, Internationally Recognized Local Markets

As global preferences shift toward greener products, the environmental impact of production processes will increasingly become a dimension of quality in certain goods or services. Consumers may be willing to pay more to ensure that the goods they purchase are of a higher green quality, but they generally lack the means to gather that information directly. Asymmetric information affects most markets in the new economy, so governments will need to invest heavily in the institutions and infrastructure that alleviate these information failures.

To accelerate the development of markets in the new economy and ensure continued access to international markets, governments should invest in an NQI. A key public good that can help reduce information asymmetries, an NQI is one of the basic foundational elements of technological activity in any country. It can be defined as a "system comprising the organizations (public and private) together with the policies, relevant legal and regulatory framework, and practices needed to support and enhance the quality, safety, and environmental soundness of goods, services, and processes."[4]

To build a green NQI, governments must first acquire the necessary capabilities and then establish standards, which are a key element of the new economy. Capabilities must be developed for measuring impact, testing, and creating quality certification processes, while also providing timely services with a minimum level of functionality. Subsequently, governments should support the development of local standards, ensuring that they comply with international requirements and contribute to the definition of international standards when relevant. Once standards are set, governments play a central role in ensuring a good understanding of standards, supporting the transitions needed to achieve those standards, and providing incentives for standards adoption when needed. Standards codify know-how and market requirements, enable interoperability between products and processes, set a minimum level of quality, and reduce variety, enabling economies of learning and scale (Racine et al. 2007). Standards can also reduce transaction costs and information asymmetries between sellers and buyers, thereby minimizing uncertainties with respect to quality and technical characteristics (Pietrobelli and Rabelloti 2009). The use of standards is key to accelerating the innovation required for success in the new economy. An effective NQI must also perform conformity assessments, given how important product certification is for the new economy. To evaluate whether a product, process, or service fulfills certain standards, procedures often involve testing and inspection, calibration, and certification.

Reliable national innovation systems and effective MRV systems can support enforcement efforts and incentivize the efficient use of natural resources. Given increased demand for sustainable products and new deforestation-free requirements in international markets, improvements in monitoring and tracing systems can help ensure continued access to markets for agricultural products. The beef sector provides an example. After the G4 Agreement on zero-deforestation cattle, ranchers moved swiftly to comply. While 36 percent of properties that supplied slaughterhouses had a recent history of deforestation before the agreement in 2009, this share had dropped to 4 percent by 2013. To preserve market access, ranchers rapidly registered their properties with the required environmental authorities after the agreement was signed. Purchases from compliant properties rose from 2 percent in 2009 to 96 percent in 2013. However, challenges remain, not least because the agreement regulates only direct suppliers. It has been estimated that 48 percent of beef exports from the Brazilian states of Mato Grosso and Pará could be from deforested land if indirect supply chains are accounted for, in contrast to 12 percent when considering only direct suppliers.[5]

Advanced information and MRV systems are also key to unlocking new markets where information failures are perhaps strongest. In addition to the general information problems found in established markets, there is additional uncertainty surrounding the effectiveness and impact of new technologies, which can hamper long-term offtake agreements. Carbon credit markets, for example, need substantial information to establish baselines for additionality, reporting, and verification requirements. Effective MRV systems minimize the reputational risks associated with greenwashing. Addressing these environmental and social concerns can help overcome this barrier to implementation (Clifford Chance 2022). Similarly, in the green hydrogen (GH_2) market, most countries lack institutionalized mechanisms to track the production and consumption of any shade of hydrogen (H_2) and identify its characteristics (for example, origin and life-cycle missions) (IEA 2020). Standards and certification mechanisms are lacking, especially for establishing internationally compatible certification and guarantees of origin for exporters.

Stronger applied skills and digital capacity are needed to improve the monitoring and management of forests and land. In a low-emissions future in which Paris Agreement goals are met, agriculture and food system jobs are expected to increase by 54 percent (Saget, Vogt-Schilb, and Luu 2020) and forestry jobs by 6 percent by 2030. While potential job growth in agriculture and forestry is significant, this growth depends on the availability of the right mix of fundamental and applied skills, as well as the flexibility of the labor force (Saget, Vogt-Schilb, and Luu 2020). Current research suggests that although many of the fundamental skills are present, there is a lack of applied skills, such as knowledge of carbon accounting, and of engineering principles for sustainable production. In the land use and forestry sector in Latin America and the Caribbean, these gaps are easy enough to close; about 60 percent of new jobs require skills that are manual and not occupation-specific, so existing skills can be reapplied. However, the other 40 percent come from gaps in management, supervisors, and financial analysts, where specialized skill requirements make the gaps harder to close (Saget, Vogt-Schilb, and Luu 2020). The carbon credit market will also require increased capacity for entrepreneurship and business development, along with investments in the applied skills needed to monitor landscape status and enforce regulations.

A range of tools to accelerate investment in more productive sustainable agricultural technologies across Latin America and the Caribbean's diverse range of farming systems is critical. At one end of the spectrum, a small number of large, well-capitalized, technologically sophisticated agribusiness enterprises dominate exports. At the other end, a vast number of much smaller family farms account for about half of the region's food production (IDB 2014). To facilitate uptake of productivity- and sustainability-enhancing technologies, governments in Latin America and the Caribbean will need to provide support for investments in areas including research and development (R&D), extension, and pilot projects, so that the benefits of innovation can be demonstrated and technical barriers overcome. Governments can also support private investment in trying out innovative financing methods that reduce risks for the private sector. This support can be particularly helpful to the small- and medium-size enterprises that produce the majority of the region's food and often struggle to access credit and financial markets.

An effective green NQI is also a prerequisite for technological innovation and upgrading of production processes. Gathering information on resource use and the environmental impact of different production processes is essential to understand how policy can then incentivize actors to innovate and push productivity and sustainability frontiers. Developing metrological (pertaining to the science of measurement), testing and inspection, calibration, and certification capabilities will be key for measuring progress in making production processes greener.

Use Investments to Complement and Coordinate Policies

The development of markets is often hampered by coordination failures. Participants in a market may benefit from investing in and developing a new technology, for example, but only if investments are coordinated. If agents lack information on each other's actions, and mechanisms to induce coordination are not available, the market may remain undeveloped. Governments can alleviate such market failures through two main channels. First, they can create institutions or design mechanisms to induce optimal coordination. It is often sufficient for governments to act as a convener through the creation of business associations in which firms, entrepreneurs, government officials, and researchers can meet (Agosin et al. 2014). Second, governments can provide enabling infrastructure or public goods that raise the productivity of private investments.

A more efficient private sector will require complementary investments in public infrastructure. These include basic transport infrastructure such as roads, highways, and trains, as well as efficient logistical infrastructure (such as ports and airports) that can make exports more competitive. They also include the development of countries' digital infrastructure, which can significantly improve productivity across a wide range of industries through multiple channels: reduced transaction costs, improved matching between producers and consumers, enhanced information flows, and increased competition (Goldfarb and Tucker 2019). Digital technologies also serve to more quickly diffuse best practices and technological innovations (Beylis et al. 2023).

Good-quality infrastructure paired with access to abundant, reliable, and affordable renewable energy (RE) can be a major advantage in attracting new investments—leveraging recent trends in greenshoring (as previously mentioned). Fostering market integration by investing in transmission lines that connect areas with high RE potential with demand centers can induce higher levels of investment in RE generation capacity (Gonzales, Ito, and Reguant 2023). But attracting manufacturing firms will also require investments in transport infrastructure, as well as low-carbon transport services and logistics, to ensure that cost savings from proximity to markets are not offset by limited connectivity, high shipping times, or other inefficiencies. Ensuring low-carbon transport will be important to maintain production value chains with a low-carbon-footprint. Access to reliable, efficient, and low-carbon supply chains, workers with the required skill sets, and effective R&D capabilities are all complementary inputs that will increase Latin America and the Caribbean's attractiveness for greenshoring.

The mining sector's efforts to push the sustainability and productivity frontier outward is a good example of the potential positive effect of complementary investments. The proximity of many lithium and copper mines to the high solar radiation areas of the Andes, for example, yields an ideal symbiotic relationship. The carbon emissions of mines can be reduced through the electrification of production processes with renewable solar energy. However, this reduction requires investment in transmission lines to connect mines with solar farms.

Given that solar electricity is available only during the day (whereas mines may operate around the clock), additional energy storage solutions or connection to the grid will be required. While the market opportunity may exist, governments may have to step in to resolve coordination failures.

Investments in roads and logistics will also be key to leveraging the critical mining sector's potential. Poor road access to mining regions persists in many countries in Latin America and the Caribbean. Additional investments in road expansion and maintenance are already needed, given the expected increased loads on roads and climate change risks. A recent assessment for Argentina suggests the main challenges lie in provincial and tertiary roads, with estimated investment needs of $1.5 million per kilometer to pave gravel roads to access lithium production areas. In addition, maintenance is needed so that roads can absorb the impact of excess loads; for national roads, this work is estimated to cost between $5.35 million and $12.48 million per 100 kilometers every 10 years (World Bank 2023).

Even as governments prioritize the construction and maintenance of roads, careful consideration of alternative transportation methods and their inherent trade-offs is warranted. In the case of mining in Argentina, improving rail networks would require additional investments but also would reduce the carbon emissions. When economic activity is close to sensitive forest ecosystems such as the Amazon rain forest, river transportation could be supported to facilitate the movement of people and goods while avoiding deforestation from road building (Hanusch 2023).

Coordinating investments across sectors can significantly lower infrastructure deployment costs. All network industries—roads, railways, electricity—can contribute to digital infrastructure by making their own infrastructure available to telecommunications operators for the installation of parallel digital networks, which can help lower deployment costs (García Zaballos and Foditsch 2014). For 5G technologies, savings in capital expenditure are estimated to be as high as 40 percent (Houngbonon et al. 2023; Tognisse and Degila 2021). For example, Internet for All, a partnership to deploy digital infrastructure between Corporación Andina de Fomento, telecommunications provider Telefónica, IDB Invest, and Facebook, plans to reach more than 6 million Peruvians in rural areas across the country. It has already reached more than 2 million people in 12 communities across 23 departments (Zaballos and Foditsh 2014).

Digital infrastructure can significantly improve the effectiveness of enforcement agencies. For example, digital MRV tools can help agencies that guard against illegal deforestation: artificial intelligence (AI) and machine learning models can be applied to data collected from satellites and drones to identify areas of deforestation and estimate carbon stocks. Automated data collection can also enable the enforcement of liability in cases of reversals, allowing agencies to monitor large tracts of land without costly and time-consuming physical inspections. In Brazil, the pioneering use of near-real-time forest monitoring greatly increased the capacity of law enforcement to apply binding and costly penalties to offenders (Assunção, Gandour, and Rocha 2023).

Digital technologies can also improve market efficiency and positively affect sustainability. One good example is farming, where digital technologies—which reduce transaction costs and ease information asymmetry problems—have been shown to positively affect productivity (Lio and Liu 2006). Farmers can better plan and resolve production issues, manage weather-related risks, and facilitate financial transactions (Baumüller 2017). There is now substantial evidence on the effect of market information and agricultural extension advisory services delivered through mobile phones. A meta-analysis of randomized control trials in Kenya and Rwanda found positive effects from text message–based agricultural extension programs on input adoption and cost-effectiveness (Fabregas, Kremer, and Schilbach 2019). Mining production may also benefit from adopting new digital technologies and AI tools: the use of satellites, drones, remotely operated vehicles, and emerging AI technologies can greatly reduce waste and improve efficiency and sustainability.

To achieve reliable, affordable, and high-quality connectivity, governments must provide not only the hard infrastructure of internet cables, towers, training data, and data centers, but also the complementary soft infrastructure. But developing soft infrastructure means both (a) developing a skilled labor force with digital capabilities and (b) establishing technology centers or business associations that include, as one party, software and AI developers and, as a second party, companies from the sector in question. Such organizations can foster the user-consumer interactions that are an essential part of successful, productivity-enhancing innovation processes. Although these interactions may emerge naturally, in the case of mining, the experience of countries in Latin America and the Caribbean suggests that interaction between knowledge-intensive service providers and mining corporations has been quite limited (Calzada Olvera 2022; Katz and Pietrobelli 2018). This limited interaction further suggests the presence of coordination failures and information challenges that require government intervention.

When developing new markets, coordination may also be important to help achieve scale. In the case of GH_2, a large enough market could lower the cost of H_2 technology through economies of scale, learning by doing, and innovation, thereby encouraging investment in H_2 production. However, market failures have led to low investment in transportation, conversion, and storage infrastructure.

Although the primary cost drivers of H_2 production are energy and electrolyzers, the additional costs incurred when it is not consumed on-site can be much higher (De Sisternes Jimenez and Jackson 2020). The goal should be to move toward a regulatory framework that facilitates cross-border trade and coordinated infrastructure investments to develop a regional market. A failure to do so could lead to duplication and unnecessary costs.

Notes

1. EITI is an international initiative aimed at improving transparency and accountability in the extractive industries through the publication, full verification, and disclosure of information on key issues relating to the management of oil, gas, and mining resources. See https://eiti.org/es/paises.
2. Resolution No. 89/2022. https://www.argentina.gob.ar/normativa/nacional/resoluci%C3%B3n-89-2022-365573.
3. Transparencia Minera, https://www.transparenciaminera.cl.
4. World Bank, "Ensuring Quality to Gain Access to Global Markets: A Reform Toolkit," online toolkit, part 2, 41, https://thedocs.worldbank.org/en/doc/122661553265338942-0090022019/original/Part2TheQualityInfrastructure.pdf.
5. Transparency for Sustainable Economies (Trase), data tool focused on trade and the sustainability of globally traded agricultural commodities, https://supplychains.trase.earth/. See SEI (Stockholm Environment Institute), "Brazilian Beef Trade's Links to Deforestation Revealed by Transparency Tool, press release, September 18, 2019, https://www.sei.org/about-sei/press-room/brazilian-beef-trades-links-to-deforestation/.

References

Agosin, M. R., E. Fernández-Arias, G. Crespi et al. 2014. *Rethinking Productive Development: Sound Policies and Institutions for Economic Transformation* (Synopsis). Washington, DC: Inter-American Development Bank. https://doi.org/10.18235/0006382.

Assunção, J., C. Gandour, and R. Rocha 2023. DETER-ing Deforestation in the Amazon: Environmental Monitoring and Law Enforcement. *American Economic Journal: Applied Economics* 15 (2): 125–56. https://doi.org/10.1257/app.20200196.

Baumüller, H. 2017. "The Little We Know: An Exploratory Literature Review on the Utility of Mobile Phone-Enabled Services for Smallholder Farmers." *Journal of International Development* 30: 134–54. https://doi.org/10.1002/jid.3314.

Beylis, G., W. Maloney, G. Vuletin, and J. A. Zambrano Riveros. 2023. "Wired: Digital Connectivity for Inclusion and Growth." Latin America and the Caribbean Economic Review (October 2023). Washington, DC: World Bank. https://doi.org/10.1596/978-1-4648-2038-0.

Brichetti, J. P., L. Mastronardi, M. E. Rivas, T. Serebrisky, and B. Solís. 2021. *The Infrastructure Gap in Latin America and the Caribbean: Investment Needed through 2030 to Meet the Sustainable Development Goals*. Washington, DC: Inter-American Development Bank. https://publications.iadb.org/en/infrastructure-gap-latin-america-and-caribbean-investment-needed-through-2030-meet-sustainable.

Calzada Olvera, B. 2022. Innovation in Mining: What Are the Challenges and Opportunities along the Value Chain for Latin American Suppliers? *Mineral Economics* 35: 35–51. https://doi.org/10.1007/s13563-021-00251-w.

Clifford Chance. 2022. *The Rise of Consumer Complaints, Litigation and Enforcement Actions to Curb Greenwashing*. London: Clifford Chance. https://www.cliffordchance.com /content/dam/cliffordchance/briefings/2022/12/The-Rise-of-Consumer-Complaints -Litigation-and-Enforcement-Actions-to-Curb-Greenwashing.pdf.

De Sisternes Jimenez, F. J., and C. P. Jackson. 2020. *Green Hydrogen in Developing Countries*. Washington, DC: World Bank. http://documents.worldbank.org/curated/en /953571597951239276/Green-Hydrogen-in-Developing-Countries.

Fabregas, R., M. Kremer, and F. Schilbach. 2019. "Realizing the Potential of Digital Development: The Case of Agricultural Advice." *Science* 366 (6471): eaay3038. https://doi.org/10.1126/science.aay3038.

García Zaballos, A., and N. Foditsch. 2014. *Universal Access to Broadband and Service Programs: A Comparative Study*. Washington, DC: Inter-American Development Bank. https://doi.org/10.18235/0012398.

Goldfarb, A., and C. Tucker. 2019. "Digital Economics." *Journal of Economic Literature* 57 (1): 3–43.

Gonzales, L. E., K. Ito, and M. Reguant. 2023. "The Investment Effects of Market Integration: Evidence from Renewable Energy Expansion in Chile." *Econometrica* 91 (5): 1659–93.

Hanusch, M., ed. 2023. *A Balancing Act for Brazil's Amazonian States: An Economic Memorandum*. Washington, DC: World Bank. https://doi.org/10.1596/978-1-4648 -1909-4.

Houngbonon, G. V., M. Ivaldi, E. Palikot, and D. Strusani. 2023. "The Impact of Shared Telecom Infrastructure on Digital Connectivity and Inclusion." Working paper. http://dx.doi.org/10.2139/ssrn.4530998.

IDB (Inter-American Development Bank). 2014. *The Next Global Breadbasket: How Latin America Can Feed the World; A Call to Action for Addressing Challenges*. Washington, DC: Inter-American Development Bank. https://publications.iadb.org/en/next-global -breadbasket-how-latin-america-can-feed-world-call-action-addressing-challenges.

IEA (International Energy Agency). 2020. *World Energy Outlook 2020*. Paris: International Energy Agency.

Katz, J., and C. Pietrobelli. 2018. "Natural Resource Based Growth, Global Value Chains and Domestic Capabilities in the Mining Industry." *Resources Policy* 58: 11–20. https://doi .org/10.1016/j.resourpol.2018.02.001.

Lio, M., and M.-C. Liu. 2006. "ICT and Agricultural Productivity: Evidence from Cross-Country Data." *Agricultural Economics* 34 (3): 221–28. https://doi.org/10.1111/j.1574 -0864.2006.00120.x.

Pietrobelli, C., and R. Rabellotti. 2009. "The Global Dimension of Innovation Systems: Linking Innovation Systems and Global Value Chains." In *Handbook of Innovation Systems and Developing Countries*, edited by B.-Å. Lundvall, K. J. Joseph, C. Chaminade, and J. Vang. Edward Elgar Publishing.

Racine, J.-L., J. L. Guasch, I. Sánchez, and M. Diop. 2007. *Quality Systems and Standards for a Competitive Edge*. Washington, DC: World Bank.

Saget, C., A. Vogt-Schilb, and T. Luu. 2020. *Jobs in a Net-Zero Emissions Future in Latin America and the Caribbean*. Washington, DC: Inter-American Development Bank and International Labour Organization.

Signoria, C., and M. Barlettani. 2023. *Environmental, Health, Safety, and Social Management of Green Hydrogen in Latin America and the Caribbean*. Washington, DC: Inter-American Development Bank.

Tognisse, I., and J. Degila. 2021. "Rural Technology Adoption and Use Model in Rural Africa: A Predictive Approach to Telephony Acceptance." International Journal of E-Adoption 13: 36–55. 10.4018/IJEA.2021010103.

World Bank. 2023. *Corredores Económicos Transformadores del Noroeste Argentino.* Washington, DC: World Bank. https://documents.worldbank.org/curated/en/0991009 23161014616/P17940301690e70200a800002036794540c.

Zaballos, A. G., and N. Foditsch. 2014. *Universal Access to Broadband and Service Programs: A Comparative Study.* Washington, DC: Inter-American Development Bank.

CHAPTER 5

Innovation

Guillermo Beylis and Nancy Lozano Gracia

Supporting the Transition to Resource Smart Requires a National Innovation System

Latin America and the Caribbean's paradigm shift toward a new economy has given the region's countries a unique opportunity to propel themselves into the lead in green technology sectors. With the right enabling environment and a capacity to quickly adopt, diffuse, and enhance emerging technologies, countries will get the chance to leapfrog ahead of developed countries. But to do so successfully, they must build their capacity to innovate.

Truly effective progress in innovation and technology comes from effective interaction between a variety of actors involved in the development, distribution, and application of new technologies. Progress and high performance in innovation therefore depend not only on research and development (R&D) but also on the strength of the links between government, the private sector, public research institutes, universities, and others. The system that supports effective interaction between creators, distributors, and technology users is often referred to as the national innovation system (NIS).

The NIS can help firms become efficient and sustainable. A better system for gathering and diffusing information on new technologies and good practices (such as climate-smart agricultural practices) can facilitate learning and adoption. Moreover, management extension programs, which provide educational tools and training, can empower managers, through technology and knowledge transfer, to be significantly more efficient. Because individuals tend to undervalue the benefits of innovation and technology adoption (Bloom and Van Reenen 2007), governments have an important role to play. The adoption of new technology, upgrading of machines, and improvements in management quality can significantly improve the allocation of resources and overall efficiency in an economy (Lundvall et al. 2002; Nelson 1993).

The smooth functioning of the NIS is also the key to developing new production processes and technologies that can expand production while also reducing its environmental impact. Through public research institutions and technology extension centers, governments can directly and indirectly support R&D efforts and simultaneously guide them in more socially or environmentally desirable directions. A central role for the NIS is to resolve coordination failures by facilitating interaction between users and developers—to accelerate and improve technology development and adoption—and by identifying specific services, skills, or public goods that may be lacking.

Perhaps most importantly, the strength of the NIS is fundamental for the development of the new frontier technologies that are needed to open new markets. Such innovation efforts require both a highly complex mix of supportive policies and the NIS's technical and managerial capability to effectively handle long-term projects with high uncertainty. It is important to note that this level of maturity and capability requires decades to build and involves not just technological and scientific know-how, but also well-functioning educational and financial markets that complement innovation.

Investments in sharpening the capabilities of firms will be central to the development of a fruitful green innovation ecosystem. Cirera and Maloney (2017, 6) note that basic managerial skills are "central to the introduction of new processes, technologies, and products as well as to patenting" and that these capabilities are sorely lacking in developing countries. The authors introduce the concept of a "capabilities escalator," in which firms advance from basic production capabilities to the ability to adopt and adapt technologies, and finally to the ability to invent. This framework of firm advancement informs this report's policy recommendations for developing an effective NIS using the green transition as a catalyst. The main message from this framework is that policies intended to support innovation efforts need to be matched with the capabilities and sophistication of firms. In other words, firms need to learn how to walk before they can run. Innovation policies, then, will increase in sophistication and complexity as firms increase their capabilities.

Unfortunately, the capacity of governments to design and implement the complex and broad-scope policies necessary to catch up to the technological frontier tends to diminish as distance from the frontier increases. Investments in developing government capabilities are therefore critical to ensure the effectiveness of innovation policy—part of resolving the "innovation paradox" (Cirera and Maloney 2017). As a government's diagnostic, design, and execution capabilities improve, the set of policies that it can effectively implement grows. In this way, the policy mix supporting innovation evolves with the capabilities of both firms and governments, as they become more sophisticated over time.

To prosper in a greener economy, the complementarity of R&D and innovation efforts must also be reinforced (Cirera and Maloney 2017). It is useful to view innovation as another factor—knowledge capital—that enters the production function (Correa, Fernandes, and Uregian 2008).[1] In this framework, then, the effectiveness of innovation efforts will depend on the stock of other factors of production—such as physical and human capital—which are generally scarcer in Latin America and the Caribbean than elsewhere globally. Therefore, implementing reforms to accumulate these complementary factors is also important for improving competitiveness in the green economy.

Currently, Latin America and the Caribbean underperforms in innovation efforts and outcomes, even considering its income level (Cirera and Maloney 2017). Average regional expenditures on R&D are low, hovering around 0.6 percent of gross domestic product (GDP). This may be the result of rational decisions by firms which, lacking innovation capabilities and facing a scarcity of complementary factors, find investments in R&D to have low or even negative returns (Cirera and Maloney 2017). Even for Brazil, the regional leader—which spends around 1.6 percent of GDP on R&D—the outcomes are underwhelming. This result is partly due to a lack of complementary factors, but it can also be attributed to Brazil's weak NIS, which mostly funds research in basic science at national universities, undervaluing the research in applied sciences that has greater potential for industrial use. Furthermore, most firms lack the managerial and entrepreneurial flair for far-reaching innovation and are out of touch with research activities (Leal and Figueiredo 2021).

Developing the NIS's robustness and the productive capabilities needed to capitalize on a greener future will therefore be a gradual process. Helping producers modernize will require sustained investments in innovation efforts and capability building; the growing sophistication of a policy mix that stretches the technological and sustainability frontier; and a more general agenda that amplifies factors that complement innovation (such as education and finance). With these elements, Latin America and the Caribbean's NISs will be able to implement the highly complex R&D and innovation efforts that produce cutting-edge technologies.

Strengthen Government Capabilities to Support Innovation in the Green Economy

Success in the new economy will be determined by Latin America and the Caribbean's effectiveness at technology adoption and innovation. In fact, technological progress explains most of the growth performance and differences in income levels across countries globally. Therefore, the appropriate design and implementation of innovation policies are fundamental to support private sector innovation capabilities and build the foundations for future growth.

The type, responsibilities, and cross-coordination of the agencies and organizations that design and implement innovation policy are crucial. Institutional organograms cannot just be imported from advanced countries without consideration of local specificities (Andrews 2015; Andrews, Pritchett, and Woolcock 2013; Rodrik 2008). There is no single successful model for an innovation agency (Glennie and Bound 2016). What matters is the function that the agency serves—that is, a clear justification for its existence and a rationale that identifies the gap or market failure the agency is intended to address, with clearly defined metrics of success (Edquist 2004; Link and Scott 2009).

The same applies to innovation policies. They also require clear rationales, defined goals, and measurable objectives, as well as considering a government's capabilities for implementation and monitoring. While reducing the complexity of a policy that doesn't require high government capabilities may lead to second-best design, this more pragmatic approach can improve outcomes (Wu and Ramesh 2014). Capturing innovation policies by interest groups—like academic departments or elite firms that may already be engaged in R&D—must also be avoided, especially in countries with less developed institutions and weaker accountability. Built-in mechanisms to avoid capture may result in better outcomes in the long run.

While there is no single model for an innovation agency, some important principles can be adapted to the local context. Boards of directors should include the representation of diverse interests and the private sector to ensure that innovation goals and business needs are aligned. For example, environmentalists and green entrepreneurs can help an agency better respond to the needs of businesses in the new economy. The representation of big mining companies and the supplier industry in a mining public research institute (PRI), for example, can ensure that innovations are responsive to industry needs and also enhance sustainability. Robust and transparent governance improves legitimacy and accountability and can shield agencies from political considerations. International partners—who can aid countries by reviewing scientific proposals, for example—can avoid undue influence and increase trust in the agency's effectiveness.

It is also important for agencies to have staff with the right skills and well-designed incentive structures that prioritize quality and output goals. Innovation agencies in technologically advanced countries generally recruit individuals from industries or those who possess particular technical experience—rather than policy generalists (Glennie and Bound 2016). This means, for example, hiring agriculture and forestry experts with backgrounds in sustainable production techniques and knowledge of carbon accounting techniques; mining experts and engineers focused on water or energy efficiency techniques; or engineers from the fossil fuel industry that have transferable skills to the green hydrogen (GH$_2$) sector. When specific skills are scarce, international partnerships can help fill the gap by developing local capabilities, cultivating the required human capital, and using global funding and knowledge networks to better design programs that follow best practices.

Long-term funding and commitment from governments are required to build effective innovation agencies. Initially, the need for government resources is greater, as they allow agencies to build capacity and streamline operations. The government resources provide stability for hiring and retaining capable staff and implementing the rigorous piloting needed to evaluate program efficiency and additionality (Aridi and Kapil 2019). Over the long run, a combination of government and private sector financing is optimal, as it ensures quality and alignment with business objectives. Financing should be predictable, long term, and able to withstand political cycles (Kapil, Piatkowsi, and Navarrete 2014), which can be achieved by ring-fencing budgets or using dedicated funds.

Policy design must also be coherent and consistent over time. This will help better target policies to resolve the specific bottlenecks identified, obtain the resources to tackle the issues appropriately, and create policies that complement other policies rather than duplicating or, worse, offsetting them. Success requires coordination across ministries and long-term commitment from the government—which generally requires support from across the political spectrum. In land markets, for example, a coherent policy would avoid directing efficiency-enhancing agricultural extension services toward regions protected for conservation.

Taxes and subsidies should be aligned with the government's land use objectives. If producers lack information or production capabilities, programs that require the adoption of sustainable practices in exchange for agricultural cash transfers should be accompanied by mentoring, technology, and agricultural management extension services. Incentives can either be adjusted broadly or in a more targeted way. In the broad approach, which is extremely useful in farming, existing subsidy regimes can be widened without distorting farmer choices relating to crops or inputs. For example, existing subsidies can be reallocated from price supports or input subsidies (which are distortionary and currently predominate) toward general services such as, innovation, education, cybersecurity, inspection, and control. This broadly benefits the sector regardless of crops or inputs used (OECD 2024). Meanwhile, targeted incentives for land use change can serve long-term productivity and sustainability goals. Brazil offers a good example, with programs to incentivize the adoption of conservation practices. Broad incentives would pay farmers to restore degraded land, while targeted incentives would offer low-interest loans to farmers who adopt sustainable agricultural practices (Sutton, Lotsch, and Prasann 2024).

Building the efficiency of the NIS takes decades of continuous investment as policy and institutions evolve. Innovation is a central element of the green agenda, so it is critical to seize the opportunity to redesign innovation agencies and policies to maximize their impact. That means building a dynamic feedback loop framework—from design, to implementation, to evaluation, and back to design. This feedback loop can include experimenting with policy instruments or implementing small-scale pilots. To improve program design and facilitate the elimination of ineffective policies, impact evaluations should be built into all policies from the beginning (Dutz et al. 2014).[2] To test and improve successful policies, monitoring and evaluation systems are essential. A greater emphasis on evaluation and policy learning also relieves pressure from interest groups and promotes policy changes that are informed by evidence, which encourages transparency (Andrews and Pritchett 2013; Krause, Yi, and Feiock 2016; Teirlink et al. 2013).

Improve Firm Capabilities to Carry Out Innovation in the Green Economy

While governments play an important role in supporting innovation, ultimately it is the private sector that must develop the capabilities necessary to adopt, diffuse, and invent new technologies for the green economy. There are striking contrasts between and within Latin American and the Caribbean countries when it comes to NIS maturity and innovation capabilities. Most of the region's firms are generally at the lower end of the capabilities spectrum (Bell and Figueiredo 2012; Bell and Pavitt 1993; Lundvall et al. 2009; Zanello et al. 2013), with just a few firms (especially in the agriculture technology sector) reaching the highest capability levels—reflected in the steady growth of patent filings for agrobiotechnologies in Latin America and the Caribbean since 2000.

Policies targeting firms should be designed to match existing managerial and innovation skills, and mechanisms should be set up to gradually strengthen capabilities. Because of significant differences in capabilities within countries, and even within economic sectors, policy interventions should be thought of as gradual and cumulative; even as some firms increase their capabilities (graduating toward more sophisticated R&D and innovation efforts), the NIS still plays a role in improving the capabilities of those lagging behind.

Governments can create investment readiness programs around green innovation that connect local innovators with foreign venture capital funds, helping to create a solid entrepreneurial pipeline. Many innovative start-ups and small and medium-sized enterprises have excellent ideas, yet they often lack the experience necessary to secure external funding. Investment readiness programs aim to bridge this gap through a combination of training, mentoring, master classes, and networking opportunities. Evidence suggests that these types of programs can be effective in improving a firm's attractiveness to investors (Dautovic, Cusolito, and McKenzie 2018).

Catching Up to the Frontier: Moving from Basic Production to the Adoption of New Technologies

For firms at the bottom of the capabilities escalator, innovation policy should focus on basic managerial and organizational practices, process improvements, and machinery upgrades, with little or no investment in complex R&D projects. Significant information asymmetries imply that firms (and sometimes governments) don't know what they don't know and hence underinvest in productivity-enhancing technology adoption. While there are diverse firms at this first stage, the agriculture, forest, and other land use (AFOLU) sector best illustrates the issues to be solved and the policies that can address underlying market and system failures.

In the AFOLU sector, there is a clear rationale for policies promoting the diffusion of best practices and the adoption of technology. There are significant information failures and externalities in land use that are not internalized by private agents. Sometimes, producers will need support to improve their efficiency. The case of Uruguay, highlighted in box 5.1 below, underlines the potential to improve both sustainability and economic outcomes through relatively simple innovations and adjustments to management practices. In another example, Argentina's Program for Rural Development and Family Agriculture (PRODAF) program helped farmers develop business plans for new technologies and covered a small share of the technology adoption costs. By reducing information and liquidity barriers, PRODAF increased the likelihood of farmers accessing credit by 47 percentage points and farmers adopting the new technology by 21 points (Schling and Pazos 2022). In other cases, policy makers may want to aid producers in changing the use of land—specifically, through a shift to sustainable forestry or afforestation projects. An innovation agency can also bolster efficiency in land use markets by filling significant information gaps. For example, sustainable forest management principles are more likely to be followed when forest technical assistance is integrated into agricultural extension programs.

Box 5.1

Agricultural Innovation for Productivity and Sustainability in Uruguay

Uruguay's agriculture sector accounts for 77 percent of its export earnings and 80 percent of its emissions, half of which come from enteric fermentation. Soil and water resources are increasingly being depleted from decades of intensive and industrial farming, leaving agricultural systems more vulnerable to the weather. Extreme weather events are increasingly affecting production, with serious social and economic consequences. The Ministry of Livestock, Agriculture and Fishing (MGAP) estimates that the 2022–2023 drought caused US$1.8 billion in direct losses from livestock, agriculture, and the dairy industry. Accounting for both direct and indirect effects, the drought resulted in a 2.8 percent fall in GDP (Giuliano, Navia, and Ruberl 2024). The government of Uruguay has expressed a strong commitment to adopt agroecological principles across the agrifood sector to stimulate growth and productivity while protecting the country's natural resources and promoting environmental sustainability and climate-smart agricultural production.

Within this context, from 2021 to 2023, the country's Livestock and Climate pilot project sought to mitigate climate change and restore degraded lands through the promotion of climate-smart practices in the livestock sector. The pilot adopted a "co-innovation approach," working with 60 small and medium-sized farmers across a total of 30,000 hectares to promote their adoption of management techniques to improve pasture growth, synchronize animal feeding with peak pasture production, improve livestock management (body fat reserves, body condition, weaning, growth speed, reproduction, fattening rates, and slaughter age), and use improved monitoring and data collection of environmental and agricultural information.

After the pilot's first year, 60 percent of participating farms experienced a 50 percent increase in net farm income, stocking rates declined by 16 percent (meaning fewer livestock per hectare), beef and sheep production both increased, and the greenhouse gas emissions intensity and gross greenhouse gas emissions declined by 27 percent and 17 percent, respectively. As a result, these innovative farm management systems are successfully being scaled up across the country with the support of the World Bank.

Sources: CCAC 2021; FAO 2022; World Bank 2021.

Governments can also support farmers by incentivizing the adoption of digital technologies. In addition to providing the necessary digital infrastructure (the "hardware"), developing "software" infrastructure is equally important. Governments can support the development of apps and services that help farmers improve their productivity, sustainability, and resilience in all the different ecosystems that the region is endowed with, as well as the digital skills to make use of them. Digital software solutions can enhance access to services like advice and financing, to markets (procurement and e-commerce), and to assets for monitoring and decision-making (Loukos and Arathoon 2020). Digital technologies can greatly increase the flow of information between research, extension services, and farmers, enhancing the role of extension agents as intermediaries and communicators. However, it is critical to emphasize that information and communication technology infrastructure cannot substitute content. Governments can also act as incubators or accelerators for entrepreneurship and digital innovation. In some countries, government backing for agricultural innovation—particularly to support small producers—is helping to expand access to agricultural technology. In Colombia, the Ministry of Technology Information and Communications runs Apps.co to foster entrepreneurship and the development of technology applications. Agricultural technology firms like Kanpo, an agritech firm targeting smallholder farmers who receive government subsidies, were established through the support of Apps.co (Loukos and Arathoon 2020). Collaborative, public-private, and regional initiatives can drive financing and investment (Saini 2023). FONTAGRO, one of the oldest regional research consortia, initially used seed funding from member governments as an investment in capital markets that could finance research initiatives in agriculture. As of 2022, the fund oversaw 58 projects (US$47 million) at over 576 pilot sites (FONTAGRO 2022). Examples of projects it has funded include research on opportunities to increase soil-based carbon sequestration, improve pest and disease management, and develop iron-rich staple foods to strengthen regional food security. Expanding these collaborative models and tightening links to the private sector can help set examples to follow and prove the profitability and effectiveness of new productivity- and sustainability-enhancing technologies.

Pricing and compensation mechanisms with the right incentives to halt deforestation are another area where governments can guide the private sector. Payments for ecosystem services (PES), for example, have a long history in the region, but they can do much more to ensure that land is better used. Reviews of the effectiveness of PES systems globally, and in Latin America and the Caribbean specifically, show small positive effects on reducing deforestation, although evidence is mixed. Part of the reason is that many deforestation PES systems are not targeted at high deforestation risk locations, leading to low overall additionality (Badgley et al. 2022; Coffield et al. 2022; Jack and Jayachandran 2019; Jayachandran et al. 2016). Existing PES systems in Latin America and the Caribbean vary widely in both range and structure. Innovative designs, implemented with underlying policy learning mechanisms, can support conservation and land use transformations or help finance the costs of productivity-enhancing technologies. Contracts with clearly defined and shorter renewal cycles can support learning by helping governments and producers to give and receive feedback, evaluate the results of current policies, and redesign them to improve effectiveness. Evidence from programs in Colombia suggests that temporary PES provisions can have lasting effects on the adoption of productive technologies as well as conservation (Blanco et al. 2023; Moros et al. 2023). In one project in Colombia, effects persisted for four years after a temporary PES scheme was implemented to encourage adoption of silvopastoral practices, particularly for productivity enhancement activities (Pagiola, Honey-Rosés, and Freire-González 2016).

Crucially, investments in science, technology, engineering, and mathematics (STEM) skills and early-stage innovation infrastructure should be made in parallel, as building these capabilities takes decades. From the very beginning, the foundations for a green national quality infrastructure (NQI), as discussed earlier in this report, should also be laid, just as general reforms must be made to the business environment to facilitate the accumulation of complementary productive factors to innovation, such as education and financial markets.

Pushing the Frontier: Moving from Adoption to Invention

When firms reach an intermediate point in the innovation capabilities spectrum, they move from being takers of knowledge to producers, and they start investing in R&D projects. In such firms, the quality and sophistication of products tends to increase—particularly in sectors exposed to trade. There will be heterogeneity across sectors; those that are more advanced should have well-established technology centers in close contact with firms, enabling them to keep up with the latest technological developments and optimal production processes. Fostering collaboration between researchers and industry actors will be key for the region.

Global innovations in technologies and agricultural practices can enable productivity to increase in tandem with sustainability—of which there are many global examples. Micro-drip irrigation technologies can reduce water use significantly while also increasing crop quality. Precision agriculture—using GPS, drones, data analytics, and increasingly AI—can minimize the use of pesticides and increase yields by tailoring interventions to specific crop and growing conditions in real time (Chomsky 2023). Drones can reduce crop losses by monitoring soil and crop conditions, identifying emerging problems such as pests or disease, and enabling intervention before problems spread. Bio-inputs can also improve agricultural productivity while supporting sustainability and biodiversity.

Effective NISs would support more advanced firms and farms, not only in adopting global innovations but also in developing home-grown innovations. For example, the NIS could support adaptation to local challenges by investing in innovation. The agriculture sector provides several examples of NISs that have supported innovation and even catch-up in past decades. The Brazilian Agricultural Research Corporation (EMBRAPA[3]) provides a successful historical example of nationally-led innovation in the region. The public research, development, and innovation company was established in 1973 to lead innovation in Brazilian farming. EMBRAPA's work in soil fertility and soybean genetics was critical for enabling the creation and adoption of soy variants that were suited to larger areas of Brazil. Prior to EMBRAPA's efforts, soy cultivation was restricted to only a few small areas of the country (Figueiredo 2014). Today EMPBRAPA acts as an open, networked innovation facilitator that promotes engagement with the private sector, deepening the innovation ecosystem. More recently, Chile has also become a hotspot for innovation in plant breeding and is the main exporter of seeds for off-season production, both for research purposes and to offset northern hemisphere production shortages (Sánchez 2020). Growing techniques and crop development (both GMO and non-GMO) remain a relative bright spot in Latin America and the Caribbean's agricultural innovation story. Patent data for agrobiotechnologies in Latin America and the Caribbean show steady growth in filings from the region since 2000. Patent family filings have also increased steadily, dominated by Brazil, with Argentina, Chile, and Mexico also contributing, although the volume remains small relative to global leaders (Government of Australia 2021).

The mining sector illustrates the challenges of this intermediate stage of innovation capabilities. Multinational corporations (MNCs) dominate this sector, and they possess significant technological absorptive capacity. While the specific dynamics of this sector mean that MNCs mostly do not actually innovate themselves,[4] they are the main catalysts for innovation. This means they serve as models for the necessary investments and policies that enable firms to climb up the capabilities escalator.

New opportunities are opening up in the mining sector for local innovation and higher-quality links between local suppliers and MNCs (Morris, Kaplinsky, and Kaplan 2012), amid pressures to reduce the environmental effect of mining, global technological advances, and geopolitical tensions. While some local firms have developed important innovations for the industry, they are not the result of rich links between suppliers and mining firms. Large mining companies have not systematically built formal long-term links or committed to joint innovation with local suppliers, especially in Chile and Peru (Molina 2018; Stubrin 2017). Local innovation seems to be infrequent and carried out by only a few firms. When production challenges arise, mining firms tend to rely on their established foreign suppliers. There is increasing consensus that the radical innovations needed to significantly improve productivity, profitability, and environmental performance will require a cooperative approach throughout a highly connected innovation ecosystem that includes mining firms, suppliers, government, industry associations, academia, and incubators (Bryant 2015; Deloitte 2016; Upstill and Hall 2006).

Moreover, there is limited communication between suppliers and mining companies, which is generally more transactional than collaborative (Figueiredo and Piana 2018; Molina 2018; Pietrobelli, Marin, and Olivari 2018). One exception is the development of the World Class Supplier Program in Chile, led by BHP Billiton and Codelco, the state mining company. The program aimed to communicate the operational problems of mining firms so local suppliers could build their organizational and technological capabilities to provide solutions. Impact reviews suggest that the program has improved innovation efforts, although it has not succeeded in providing large-scale solutions or generating exports of services from local suppliers (Navarro 2017). Another barrier to innovation is the lack of facilities for piloting and testing during the scaling-up phase of technologies. Access to such facilities is essential for providing proof of concept and measuring the effectiveness of prototypes and new technologies, while also providing important feedback for further development of the technology.

The lack of support in key areas—such as research, education, and training centers—as well as the absence of coordination and communication channels puts Latin America and the Caribbean's suppliers at a major disadvantage. All of these issues point toward a weak innovation system in mining, which can be addressed with the right incentives and policy design. In Australia, the United States, and Canada, where most successful supplier firms originate, a broad ecosystem for innovation exists. There are coordinating agencies, research centers, and industrial organizations that support innovation by creating spaces for communication, addressing common problems, and sharing the risk and cost for innovators (Bryant 2015; Deloitte 2016).

When designing institutions and policies to incentivize innovation, there are two important lessons to keep in mind (Cirera and Maloney 2017). First, technology extension centers and business associations are more effective when they are the result of public-private partnerships. This ensures communication and helps address coordination issues while keeping services aligned with business needs. Second, successful institutions tend to be subnational and close to specific sector clusters. Local knowledge and proximity facilitate effective and frequent interaction with local firms.

Governments can also provide services that help local firms connect internationally—through exports or by participating in global value chains. Export promotion agencies help develop the skills needed to participate in the export market while also addressing the externalities associated with foreign market intelligence related to consumer preferences, business opportunities, quality and technical requirements, and so on. Technology centers can provide information to firms and help them upgrade their production capabilities to meet the quality requirements of MNCs.

Arriving at New Frontiers: Leadership in Invention and New Technology

When a critical mass of firms has reached the technological frontier, innovation policy can focus on enabling advanced technological development capabilities and invention, promoting the generation of new technologies and increasingly complex innovative projects. Effective government support consists of three types of instruments carefully designed to promote R&D: (a) tax incentives, (b) direct grants, and (c) creation of PRIs.

Tax incentives are frequently used in advanced and middle-income countries. While they support additional investments in R&D, the beneficiaries are primarily larger firms, which already conduct R&D. Moreover, such incentives require tax authorities to develop complementary monitoring capabilities to ensure that resources are well spent. An additional drawback is that tax incentives tend not to promote interaction within the innovation system (Cirera and Maloney 2017).

Grants and matching grants are another popular tool to support continued innovation in technologically advanced firms. They usually finance specific types of innovation projects, including proofs of concept, prototyping, testing, advanced machinery, technical assistance, and so on. With matching grants, governments contribute a percentage of the applicant's project cost outlay. Agencies should design these programs with a keen understanding of the receiving firm's capabilities. When they are weaker, effectiveness can be boosted by accompanying grants with mentoring or technical assistance. Policy makers may want to design such programs to incentivize partnerships, which can improve links between firms and research centers.

While the effectiveness of grant programs varies, a number of studies find a positive effect, particularly on input and behavioral additionality (Becker 2015; Garcia-Quevedo 2004; Zúñiga-Vicente et al. 2014).[5] There is much less evidence regarding output and output additionality.[6] When comparing the effectiveness of tax incentives and grants, some evaluations of grants in the Organisation for Economic Co-operation and Development (OECD) suggest that they can be more effective in supporting R&D projects than tax incentives (Arqué-Castells and Mohnen 2015).

PRIs tend to be sector specific and can support both applied and basic R&D, generally on demand. Developing successful PRIs is difficult, as they require the existence of significant technological capabilities. While there are some successful institutes in Latin America and the Caribbean—such as EMBRAPA in Brazil—evidence on their effect is thin. Link and Scott (2009), looking at case studies of similar institutes in the region, found that they were poorly conceived and had unclear missions and goals, hinting at limited effectiveness.

The complexity of the innovation challenge at this stage is perhaps best illustrated by the development of the GH_2 sector. The technology is new, carries high costs, and has uncertain outcomes—although costs are expected to fall through economies of scale, innovation, and learning. Its development, however, is a medium- to long-term project requiring sustained investment and complex innovation capabilities. Latin America and the Caribbean's abundance of affordable renewable energy can be a major advantage if governments invest in innovation systems that harness the learning-by-doing opportunities that may arise. International partnerships can help countries in which capabilities are still low. However, governments can support efforts to fill niches up and down the GH_2 value chain. For example, while some fossil fuel infrastructure can be repurposed, the design of specific GH_2 infrastructure for optimal storage, conversion, and transportation can be a source of future industrial development.

The design of carbon credit markets, as they are completely new, can also be approached through a government learning framework. Using a "regulatory sandbox" approach can, for example, inform policy makers about a policy's effectiveness and the adjustments that could address potential pitfalls or curb inefficient rent-seeking. Carbon credit markets can be considered part of an integrated approach to land use, development, and environmental considerations. As an emerging market, however, there is much to be learned about how different regulatory frameworks may affect incentives and outcomes. The learning process may also include incentivizing green entrepreneurs who can develop innovative business models based on land recovery or protection while creating commercially viable high-quality carbon credits.

The region has several important advantages that it could leverage to leapfrog ahead in green-technology sectors. The most enduring and potent investment, however, will be the consolidation of the effective NIS with the ability to manage complex projects and bring new technologies to the world—a source of "Schumpeterian" or "innovation" rents that is the foundation for sustained and inclusive growth.

Notes

1. Correa, Fernandes, and Uregian (2008) find that the technology choices of firms in Europe and Central Asia are related to access to appropriate complementary inputs such as skilled labor, managerial capacity, R&D, finance, and to a lesser extent good infrastructure.
2. See Dutz et al. (2014) for a description of learning and experimentation in innovation policy.
3. Empresa Brasileira de Pesquisa Agropecuária.
4. Since the 1990s the global mining industry has gone through a process of de-verticalization and outsourcing of many activities, transforming the dynamics of innovation in the industry. Big multinational mining corporations are more focused on core activities, outsourcing more activities and thus pushing innovation efforts toward the mining equipment and knowledge service providers.
5. Studies have found positive effects of grant programs resulting in additional R&D spending, more researchers hired by the firms, and firms spending more worker hours in R&D projects (Garcia-Quevedo 2004).
6. Syntheses and meta-analyses, such as Becker (2015), Garcia-Quevedo (2004), and Zúñiga-Vicente et al. (2014), all conclude that most of the evidence focuses on input additionalities—impact on innovation expenditure—and hardly any evidence focuses on innovation outcomes and firm performance.

References

Andrews, M. 2015. "Explaining Positive Deviance in Public Sector Reforms in Development." *World Development* 74: 197–208.

Andrews, M., and L. Pritchett. 2013. "Escaping Capability Traps through Problem Driven Iterative Adaptation (PDIA)." *World Development* 51: 234–44.

Andrews, M., L. Pritchett, and M. Woolcock. 2013. "Looking Like a State: Techniques of Persistent Failure in State Capability for Implementation." *Journal of Development Studies* 49 (1): 1–18.

Aridi, A., and N. Kapil. 2019. *Innovation Agencies: Cases from Developing Economies.* Washington, DC: World Bank.

Arqué-Castells, P., and P. Mohnen. 2015. "Sunk Costs, Extensive R&D Subsidies and Permanent Inducement Effects." *Journal of Industrial Economics* 63 (3): 458–94.

Badgley, G., J. Freeman, J. J. Hamman et al. 2022. "Systematic Over-Crediting in California's Forest Carbon Offsets Program." *Global Change Biology* 28 (4): 1433–45.

Becker, B. 2015. "Public R&D Policies and Private R&D Investment: A Survey of the Empirical Evidence." *Journal of Economic Surveys* 29: 917–42.

Bell, M., and P. N. Figueiredo. 2012. "Innovation Capability Building and Learning Mechanisms in Latecomer Firms: Recent Empirical Contributions and Implications for Research." *Revue Canadienne d'Études du Développement* 33 (1): 14–40.

Bell, M., and K. Pavitt. 1993. "Technological Accumulation and Industrial Growth: Contrasts Between Developed and Developing Countries." *Industrial and Corporate Change* 2 (2): 157–210.

Blanco, E., L. Moros, A. Pfaff, I. Steimanis, M. A. Velez, and B. Vollan. 2023. "No Crowding Out among Those Terminated from an Ongoing PES Program in Colombia." *Journal of Environmental Economics and Management* 120: 102826.

Bloom, N., and J. Van Reenen. 2007. "Measuring and Explaining Management Practices across Firms and Countries." *Quarterly Journal of Economics* 122 (4): 1351–408.

Bryant, Peter. 2015. "The Case for Innovation in the Mining Industry." White paper, Clareo, Fort Lauderdale, FL. https://clareo.com/wp-content/uploads/2020/05/Clareo-Case -for-Innovation-in-Mining-0615.pdf.

CCAC (Climate and Clean Air Coalition). 2021. *Government Action to Reduce Methane from the Livestock Sector*. Presentation. https://www.ccacoalition.org/sites/default/files /resources//2021_Government-action-livestock-webinar.pdf.

Chomsky, Raf. 2023. "Tech Innovations in Sustainable Agriculture." *Sustainable Review*, August 20, 2023. https://sustainablereview.com/tech-innovations-in-sustainable -agriculture/.

Cirera, X., and W. F. Maloney. 2017. *The Innovation Paradox: Developing-Country Capabilities and the Unrealized Promise of Technological Catch-Up*. Washington, DC: World Bank.

Coffield, S. R., C. D. Vo, J. A. Wang et al. 2022. "Using Remote Sensing to Quantify the Additional Climate Benefits of California Forest Carbon Offset Projects." *Global Change Biology* 28 (22): 6789–806.

Correa, P. G., A. M. Fernandes, and C. J. Uregian. 2008. "Technology Adoption and the Investment Climate: Firm-Level Evidence for Eastern Europe and Central Asia." *World Bank Economic Review* 24 (1): 121–47.

Dautovic, E., A. P. Cusolito, and D. McKenzie. 2018. "Can Government Intervention Make Firms More Investment-Ready? A Randomized Experiment in the Western Balkans." Policy Research Working Paper 8541, World Bank, Washington, DC.

Deloitte. 2016. "Business Ecosystems in Exploration." https://www.deloitte.com/ca/en /Industries/mining-metals/research/business-ecosystem-in-exploration.html.

Dutz, M. A., Y. Kuznetsov, E. Lasagabaster, and D. Pilat, eds. 2014. *Making Innovation Policy Work: Learning from Experimentation*. Paris: OECD and World Bank.

Edquist, C. 2004. "Final Remarks: Reflections on the Systems of Innovation Approach." *Science and Public Policy* 31 (6): 485–89.

FAO (Food and Agriculture Organization of the United Nations). 2022. "Agroecology a Win-Win for Uruguay's Farmers, Environment and Economy." FAO Investment Centre, March 8, 2022. https://www.fao.org/support-to-investment/news/detail/en/c /1601307/.

Figueiredo, P. N. 2014. "Technological Catch-Up and Indigenous Institutional Infrastructures in Latecomer Natural Resource-Related Industries: An Exploration of the Role of EMBRAPA in Brazil's Soybean and Forestry-Based Pulp and Paper Industries." IRIBA Working Paper: 03, International Research Initiative on Brazil and Africa, University of Manchester.

Figueiredo, P. N., and Janaina Piana. 2018. "Innovative Capability Building and Learning Linkages in Knowledge-Intensive Service SMEs in Brazil's Mining Industry." *Resources Policy* 58: 21–33.

FONTAGRO. 2022. "Annual Report 2022." Inter-American Development Bank, Washington, DC.

Garcia-Quevedo, J. 2004. "Do Public Subsidies Complement Business R&D? A Meta-Analysis of the Econometric Evidence." *Kyklos* 57 (1): 87–102.

Giuliano, F., D. Navia, and H. Ruberl. 2024. "The Macroeconomic Impact of Climate Shocks in Uruguay." Policy Research Working Paper 10740, World Bank, Washington, DC.

Glennie, A., and K. Bound. 2016. *How Innovation Agencies Work: International Lessons to Inspire and Inform National Strategies*. London: Nesta. https://media.nesta.org.uk /documents/how_innovation_agencies_work.pdf.

Government of Australia. 2021. *A Growing South: Patent Analytics on Plant Biotechnology in Latin America*, by IP Australia. Report. https://www.ipaustralia.gov.au/tools-and -research/professional-resources/data-research-and-reports/publications-and -reports/~/-/media/Project/IPA/IPAustralia/PDF/a-growing-south-patent-analytics -on-plant-biotechnology-in-latin-america.pdf.

Jack, B. K., and S. Jayachandran. 2019. "Self-Selection into Payments for Ecosystem Services Programs." *Proceedings of the National Academy of Sciences* 116 (12): 5326–33.

Jayachandran, S., J. de Laat, E. F. Lambin, and C. Y. Stanton. 2016. "Cash for Carbon: A Randomized Controlled Trial of Payments for Ecosystem Services to Reduce Deforestation." NBER Working Paper 22378, National Bureau of Economic Research, Cambridge, MA.

Kapil, N., M. Piatkowsi, and C. Navarrete. 2014. "Poland: Smart Growth Operational Program Review." Washington, DC: World Bank.

Krause, R. M., H. Yi, and R. C. Feiock. 2016. "Applying Policy Termination Theory to the Abandonment of Climate Protection Initiatives by US Local Governments." *Policy Studies Journal* 44 (2): 176–95.

Leal, C. I. S., and P. N. Figueiredo. 2021. "Technological Innovation in Brazil: Challenges and Inputs for Public Policies." *Brazilian Journal of Public Administration* 55 (3): 512–37.

Link, A. N., and J. T. Scott. 2009. "The Role of Public Research Institutions in a National Innovation System: An Economic Perspective." Working paper. World Bank, Washington, DC.

Loukos, P., and L. Arathoon. 2020. "Landscaping the Agritech Ecosystem for Smallholder Farmers in Latin America and the Caribbean." GSMA AgriTech Programme and Inter-American Development Bank (IDB) Lab, IDB, Washington, DC. https://www.gsma .com/solutions-and-impact/connectivity-for-good/mobile-for-development/wp -content/uploads/2020/11/Landscaping_the_agritech_ecosystem_for_smallholder _farmers_in_Latin_America_and_the_Caribbean_1.pdf

Lundvall, B.-Å., B. Johnson, E. S. Andersen, and B. Dalum. 2002. "National Systems of Production, Innovation, and Competence Building." *Research Policy* 31 (2): 213–31.

Lundvall, B.-Å., K. J. Joseph, C. Chaminade, and J. Vang, eds. 2009. *Handbook of Innovation Systems and Developing Countries: Building Domestic Capabilities in a Global Setting*. Cheltenham: Edward Elgar.

Molina, O. 2018. "Innovation in an Unfavorable Context: Local Mining Suppliers in Peru." *Resources Policy* 58: 34–48.

Moros, L., M. A. Vélez, D. Quintero, D. Tobin, and A. Pfaff. 2023. "Temporary PES Do Not Crowd Out and May Crowd In Lab-in-the-Field Forest Conservation in Colombia." *Ecological Economics* 204 (Part A): 107652.

Morris, M., R. Kaplinsky, and D. Kaplan. 2012. "'One Thing Leads to Another'—Commodities, Linkages and Industrial Development." *Resources Policy* 37 (4): 408–16.

Navarro, L. 2017. "The World Class Supplier Program for Mining in Chile: Assessment and Perspectives." *Resources Policy* 58: 49–61.

Nelson, R. R., ed. 1993. *National Innovation Systems: A Comparative Analysis*. New York: Oxford University Press.

OECD (Organisation for Economic Co-operation and Development). 2024. *Agricultural Policy Monitoring and Evaluation 2024: Innovation for Sustainable Productivity Growth*. https://www.oecd.org/en/publications/2024/11/agricultural-policy-monitoring-and -evaluation-2024_b4c72370.html.

Pagiola, S., J. Honey-Rosés, and J. Freire-González. 2016. "Evaluation of the Permanence of Land Use Change Induced by Payments for Environmental Services in Quindío, Colombia." *PLoS One* 11 (3): e0147829.

Pietrobelli, C., A. Marin, and J. Olivari. 2018. "Innovation in Mining Value Chains: New Evidence from Latin America." *Resources Policy* 58: 1–10.

Rodrik, D. 2008. "Second-Best Institutions." *American Economic Review* 98 (2): 100–104.

Saini, E. 2023. "Leveraging Investment in Agricultural Science, Technology, and Innovation in Latin America and the Caribbean." *Science* 382 (6669): eadl0654. https://doi.org/10.1126/science.adl0654.

Sánchez, M. A. 2020. "Chile as a Key Enabler Country for Global Plant Breeding, Agricultural Innovation, and Biotechnology." *GM Crops and Food* 11 (3): 130–39. https://doi.org/10.1080/21645698.2020.1761757.

Schling, M., and N. Pazos. 2022. "The Impact of Smart Subsidies on Agricultural Production: Innovative Evidence from Argentina Using Survey and Remote Sensing Data." IDB Working Paper Series 01358, Inter-American Development Bank, Washington, DC.

Stubrin, L. 2017. "Innovation, Learning and Competence Building in the Mining Industry. The Case of Knowledge Intensive Mining Suppliers (KIMS) in Chile." *Resources Policy* 54: 167–75.

Sutton, W. R., A. Lotsch, and A. Prasann. 2024. *Recipe for a Livable Planet: Achieving Net Zero Emissions in the Agrifood System.* Agriculture and Food Series, Conference edition. Washington, DC: World Bank. http://hdl.handle.net/10986/41468.

Teirlink, P., H. Delanghe, P. Padilla, and A. Verbeek. 2013. "Closing the Policy Cycle: Increasing the Utilization of Evaluation Findings in Research, Technological Development and Innovation Policy Design." *Science and Public Policy* 40 (3): 366–77.

Upstill, G., and P. Hall. 2006. "Innovation in the Minerals Industry: Australia in a Global Context." *Resources Policy* 31 (3): 137–45.

World Bank. 2021. *Agro-ecological and Climate Resilient Systems in Uruguay (P176232).* Project information document. https://documents1.worldbank.org/curated/en/710401633541528912/pdf/Project-Information-Document-Agro-ecological-and-Climate-Resilient-Systems-in-Uruguay-P176232.pdf.

Wu, X., and M. Ramesh. 2014. "Market Imperfections, Government Imperfections, and Policy Mixes: Policy Innovations in Singapore." *Policy Sciences* 47 (3): 305–20.

Zanello, G., X. Fu, P. Mohnen, and M. Ventresca. 2013. "The Diffusion of Innovation in the Private Sectors in Low-Income Countries (LICs): A Systematic Literature Review." TMD Working Paper 62, Technology and Management for Development Centre, University of Oxford.

Zúñiga-Vicente, J. Á., C. Alonso-Borrego, F. J. Forcadell, and J. I. Galán. 2014. "Assessing the Effect of Public Subsidies on Firm R&D Investment: A Survey." *Journal of Economic Surveys* 28 (1): 36–67.